THE PRIN

2000

CRACKING THE REGENTS

SEQUENTIAL MATH II

DOUGLAS FRENCH

2000 Edition

Random House, Inc.

New York

www.randomhouse.com/princetonreview

Princeton Review Publishing, L.L.C.
2315 Broadway
New York, NY 10024

E-mail: comments@review.com

Published in the United States by Random House, Inc., New York.

ISBN 0-375-75546-2

Editor: Gretchen Feder
Design: Chris J. Thomas
Production Coordinator: Robert McCormack
Production Editor: Julieanna Lambert

Manufactured in the United States of America

9 8 7 6 5 4 3 2 1

2000 edition

CRACKING THE REGENTS

REGENTS

SEQUENTIAL
MATH II

ACKNOWLEDGMENTS

I'm especially grateful to Carl Hostnik and Frank Quinn, two of the best math professors of all time. (When working through really long calculus problems, Mr. Hostnik would routinely write on bulletin boards, walls, and posters when he ran out of space on the blackboard.) They taught me that a math teacher can be completely nuts and still be a great teacher.

Thanks to Melanie Sponholz and Evan Schnittman, the powers who got me involved with this project. My editors at The Princeton Review, including Lesly Atlas, Amy Zavatto, and Kristen Azzara, were a great help. Thanks also to the PageMakers, Chris J. Thomas, Robert McCormack, Dave Spalding, and Neil McMahon, who made sure all the diagrams looked good, and to the expert reviewers, Sasha Alcott, Kenneth Butka, Blase Caruana, and Nancy Schneider, who made sure it all made sense.

Thanks to my family (especially Mom, who convinced me that I could sit down long enough to write a book), and to Agnes Dee, who is my favorite favorite.

And most of all, I'd like to thank all the math students I've tutored over the years. There's nothing better than getting a phone call from an ecstatic student who has just aced a final exam.

And special thanks for the 2000 edition to Les Groman.

CONTENTS

PART I

HOW TO
CRACK THE SYSTEM

INTRODUCTION

WHAT IS THE PRINCETON REVIEW?

The Princeton Review is an international test preparation company with branches in all major U.S. cities and several cities abroad. In 1981 John Katzman started teaching an SAT prep course in his parents' living room. Within five years The Princeton Review had become the largest SAT coaching program in the country.

The Princeton Review's phenomenal success in improving students' scores on standardized tests was (and continues to be) the result of a simple, innovative, and radically effective approach: Study the test, not what the test *claims* to test. This approach has led to the development of techniques for taking standardized tests based on the principles the test writers themselves use to write the tests.

The Princeton Review has found that its methods work not for cracking the SAT, but for any standardized test. We've successfully applied our system to the SAT II, AP, ACT, GMAT, and LSAT, to name just a few. As a result of hundreds of hours of exhaustive study, we are now applying that system to the New York State Regents exam. This book uses our time-tested principle: Figure out what the test-givers want, then teach that to the test-takers in a comprehensive *and* fun way.

We also publish books and CD-ROMs on an enormous variety of education- and career-related topics. If you're interested, check out our Web site at www.review.com.

WHAT IS THE REGENTS EXAMINATION?

The Regents are annual exams given in a variety of subjects—math, English, history, sciences, and foreign languages. To get a Regents Diploma, you must pass a certain number of these exams in required subjects. Among other things, you must pass the math exams. You have probably already taken the Regents examination in Sequential Math I and passed it. Thus, in this book, we will assume that you are familiar with a few basic aspects of taking the Regents.

You usually take the Regents in June, in lieu of or in addition to finals, but they are also offered in January and August. Most of you will take the Sequential II exam in tenth grade, but some of you take it earlier or later.

The test is administered in school by your teachers and graded by them as well. The New York State Department of Education sets guidelines for grading these exams. These guidelines maintain uniformity in the grading process and give your teacher specific rules to follow, particularly when it comes to awarding partial credit for answers. For more information visit the Regents Board web site at www.nysed.gov.

THE FUTURE OF THE REGENTS

In the next few years the Regents are going to change the exams. Fortunately, you probably will have graduated before then, so you won't have to worry about it. But you can tell your younger friends and siblings that big changes are on the horizon—this will make you sound well-informed and will invite people to seek your advice in many other matters. In 1999 the mathematics and English exams became mandatory, and eventually there will be only two versions of the math exams (Regents Math A and Math B). In 2001 the Regents board plans to release two new exams—the Integrated Science Exam and the Social Studies Exam—which will also be mandatory. We would not be surprised if there were delays in these release dates, but these changes are definitely coming, so be ready!

HOW TO USE THIS BOOK

This book contains twelve past Regents exams and explanations for how to arrive at the correct answer for each question. Taking these practice exams can help you dramatically improve your performance on the exam and, along with Princeton Review test-taking tips, will help you become a better standardized test taker. This book also contains an overview of the material that is on the exam. You should study this material before you take any of the exams and review it again when you discover which areas are your weak points. If you find that you want a more in-depth review of the material, we suggest that you consult The Princeton Review's *High School Math II Review*. It covers all of these topics in more detail and depth and includes lots of practice problems.

The primary value of *Cracking the Regents Math II* is that it contains the most recent exams with their explanations. Pay careful attention to the explanations to your wrong answers. We attack each particular question type the same way so that you can develop a uniform approach to cracking each type of problem found on the test. We have also included a section that we call Target Practice. If you want to work on a particular weak area, refer to this section to find the questions that specifically target that area.

When you take each test, be sure to have the following:

- Scrap paper
- Graph paper
- Extra pencils
- Blue or black pen
- Ruler or straightedge
- Compass (the kind you draw with)
- Calculator (but not a graphing calculator, like a TI-82/83)
- This book

There's also a glossary and a brief chapter listing most of the stuff that shows up on the test year in and year out. If you can take every one of the tests in this book, you'll have a very good idea of what to expect on your exam.

ABOUT THE EXAM

THE TEST FORMAT

The Sequential II Regents Exam takes three hours, and it's composed of three parts:

	Number of Questions	Number to Do	Points Each	Total Points
Part I	35	30	2	60
Part II	6	3	10	30
Part III	2	1	10	10
			Total:	**100**

Grading Part I is easy: Two points if you're right, zero if you're not. Parts II and III, though, are a bit trickier. If possible, ask your teacher to grade them for you. (Chances are, you'll be taking a lot of these tests in class anyway, as the test nears.) Because this test differs very little from session to session, your scores on these practice exams will be an excellent indicator of the score you can expect on the Real Deal.

IT'S THE SAME OLD STUFF

The great thing about this test is that the same types of questions show up over and over again. There are very few surprises, and if you see something new, you can skip it. In fact, you may notice that some of the explanations in the book look a lot alike. That's because the questions are so alike!

DO'S AND DON'TS

The Board of Regents has some pretty stiff grading guidelines, which are published in a booklet that every test grader must read. Here are some rules of thumb you should know about.

Graphing

This test requires a lot of work with the x- and y-axes. Whenever you draw them, make sure they look like this:

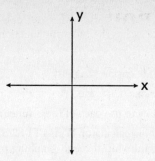

Also be sure to label each axis, so the grader knows that you know what you're talking about.

Graphing Parabolas

In Part II, you'll usually have the option of graphing a parabola on the coordinate axes.

Most of the time, they'll give you the values of x to plug into the equation. When they do, you'll always get seven coordinates—three on either side of the axis of symmetry. (For example, if the domain that you're given is $0 \le x \le 6$, you can bet your last buck that the axis of symmetry of the parabola is the line $x = 3$.)

Plug each of the seven x-coordinates into the equation, and you'll have seven points to plot on the coordinate axes. Once you're through plotting, the curve should be symmetrical (otherwise, you may have plotted a point incorrectly). When you connect them, don't just play connect-the-dots; you'll likely be penalized. Call upon whatever artistic skills you possess and make the line curved:

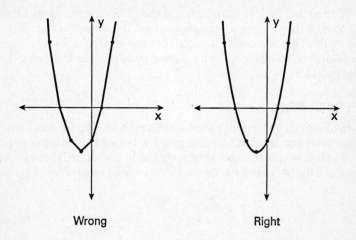

Wrong   Right

Calculators

Make sure your calculator has the following functions:

- Square root
- Trig functions (sine, cosine, tangent)
- Inverse trig functions ($\sin^{-1}$, etc.)

Be sure you know how to use each of these functions comfortably.

Do *not* bring a graphing calculator. With a TI-82/83 (or a comparable piece of machinery), you could whip through graphing problems in nothing flat. This makes the Regents people uneasy, since much of the test involves graphing on the coordinate axes.

Read Carefully and Follow Directions

Make sure you clearly indicate which questions you omit by writing "OMIT" on your answer sheet in the space provided. If they say "round to the nearest tenth," do it. If they want the positive root only, don't give them the negative root.

You're not under a lot of time pressure, so read each question completely and be sure to provide exactly what they ask for—no more, no less. You could lose full credit if you don't.

Example:

5. What is the positive root of the equation $x^2 - 3x - 10 = 0$?

There are two roots to this equation: 5 and –2. The correct answer, though, is 5 because they ask only for the positive root. If your answer was $x = \{5, -2\}$, you wouldn't get any credit (0 points!) because you didn't follow directions. So, before you start looking for the answer, make sure you know what they're asking you for.

THE GOOD NEWS

Even though the graders of this test are notorious sticklers for detail, fear not. If you think you bombed an entire problem in Part II or III, you might be better off than you thought. Most problems in Part II or III involve many steps, and the later work you do usually depends on an answer you got previously. Well, the Regents folks don't want you to be punished twice for one mistake. Even if the numbers you used on a question are wrong, you could still get full credit if you did the math correctly.

Here's a sample problem from Part II:

39. In the accompanying diagram of trapezoid $ABCD$, $\overline{CD} \perp \overline{AD}$, $BC = 9$, $AD = 15$, and m$\angle A = 35$.

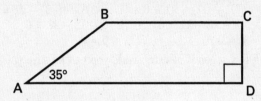

Find, to the *nearest tenth*, the

a   area of $ABCD$ [5]
b   perimeter of $ABCD$ [5]

To find the area of the trapezoid, you need to find the length of $\overline{CD}$ using trigonometry. (The answer is 4.2.) Suppose you made a mathematical mistake and got 8.4 instead, then you used this to figure out the answer to part *b*. You would lose the first five points, but the grader might give you the five points in part *b* if you did the math right.

THE PRINCETON REVIEW TECHNIQUES

The people who write the Sequential Math II exam like to think of themselves as The Big Bad Regents Board. Well, we're here to tell you that this test can be really easy—if you take the time to prepare. Here are some tips to help you perform at your best.

Relax!

Unlike most other timed exams, including the SAT and PSAT, you probably won't find yourself having to rush. They give you three hours to finish the exam, and most students don't need more than two. This lack of time pressure gives you the chance to check your work.

Always Double-Check

Errors happen, so check everything twice. (After all, you've got the time.) A typical question might involve finding the roots of an equation, like so:

$$x^2 - 4x - 21 = 0$$
$$(x - 7)(x + 3) = 0$$
$$x = \{7, -3\}$$

When you've finished with the algebra, take the time to check your answers by plugging them back into the equation:

$(7)^2 - 4(7) - 21 = 0$ $(-3)^2 - 4(-3) - 21 = 0$

$49 - 28 - 21 = 0$ $9 + 12 - 21 = 0$

$0 = 0$ $0 = 0$

With just a few seconds of extra work, you can be sure you did the work correctly.

Backsolving

This test-taking technique will help you to check your work. Sometimes you can find the right answer by plugging the answer choices you're given back into the question. Here's a sample problem:

17. The roots of the equation $2x^2 - 7x - 4 = 0$ are

(1) $\dfrac{7 \pm \sqrt{17}}{4}$ (3) $\dfrac{1}{2}, -4$

(2) $-\dfrac{1}{2}, 4$ (4) $\dfrac{-7 \pm \sqrt{17}}{2}$

Rather than factor this right away, try a little backsolving. One of the answer choices has to work, so try one of the easier numbers first. (Don't bother with (1) and (4) yet—they're too hard!)

Since 4 is the only root given that is an integer, try it first (use your calculator if you feel the urge):

$$2(4)^2 - 7(4) - 4 = 0$$
$$2(16) - 28 - 4 = 0$$
$$32 - 32 = 0$$

Bingo! Since answer choice (2) is the only choice that has 4 in it, you know that (2) is the correct answer. And all you did was a little simple arithmetic!

Note: This technique works ONLY in the multiple-choice section of Part I. Parts II and III require you to show all your work, so you can't take short cuts.

Process of Elimination (POE)

The questions on the second portion of Part I have four answer choices. On these questions, you can sometimes choose the right answer just by eliminating the other three possibilities.

18. The coordinates of two points are $X(2,5)$ and $Y(6,5)$. Which of the following equations represents the locus of points that is the perpendicular bisector of $\overline{XY}$?

(1) $x = 4$ (3) $x = 8$
(2) $y = 4$ (4) $y = 8$

If the answer to this one eludes you for the moment, don't panic. Graph the points first:

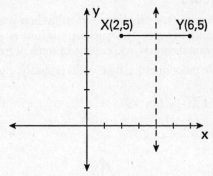

Your first instinct might be to find the midpoint of the segment. Don't bother; there's a way to solve this without doing any mathematical calculation.

From the diagram, you can see that segment $\overline{XY}$ is horizontal; the perpendicular bisector must be vertical. Therefore, you can eliminate answer choices (2) and (4), which are also horizontal. If you guess at this point, you have a 50-50 chance. Those odds aren't bad.

If you look further, you'll realize that the perpendicular bisector has to be between the two points. Since answer choice (4) is too far to the right, you can eliminate it. The only answer left is choice (1).

This is why you should take a long look at every question in the multiple-choice section of Part I. If you don't see a method right away, you still have a chance using POE.

WHEN TO OMIT

Whatever you do, don't be too quick to skip a question. If you're not quite sure how to answer something, come back to it later. Don't rush to omit a question unless you have absolutely no clue.

LOGIC

Geometric and logical proofs are the reason why this is the only Regents math test with a Part III.

It would be very hard to escape this test without having to construct a proof, so study your theorems. As you'll see from the proofs in this book, there are only a couple dozen or so theorems, postulates, and definitions to know. As far as logical proofs go, there are seven things to know (see the Math Review chapter). Becoming familiar with them shouldn't be too difficult—so do it!

GEOMETRIC PROOFS

When you plan a geometric proof, try to visualize how you're going to end it before you put pencil to paper. This will keep you from rambling on, spouting a bunch of irrelevant theorems, and hoping for some degree of partial credit.

Here's a sample proof question that would probably appear in Part III:

Given: $\overline{DB} \perp \overline{AC}$; $\angle 1 \cong \angle 2$

Prove: $\overline{AB} \cong \overline{BC}$

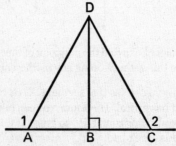

Analyze the given statements. $\overline{AB}$ and $\overline{BC}$ are corresponding parts of $\triangle ABD$ and $\triangle CBD$, so how can you prove that the two triangles are congruent? You can prove that $\angle DAB$ is congruent to $\angle DCB$, because they're supplemental to $\angle 1$ and $\angle 2$, respectively. Since $\overline{DB}$ is perpendicular to $\overline{AC}$, angles DBA and DBC are right angles, which are always congruent. Further, the triangles share a common side, $\overline{DB}$.

From this information, you can plan to prove that $\triangle ABD$ and $\triangle CBD$ are congruent using Angle-Angle-Side, then use CPCTC. Write that on the page first, and don't worry about numbering. You can number everything when you're finished.

Statements	Reasons
$\triangle DBA \cong \triangle DBC$	$AAS \cong AAS$
$\overline{AB} \cong \overline{BC}$	CPCTC

Now that you have a clear objective, you can fill in the blanks as you go along. This minimizes the chance that you'll include a lot of stuff you don't need. Here's the final proof:

Statements	Reasons
1. $\angle 1 \cong \angle 2$	1. Given
2. $\angle 1$ and $\angle DAB$ are supplemental; $\angle 2$ and $\angle DCB$ are supplemental	2. Definition of supplemental angles
3. $\angle DAB \cong \angle DCB$	3. Angles that are supplemental to congruent angles are congruent.
4. $\overline{DB} \perp \overline{AC}$	4. Given
5. $\angle DBA$ and $\angle DBC$ are right angles	5. Definition of perpendicular lines
6. $\angle DBA \cong \angle DBC$	6. All right angles are congruent
7. $\overline{DB} \cong \overline{DB}$	7. Reflexive property of equality
8. $\triangle DBA \cong \triangle DBC$	8. $AAS \cong AAS$
9. $\overline{AB} \cong \overline{BC}$	9. CPCTC

Look at Reason 5. Some teachers might want you to write that "perpendicular lines intersect to form four right angles," while others are just as happy with "definition of perpendicular lines." When you list your reasons, phrase them in the same way that your instructor has taught you all year. This is no time to get creative.

PREPARING FOR THE TEST

The Day Before the Test

Don't try to cram a lot of information into your brain the night before you take the test. After all, what extra bit of magic can you learn that you didn't learn all year? Look over a few formulas, make sure you have everything you need to take to the test site, and get a good night's sleep. Cramming the night before just makes you flaky and burns you out the next day.

The Day of the Test

There's a big difference between "awake" and "alert." Get up early and have something to eat. Your body wakes up when it has to digest food, and your breakfast will serve as an energy source throughout the morning.

Bring several layers of clothing to the test. You don't know if it will be too warm or too cold at the test site, so be prepared. You'll do much better if you're comfortable.

Get to the test site early. While you're waiting, take out this book and look over a few problems you did well on. (*Don't* try anything new.) As you familiarize yourself with the material once again, you'll get your mind ready to do math for three hours.

Take your time, be thorough, and crush this test. It'll be over before you know it.

Good luck!

MATH REVIEW:
WHAT YOU SHOULD KNOW

This chapter lists the formulas and other calculations you should be familiar with for the Sequential Math II exam, as well as a few handy ways to remember them. If a complete explanation of something doesn't appear here, it probably appears in full within the explanations of one of the tests. You can also check the Glossary.

Some teachers let their students bring a sheet of formulas in with them to the exam. Ask your teacher if he or she will let you do so. Otherwise, *memorize*.

ALGEBRA

You should have a good sense of factoring quadratics in order to determine their roots. For example:

$$x^2 - 4x - 12 = 0$$
$$(x - 6)(x + 2) = 0$$
$$x = \{6, -2\}$$

If you can't factor a quadratic equation, you can always use the Quadratic Formula. Given the equation $ax^2 + bx + c = 0$, you can find the roots using this:

$$x = \frac{-b \pm \sqrt{b^2 - 4ac}}{2a}$$

It's not mandatory, but it might be helpful in some places to remember that the sum of the roots of a quadratic in standard form is $-\dfrac{b}{a}$, and the product is $\dfrac{c}{a}$.

AREAS

Know these area formulas:

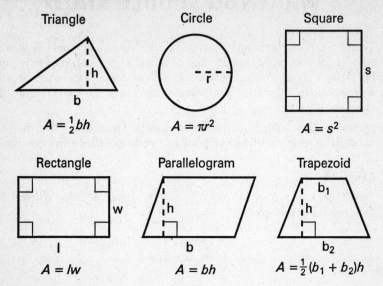

Triangle	Circle	Square
$A = \frac{1}{2}bh$	$A = \pi r^2$	$A = s^2$

Rectangle	Parallelogram	Trapezoid
$A = lw$	$A = bh$	$A = \frac{1}{2}(b_1 + b_2)h$

CONSTRUCTIONS

The following constructions have appeared on the Regents Exam:

- Perpendicular bisector of a segment
- Angle bisector
- Duplicate angle
- Parallel line through a point
- Perpendicular line though a point

Each of these is explained fully, with diagrams, in the test explanations.

EQUATIONS

The most basic graphic equation you should be able to recognize is the standard form of a line, in which m represents the slope of the line and b is the y-intercept:

$$y = mx + b$$

We use this formula in this book (instead of the form $y - y_1 = m(x - x_1)$, which you might have used throughout your school year) because the exam always uses standard form. The same is true for the equation of a parabola; the standard form looks like this:

$$y = ax^2 + bx + c$$

This format is used on the exam instead of the form $y - k = a(x - h)^2$ because it's easier to factor. You won't have to worry about foci or the directrix.

The formula for a circle, however, does use the (h,k) format:

$$(x - h)^2 + (y - k)^2 = r^2$$

in which (h,k) is the center of the circle and r is the radius.

FORMULAS

Here are the three big formulas you need to know, given the points (x_1, y_1) and (x_2, y_2):

The distance between them is:

$$d = \sqrt{(x_2 - x_1)^2 + (y_2 - y_1)^2}$$

Think of the distance formula as a manifestation of the Pythagorean theorem. The distance between the points is the hypotenuse of a right triangle:

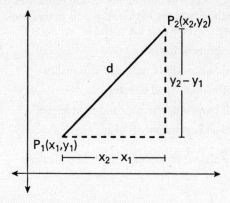

The formula for the slope between the points is:

$$m = \frac{y_2 - y_1}{x_2 - x_1}$$

The slope of a line represents the $\frac{rise}{run}$. If you remember that "the rise is the y's," you'll remember to put the difference of the y's on top and the difference of the x's on the bottom.

The midpoint formula is:

$$(\overline{x}, \overline{y}) = \left(\frac{x_1 + x_2}{2}, \frac{y_1 + y_2}{2} \right)$$

This one's easy to remember, because it makes sense that the point equidistant from two others is just the average of their x- and y-coordinates.

GEOMETRIC PROOFS

Know how to use each of these triangle congruence theorems:

- Angle-Angle-Side (AAS)
- Angle-Side-Angle (ASA)
- Side-Angle-Side (SAS)
- Side-Side-Side (SSS)
- Hypotenuse-Leg (HL)—for right angles only

You should also be familiar with the Angle-Angle theorem for similarity, as well as the theorem that "corresponding parts of congruent triangles are congruent" (CPCTC). As far as the definitions and properties you need to know, consult your textbook and the explained proofs in this book. You'll see that a select few properties show up a lot, such as:

- Reflexive Property of Equality
- Addition and Subtraction Properties of Equality
- Definition of midpoint and bisector
- Definition of perpendicular lines and right angles
- Supplements and complements of angles

Memorize the characteristics of each of the following:

- Squares
- Rectangles
- Rhombuses (or Rhombi)
- Parallelograms
- Isosceles triangles
- Isosceles trapezoids

The introduction contains some helpful hints for writing geometric proofs.

GRAPHING

Obviously, knowing how to plot a point (x,y) on the coordinate axes is a must. You'll use this knowledge to plot parabolas and the vertices of various polygons.

Remember that the formula for the axis of symmetry of the parabola $y = ax^2 + bx + c$ is:

$$x = -\frac{b}{2a}$$

You should also recognize the various formulas for transformations, including:

- Translations, under which a point (x,y) "slides" to the point $(x + h, y + k)$
- Dilations, under which a point (x,y) "expands" to the point (kx, ky)
- Reflections in the following:
  1. $r_{x-axis}(x,y) \rightarrow (x,-y)$
  2. $r_{y-axis}(x,y) \rightarrow (-x,y)$
  3. $r_{(0,0)}(x,y) \rightarrow (-x,-y)$
  4. $r_{y=x}(x,y) \rightarrow (y,x)$

As you'll see, there's been nothing on any of these 12 tests involving rotations. That stuff usually appears on the Sequential III exam.

LOGIC

Know these rules (and their translations), and you'll be fine:

- **Law of Contrapositive Inference:** if $A \rightarrow B$, then $\sim B \rightarrow \sim A$ (if A leads to B, then without B there is no A)
- **The Chain Rule:** if $A \rightarrow B$ and $B \rightarrow C$, then $A \rightarrow C$
- **The Law of Detachment (*Modus Ponens*):** $[(A \rightarrow B) \wedge A] \rightarrow B$ (if A leads to B, and A is true, then B is true)
- **The Law of *Modus Tollens*:** $[(A \rightarrow B) \wedge \sim B] \rightarrow \sim A$ (if A leads to B, and B is not true, then A is not true; this is related to the contrapositive)
- **De Morgan's Laws:** $\sim(A \wedge B) \rightarrow \sim A \vee \sim B$ (if A and B are not both true, then either A is false or B is false or both); $\sim(A \vee B) \rightarrow \sim A \wedge \sim B$ (if neither A nor B is true, then both A and B must be false)
- **Law of Disjunctive Inference:** $[(A \vee B) \wedge \sim A] \rightarrow B$ (if either A or B is true and A is false, then B is true)
- **Law of Double Negation:** $\sim(\sim A) \rightarrow A$

See the logic proofs in this book for more practice.

PARALLEL LINES

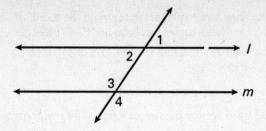

Given two parallel lines cut by a transversal, you should know that:

- Alternate interior angles are congruent ($\angle 2 \cong \angle 4$)

- Corresponding angles are congruent ($\angle 1 \cong \angle 4$)

- Interior angles on the same side of a transversal are supplementary ($m\angle 2 + m\angle 3 = 180$)

PROBABILITY AND PERMUTATIONS

Probability shows up on a few questions on each exam. Remember that the probability that something will happen is denoted by the number of favorable outcomes divided by the number of possible outcomes. For example, the probability that you'll get an even number when you roll an ordinary, six-sided die is

$\frac{3}{6}$, because there are six possible rolls and three even numbers (2, 4, and 6).

When something is certain to happen, the probability that it will happen is one. When something can't happen, the probability is zero.

Combinations show up a lot more than permutations, because order rarely matters on Sequential II test questions. For the record, though, here are the formulas:

$$_nP_r = \frac{n!}{r!} \qquad\qquad _nC_r = \frac{n!}{r!(n-r)!}$$

Problems involving combinations of letters in a word occur rather frequently. In a word with n letters, in which one letter appears p times and another appears q times (given that p and q are greater than 1), the formula is:

$$\frac{n!}{p!\,q!}$$

TRIANGLES

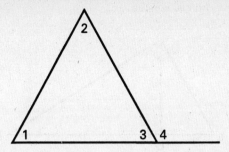

The Rule of 180 (m∠1 + m∠2 + m∠3 = 180) is tested often; and don't forget that the measure of an exterior angle equals the sum of the measures of the two non-adjacent interior angles (m∠4 = m∠1 + m∠2).

Also, remember that the length of a side of a triangle must be greater than the difference between the lengths of the two other sides and less than their sum:

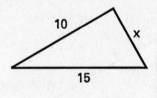

$$5 < x < 25$$

As far as right triangles are concerned, the Pythagorean Theorem comes up a lot. It's also helpful to know the relationships between the sides of 30:60:90 and 45:45:90 triangles:

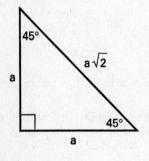 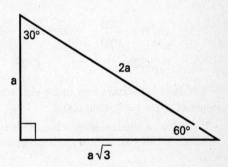

When an altitude in a right triangle is drawn, three similar triangles are created with proportional lengths:

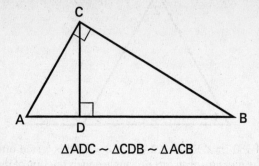

$$\triangle ADC \sim \triangle CDB \sim \triangle ACB$$

You'll usually get a question about the largest side or angle of a triangle. In any triangle, the biggest side is always opposite the biggest angle, and the smallest side is opposite the smallest angle.

TRIGONOMETRY

On this exam, trig is limited to SOHCAHTOA:

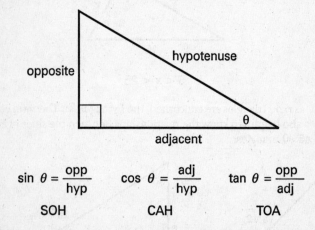

$$\sin\theta = \frac{\text{opp}}{\text{hyp}} \qquad \cos\theta = \frac{\text{adj}}{\text{hyp}} \qquad \tan\theta = \frac{\text{opp}}{\text{adj}}$$

$$\text{SOH} \qquad\qquad \text{CAH} \qquad\qquad \text{TOA}$$

You should also know how to use your calculator to find values and inverse values of trigonometric functions.

If you have a good understanding of the terms and formulas in this chapter, you are well on your way to getting the score you want on the Sequential II test.

TARGET PRACTICE

If you've pinpointed a problem area as you prepare for the Math II Regents exam, we've categorized the questions in the 12 tests from this book. As you look at these categories, you can see how the test structure doesn't vary all that much. If there's a construction, for example, it's question No. 35.

The more involved and complicated questions that appear in Parts II and III are in **bold**, and questions numbered **41** or **42** appear in Part III. Again, you can see where all the bold numbers are and predict what kinds of questions you'll see on the second half of the test.

LOGIC

Basic Concepts
June 96: 21, 27
August 96: 23, 25
January 97: 19, 27
June 97: 20
August 97: 14, 19, 25
January 98: 15, 28
June 98: 16, 22, 30
August 98: 14, 17, 32
January 99: 18, 27, 32
June 99: 13, 14

Logic Proofs
June 96: **42**
August 96: **38**
June 97: **41**
August 97: **39a**
January 98: **41**
June 98: **41**
January 99: **42**
June 99: **41**

MATHEMATICAL CONCEPTS AND SYSTEMS

Identity Element
June 96: 3
August 97: **37b**
June 98: 7
August 98: **39b**
January 99: 3

Inverse Element
August 97: **37c**
August 98: **39c, 39e**
June 99: **39a**

Systems
August 96: 1
January 97: 1

Angle Measures
June 96: 19, 25, 28
August 96: 12, 26
January 97: 18, 20
June 97: 7, 8, 9, 16
August 97: 6
June 98: 2, 6
August 98: 5
January 99: 7, 17, 20, 30

Area of a Triangle
June 97: **40b(1)**
June 98: 28, **40a**
January 99: 8

Exterior Angles
June 96: 19
January 97: 6, 18
June 97: 7
August 97: 6
January 98: 6
June 98: 25
August 98: 5
January 99: 7, 16

Isosceles Triangles
January 97: 12
June 97: 19
August 98: 30
January 99: 17

Longest Side/Largest Angle
June 96: 9
August 96: 6
June 97: 9
January 98: 6
June 98: 5
June 99: 3

Midpoints of Sides
June 96: 33
August 96: 4
January 97: 10
August 97: 5
August 98: 7
June 99: 9

Possible Length of a Third Side
August 96: 20
January 97: 23
August 97: 30
January 98: 29
August 98: 16

PART II

EXAMS AND EXPLANATIONS

EXAMINATION
JUNE 1996

Part I

Answer 30 questions from this part. Each correct answer will receive 2 credits. No partial credit will be allowed. Write your answers in the spaces provided on the separate answer sheet. Where applicable, answers may be left in terms of π or in radical form. [60]

1 If $a \otimes b$ is defined as $a^2 - 2b$, find the value of $5 \otimes 7$.

2 If tan A = 1.3400, find the measure of $\angle A$ to the *nearest degree*.

3 What is the identity element in the system defined by the table below?

★	2	4	6	8
2	4	8	2	6
4	8	6	4	2
6	2	4	6	8
8	6	2	8	4

4   In the accompanying figure, $\overline{DE} \parallel \overline{BC}$, $AD = 10$,
    $AB = 24$, and $AC = 36$. Find AE.

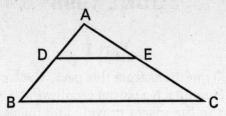

5   Evaluate: $_7C_3$

6   If one the roots of the equation $x^2 + kx = 6$ is 2,
    what is the value of k?

7   Solve for the positive value of y: $\dfrac{16}{y} = \dfrac{y}{4}$

8   How many different 4-letter arrangements can be
    formed from the letters in the word "NINE"?

9   In $\triangle ABC$, $m\angle B > m\angle C$ and $m\angle C > m\angle A$. Which
    side of $\triangle ABC$ is the longest?

10 In the accompanying diagram of rhombus $ABCD$,
    diagonal $\overline{AC}$ is drawn. If $m\angle CAB = 35$, find
    $m\angle ADC$.

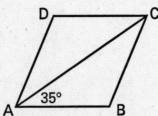

11 What is the slope of the line whose equation is $3x + y = 4$?

12 The graph of the equation $x^2 + y^2 = 9$ represents the locus of points at a given distance, d, from the origin. Find the value of d.

13 Find the area of the parallelogram whose vertices are $(2,1)$, $(7,1)$, $(9,5)$, and $(4,5)$.

14 Express $\dfrac{5x}{6} - \dfrac{x}{3}$ in simplest form.

15 The line that passes through points $(1,3)$ and $(2,y)$ has a slope of 2. What is the value of y?

16 What is the length of a side of a square whose diagonal measures $4\sqrt{2}$?

Directions (17–35): For *each* question chosen, write on the separate answer sheet the *numeral* preceding the word or expression that best completes the statement or answers the question.

17 When factored completely, $x^3 - 9x$ is equivalent to
(1) $x(x - 3)$ (3) $(x + 3)(x - 3)$
(2) $x(x + 3)(x - 3)$ (4) $x(x + 3)$

18 If $(x + 2)^2 + (y - 3)^2 = 25$ is an equation of a circle whose center is $(-2,k)$, then k equals

(1) 1   (3) 3
(2) 2   (4) 4

19 In the accompanying diagram of $\triangle ABC$, side $\overline{BC}$ is extended to D, $m\angle B = 2y$, $m\angle BCA = 6y$, and $m\angle ACD = 3y$.

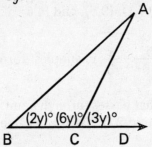

What is $m\angle A$?

(1) 15   (3) 20
(2) 17   (4) 24

20 The coordinates of $\triangle ABC$ are $A(0,0)$, $B(6,0)$, and $C(0,4)$. What are the coordinates of the point at which the median from vertex A intersects side $\overline{BC}$?

(1) $(1,4)$ (3) $(3,0)$
(2) $(2,3)$ (4) $(3,2)$

21 Which statement is the equivalent of $\sim(\sim m \wedge n)$?

(1) $m \wedge n$ (3) $m \vee \sim n$
(2) $m \wedge \sim n$ (4) $\sim m \vee \sim n$

22 The translation $(x,y) \rightarrow (x-2, y+3)$ maps the point (7,2) onto the point whose coordinates are

(1) (9,5)   (3) (5,–1)
(2) (5,5)   (4) (–14,6)

23 In the accompanying diagram, $\triangle FUN$ is a right triangle, $\overline{UR}$ is the altitude to hypotenuse $\overline{FN}$, UR = 12, and the lengths of $\overline{FR}$ and $\overline{RN}$ are in the ratio 1:9.

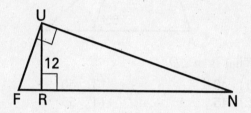

What is the length of $\overline{FR}$?

(1) 1   (3) 36
(2) $1\frac{1}{3}$ (4) 4

24 Lines l and m are perpendicular. The slope of l is $\frac{3}{5}$. What is the slope of m?

(1) $-\frac{3}{5}$ (3) $\frac{3}{5}$

(2) $-\frac{5}{3}$ (4) $\frac{5}{3}$

25 In the accompanying diagram of $\triangle ABC$, $\overline{AC}$ is extended to D, $\overline{DEF}$, $\overline{BEC}$, $\overline{AFB}$, m$\angle B$ = 50, m$\angle BEF$ = 25, and m$\angle ACB$ = 65.

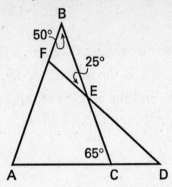

What is m$\angle D$?

(1) 40   (3) 50

(2) 45   (4) 55

26 In the accompanying diagram, parallel lines l and m are cut by transversal t.

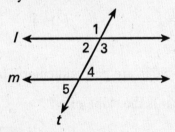

Which statement is true?

(1)   m$\angle 1$ + m$\angle 2$ + m$\angle 5$ = 360

(2)   m$\angle 1$ + m$\angle 2$ + m$\angle 3$ = 180

(3)   m$\angle 1$ + m$\angle 2$ = m$\angle 2$ + m$\angle 3$

(4)   m$\angle 1$ + m$\angle 3$ = m$\angle 4$ + m$\angle 5$

27 Which argument below is *not* valid?

(1) Given: $a \rightarrow b$
         a
    Conclusion: b

(2) Given: $a \lor b$
         $\sim b$
    Conclusion: $\sim a$

(3) Given: $a \rightarrow b$
         $\sim b$
    Conclusion: $\sim a$

(4) Given: $a \rightarrow b$
         $b \rightarrow \sim c$
    Conclusion: $a \rightarrow \sim c$

28 The measure of a base angle of an isosceles triangle is 4 times the measure of the vertex angle. The number of degrees in the vertex angle is

(1) 20 (3) 36
(2) 30 (4) 135

29 What are the coordinates of R', the image of $R(-4,3)$ after a reflection in the line whose equation is $y = x$?

(1) $(-4,-3)$ (3) $(4,3)$
(2) $(3,-4)$ (4) $(-3,4)$

30 The equation $y = 4$ represents the locus of points that are equidistant from which two points?

(1) $(0,0)$ and $(0,8)$ (3) $(4,0)$ and $(0,4)$
(2) $(0,3)$ and $(0,1)$ (4) $(4,4)$ and $(-4,4)$

31 In equilateral triangle ABC, $\overline{AD}$ is drawn to $\overline{BC}$ such that $BD < DC$. Which inequality is true?

(1) $DC > AC$ (3) $AD > AB$
(2) $BD > AD$ (4) $AC > AD$

32 Which equation represents the axis of symmetry of the graph of the equation $y = 2x^2 + 7x - 5$?

(1) $x = -\dfrac{5}{4}$ (3) $x = \dfrac{7}{4}$

(2) $x = \dfrac{5}{4}$ (4) $x = -\dfrac{7}{4}$

33 How many congruent triangles are formed by connecting the midpoints of the three sides of a scalene triangle?

(1) 1   (3) 3

(2) 2   (4) 4

34 What are the roots of the equation $2x^2 - 7x + 4 = 0$?

(1) $\dfrac{7 \pm \sqrt{17}}{4}$ (3) $4, -\dfrac{1}{2}$

(2) $\dfrac{-7 \pm \sqrt{17}}{4}$ (4) $-4, \dfrac{1}{2}$

35 In the accompanying diagram of quadrilateral $QRST$, $\overline{RS} \cong \overline{ST}$, $\overline{SR} \perp \overline{QR}$, and $\overline{ST} \perp \overline{QT}$.

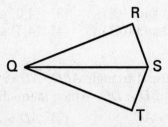

Which method of proof may be used to prove $\triangle QRS \cong \triangle QTS$?

(1) HL   (3) AAS

(2) SAS   (4) ASA

Part II

Answer *three* questions from this part. Clearly indicate the necessary steps, including appropriate formula substitutions, diagrams, graphs, charts, etc. Calculations that may be obtained by mental arithmetic or the calculator do not need to be shown. [30]

36 Answer *a*, *b*, and *c* for all values of *x* for which these expressions are defined.

a Find the value of $\dfrac{(x+1)^2}{x^2-1}$ if $x = 1.02$. [2]

b Find the positive value of *x* to the *nearest thousandth*:
$$\frac{1}{x} = \frac{x+1}{1}$$ [5]

c Solve for all values of *x* in simplest radical form:
$$\frac{x+2}{4} = \frac{2}{x-2}$$ [3]

37 Triangle *ABC* has coordinates *A*(1,0), *B*(7,4), and *C*(5,7).

a On graph paper, draw and label $\triangle ABC$. [1]

b Graph and state the coordinates of $\triangle A'B'C'$, the image of $\triangle ABC$ after a reflection in the origin. [3]

c Graph and state the coordinates of $\triangle A''B''C''$, the image of $\triangle A'B'C'$ under the translation $(x,y) \rightarrow (x+1, y+5)$. [3]

d Write an equation of the line containing $\overline{A''B''}$. [3]

38 Solve the following system of equations algebraically or graphically and check:

$$y = x^2 - 6x + 5$$
$$y + 7 = 2x \qquad [8,2]$$

39 In the accompanying diagram of rhombus $ABCD$, m$\angle CAB = 25$ and $AC = 18$.

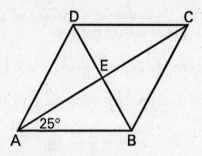

Find, to the *nearest tenth*, the

a perimeter of $ABCD$ [6]

b length of $\overline{BD}$ [4]

40 The vertices of $\triangle NYS$ are $N(-2,-1)$, $Y(0,10)$, and $S(10,5)$. The coordinates of point T are $(4,2)$.

a Prove that $\overline{YT}$ is a median.   [2]

b Prove that $\overline{YT}$ is an altitude.   [4]

c Find the area of $\triangle NYS$.   [4]

Part III

Answer *one* question from this part. Clearly indicate the necessary steps, including appropriate formula substitutions, diagrams, graphs, charts, etc. Calculations that may be obtained by mental arithmetic or the calculator do not need to be shown. [10]

41 Given: $\angle 1 \cong \angle 2$ and $\overline{DB} \perp \overline{AC}$.

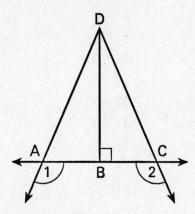

Prove: $\triangle ABD \cong \triangle CBD$ [10]

42 Given: $\sim G \rightarrow F$
              $\sim(E \wedge F)$
              $\sim E \rightarrow \sim D$
              A
              $(B \wedge C) \rightarrow D$
              $A \rightarrow (B \wedge C)$

    Prove: G [10]

ANSWERS AND EXPLANATIONS
JUNE 1996
ANSWER KEY

Part I

1. 11
2. 53
3. 6
4. 15
5. 35
6. 1
7. 8
8. 12
9. $\overline{AC}$
10. 110
11. –3
12. 3

13. 20
14. $\dfrac{x}{2}$
15. 5
16. 4
17. (2)
18. (3)
19. (3)
20. (4)
21. (3)
22. (2)
23. (4)
24. (2)

25. (1)
26. (3)
27. (2)
28. (1)
29. (2)
30. (1)
31. (4)
32. (4)
33. (4)
34. (1)
35. (1)

Part II

36. *a* 101
    b 0.618
    c $\pm 2\sqrt{3}$
37. *a* see explanations
    b $A'(-1, 0), B'(-7, -4),$
       $C'(-5, -7)$
    c $A''(0, 5), B''(-6, 1),$
       $C''(-4, -2)$
    d $y = \dfrac{2}{3}x + 5$

38. (2,–3) and (6,5)
39. *a* 39.7
    b 8.4
40. *a* see explanations
    b see explanations
    c 60

Part III

41. see explanations
42. see explanations

EXPLANATIONS
Part I

1. 11

Don't let the symbols freak you out. This function question defines what the little sun symbol means, so all you have to do is plug in $a = 5$ and $b = 7$:

$$a \odot b = a^2 - 2b$$
$$5 \odot 7 = 5^2 - 2(7) = 25 - 14 = 11$$

2. 53

Use the "inverse tangent" button on your calculator. (It usually says "$\tan^{-1}$" and involves the "second function" button.) Type 1.34 into your calculator and press "$\tan^{-1}$." You should get 53.267. When you round this off to the nearest degree, as instructed, you get 53°.

3. 6

The identity element of a system is the one that never changes any of the characters in the original row. Look at the diagram below:

★	2	4	6	8
2	4	8	2	6
4	8	6	4	2
6	2	4	6	8
8	6	2	8	4

The row of numbers at the top of the chart is identical to the row that lines up with the number 6. (The same is true about the column headed by the 6.) Therefore, 6 is the identity element.

4. 15

The first thing to realize is that $\triangle ABC$ and $\triangle ADE$ are similar. This is true because $\overline{DE}$ is parallel to $\overline{BC}$; there are two pairs of corresponding angles: $\angle ADE$ and $\angle ABC$, and $\angle AED$ and $\angle ACB$:

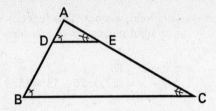

The two triangles are similar because of the Angle-Angle Rule of Similarity.

Corresponding sides of the two triangles are proportional. Set up the following proportion:

$$\frac{AD}{AB} = \frac{AE}{AC}$$
$$\frac{10}{24} = \frac{AE}{36}$$

Cross-multiply, and you're done:

$$24 \bullet (AE) = 36 \bullet 10$$
$$24(AE) = 360$$
$$AE = 15$$

5. 35

You should recognize this term as a calculation involving the Combinations Formula, which looks like this:

$$_nC_r$$

To find the value of $_7C_3$, plug in $n = 7$ and $r = 3$:

$$_7C_3 = \frac{7!}{3!\,4!} = \frac{7 \bullet 6 \bullet 5 \bullet 4 \bullet 3 \bullet 2 \bullet 1}{3 \bullet 2 \bullet 1 \bullet (4 \bullet 3 \bullet 2 \bullet 1)}$$
$$= \frac{7 \bullet 6 \bullet 5}{3 \bullet 2 \bullet 1} = \frac{210}{6} = 35$$

6. 1

Since 2 is a root of the equation, you can plug in 2 for x to determine the value of k:

$$x^2 + kx = 6$$
$$(2)^2 + k(2) = 6$$
$$4 + 2k = 6$$
$$2k = 2$$
$$k = 1$$

7. 8

Whenever two fractions are equal to each other, you can cross-multiply:

$$\frac{16}{y} = \frac{y}{4}$$
$$y(y) = 16 \bullet 4$$
$$y^2 = 64$$
$$y = \{8, -8\}$$

Since they only want the positive root, toss out −8. To check your work, plug 8 back into the equation and make sure it works.

8. 12

The formula to follow is a variation of the permutations rule. To find the number of possible arrangements of the letters in a word with n letters, in which one letter appears p times (remember that p is greater than 1), the formula looks like this:

$$\frac{n!}{p!}$$

NINE has 4 letters, but there are two N's. Therefore, you can express the number of arrangements as:

$$\frac{4!}{2!} = \frac{4 \bullet 3 \bullet 2 \bullet 1}{2 \bullet 1} = 4 \bullet 3 = 12$$

9. $\overline{AC}$

You can combine the two inequalities in the question like this:

$$m\angle B > m\angle C > m\angle A$$

From this, you can tell that $\angle B$ is the biggest angle in the triangle, which might look something like this:

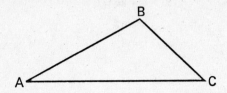

Since $\angle B$ is the biggest angle, the side opposite $\angle B$, or side $\overline{AC}$, is the biggest side.

10. 110

It's important to note two things here: (1) the diagonals of a rhombus bisect the angles from which they're drawn, and (2) opposite sides of a rhombus are parallel. Since $\overline{AC}$ is a diagonal, it bisects $\angle DAB$. Therefore, m$\angle DAC$ = 35.

Since $\overline{DC}$ is parallel to $\overline{AB}$, $\angle DCA$ and $\angle CAB$ are alternate interior angles—which always have the same measure. Therefore, m$\angle DCA$ = 35.

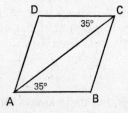

Now use the Rule of 180 to solve for the measure of $\angle ADC$:

$$m\angle ADC + m\angle DCA + m\angle CAD = 180$$
$$m\angle ADC + 35 + 35 = 180$$
$$m\angle ADC = 110$$

11. −3

Put the equation into $y = mx + b$ format, and you'll be able to figure out the slope of the line (the m) right away.

$$3x + y = 4$$
$$y = -3x + 4$$

The slope of this line is −3 (and the y-intercept, in case you were wondering, is 4).

12. 3

If you don't recognize the equation of a circle in the question, the phrase "locus of points at a given distance . . . from the origin" should have given you a hint. The distance, d, represents the radius of the circle. Since the equation of a circle centered at the origin is $x^2 + y^2 = r^2$ (in which r is the radius), $r^2 = 9$. Although r could equal 3 or −3, you're looking for a distance, which can't be negative. Therefore, $d = 3$.

13. 20

Plot your points on the coordinate axes like this:

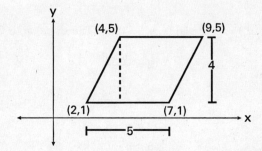

The formula for the area of a parallelogram is bh, in which b is the base and h is the perpendicular height. The base equals the distance between (2,1) and (7,1), or 5 units. (Don't bother with the distance formula here; just count the boxes on the graph paper.) The height of the parallelogram is 4 units (see diagram). The area equals 5 × 4, or 20 square units.

14. $\dfrac{x}{2}$

You can't do anything until the two fractions have the same denominator, which is the lowest common denominator (LCD) of 6 and 3. The LCD is 6, so you don't have to do anything to the first fraction. To make the second fraction compatible, multiply both the top and bottom by 2:

$$\frac{x(2)}{3(2)} = \frac{2x}{6}$$

Now you can subtract the fractions and reduce:

$$\frac{5x}{6} - \frac{2x}{6} = \frac{3x}{6}$$

$$\frac{3x}{6} = \frac{x}{2}$$

15. 5

This question gives you all but one component of the slope formula, so use it to figure out the value of y. The slope formula is:

$$m = \frac{y_2 - y_1}{x_2 - x_1}$$

Let $(x_1, y_1) = (1,3)$ and $(x_2, y_2) = (2,y)$. The slope, m, is 2:

$$2 = \frac{y - 3}{2 - 1}$$

$$2 = \frac{y - 3}{1}$$

$$2 = y - 3$$

$$5 = y$$

Check your work by plugging 5 back into the original equation.

16. 4

The diagonal of a square bisects the square into two 45:45:90 triangles. Since the ratio of the sides of a 45:45:90 triangle is $1:1:\sqrt{2}$, the legs of the triangle (which are also the sides of the square) must be 4 units long.

If you never studied 45:45:90 triangles (or you forgot the ratio), there's another way to solve this:

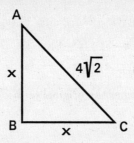

Diagonal $\overline{AC}$ is the hypotenuse of $\triangle ABC$. Since the sides of a square have equal length, $AB = BC$. Label each of these x, then use the Pythagorean Theorem:

$$(AB)^2 + (BC)^2 = (AC)^2$$
$$x^2 + x^2 = (4\sqrt{2})^2$$
$$2x^2 = 32$$
$$x^2 = 16$$
$$x = \{4, -4\}$$

Since all distances are positive, toss out −4.

Multiple Choice

17. (2)

First, factor out an x:

$$x^3 - 9x = x(x^2 - 9)$$

This doesn't match any of the answer choices, so keep going. The term $x^2 - 9$ is a difference of squares:

$$(x^2 - 9) = (x + 3)(x - 3)$$

The complete factorization looks like this:

$$x(x^2 - 9) = x(x + 3)(x - 3)$$

Note: You're in Process Of Elimination country now. One of the best ways to arrive at the right answer is to prove the others wrong.

Combine the terms in each of the other answer choices and see what you get:

(1) $x(x - 3) = x^2 - 3x$

(3) $(x + 3)(x - 3) = (x^2 - 9)$

(4) $x(x + 3) = x^2 + 3x$

None of these matches the original term $x^3 - 9x$, so cross 'em off.

18. (3)

The formula for a circle with center (h,k) and radius r is:

$$(x - h)^2 + (y - k)^2 = r^2$$

The key to the rest of this question is remembering the minus signs in the formula above. If you substitute $(-2,k)$ for (h,k) in the formula, you get:

$$[x - (-2)]^2 + (y - k)^2 = 25$$
$$(x + 2)^2 + (y - k)^2 = 25$$

When you compare this equation to the one in the problem, k must equal 3.

19. (3)

Once you determine the value of y, the rest of the problem falls into place. Since $\angle BCA$ and $\angle ACD$ are supplementary, their sum must be 180:

$$6y + 3y = 180$$
$$9y = 180$$
$$y = 20$$

Now you know that m$\angle BCA = 6 \cdot 20$, or $120°$, and m$\angle B = 2 \cdot 20$, or $40°$.

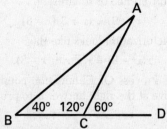

Use the Rule of 180:
$$m\angle A + m\angle B + m\angle BCA = 180$$
$$m\angle A + 40 + 120 = 180$$
$$m\angle A = 20$$

20. (4)

The median of a triangle connects a vertex to the midpoint of the side opposite that vertex. The median from vertex A, therefore, connects point A to the midpoint of $\overline{BC}$.

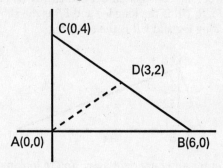

You can find the midpoint by using the midpoint formula:

$$(\bar{x}, \bar{y}) = \left(\frac{x_1 + x_2}{2}, \frac{y_1 + y_2}{2} \right)$$

Let $(x_1, y_1) = B(6,0)$ and $(x_2, y_2) = C(0,4)$:

$$(\bar{x}, \bar{y}) = \left(\frac{6+0}{2}, \frac{0+4}{2} \right) = \left(\frac{6}{2}, \frac{4}{2} \right) = (3,2)$$

21. (3)

Whenever you see the negation of a logic statement in parentheses, think of De Morgan's Laws.

$$\sim(a \wedge b) \rightarrow \sim a \vee \sim b$$

This basically means that when you negate a parenthetical statement with a "$\wedge$" or "$\vee$" in it, negate each symbol and turn the symbol upside down:

$$\sim(\sim m \wedge n) \rightarrow \sim(\sim m) \vee \sim n$$

Since $\sim(\sim m)$ is the same thing as m (because of the rule of double negation), you can rewrite the statement as: $m \vee \sim n$.

22. (2)

In order to find the image of a point (x,y) after a translation that maps it onto its image $(x - 2, y + 3)$, subtract 2 from the x-coordinate and add 3 to the y-coordinate. Under this translation, the point $(7,2)$ would be mapped onto point $(7 - 2, 2 + 3)$, or $(5,5)$.

23. (4)

This figure represents three similar right triangles (*FUR*, *URN*, and *FUN*), and all their corresponding sides are proportional to each other. For this problem, consider $\triangle FUR$ and $\triangle URN$ and set up a proportion. In $\triangle FUR$, *UR* is the long leg and *FR* is the short leg; in $\triangle URN$, *RN* is the long leg and *UR* is the short leg.

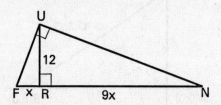

You can't enter numbers right away. You're looking for *FR*, so label it x. The ratio of *FR* to *RN* is 1:9, so the length of *RN* is $9x$. Now you can set up the proportion:

$$\frac{FR}{UR} = \frac{UR}{RN}$$

$$\frac{x}{12} = \frac{12}{9x}$$

When you cross-multiply, you'll get:

$$9x(x) = 12 \bullet 12$$
$$9x^2 = 144$$
$$x^2 = 16$$
$$x = \{4, -4\}$$

Since you're looking for a distance, which can't be a negative value, eliminate -4.

24. **(2)**

When two lines are perpendicular, their slopes are negative reciprocals. That is, their product is –1. Therefore, if line l has a slope of $\frac{3}{5}$, the slope of line m is the negative reciprocal of $\frac{3}{5}$, or $-\frac{5}{3}$.

25. **(1)**

Consider the angles of $\triangle ECD$ to figure out this one. Start with $\angle ECD$, which is supplementary to $\angle ECA$. Since m$\angle ECA = 65$, it must be true that m$\angle ECD = 115$. Further, $\angle FEB$ and $\angle CED$ are vertical angles, so they have the same measure, 25°.

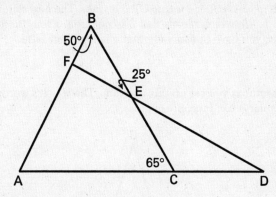

Use the Rule of 180 to determine m$\angle D$:

$$\text{m}\angle ECD + \text{m}\angle CED + \text{m}\angle D = 180$$
$$115 + 25 + \text{m}\angle D = 180$$
$$\text{m}\angle D = 40$$

26. **(3)**

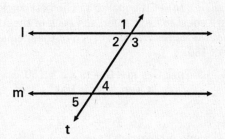

In this diagram, $\angle 1$ and $\angle 2$ are supplementary, so m $\angle 1$ + m $\angle 2$ = 180. Similarly, $\angle 2$ and $\angle 3$ are supplementary, so m $\angle 2$ + m $\angle 3$ = 180. Using the transitive property of addition, you can prove that m$\angle 1$ + m$\angle 2$ = m$\angle 2$ + m$\angle 3$; both quantities equal 180, so they must be equal to each other.

Process Of Elimination can help you eliminate the other choices rather easily.

27. (2)

Answer choice (2) has the problem. You're given the expression $a \vee b$, which means "either a is true OR b is true." The next statement you're given is $\sim b$, which means that b is not true. From these two statements, you have to conclude that a is true, not false.

28. (1)

Be careful as you set up this diagram. The way it's worded (and the vocabulary) can be confusing:

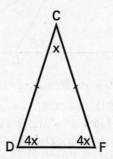

You want the measure of the vertex angle (which is $\angle C$, at the top of the triangle), so set it equal to x. The base angles of an isosceles triangle are equal to each other, and each of them is four times the measure of the vertex angle; set each of them equal to $4x$. Now use the Rule of 180:

$$\text{m}\angle C + \text{m}\angle D + \text{m}\angle F = 180$$
$$x + 4x + 4x = 180$$
$$9x = 180$$
$$x = 20$$

The vertex angle measures 20°, and each of the base angles measures 4 • 20, or 80°

29. (2)

After a reflection in the line $y = x$, the x- and y-coordinates are interchanged. In other words, $r_{y = x}(x,y) \rightarrow (y,x)$. The image of point $R(-4,3)$ is $R'(3,-4)$.

30. (1)

The locus of points that are equidistant from two points A and B is another name for the perpendicular bisector of $\overline{AB}$. The line $y = 4$ is horizontal and passes through the point $(0,4)$. If you plot each pair of points on the same coordinate axes, you'll see that the line is equidistant from points $(0,0)$ and $(0,8)$:

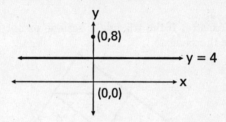

31. (4)

Make your diagram look something like this, and be sure to make $\overline{BD}$ *smaller* than $\overline{DC}$:

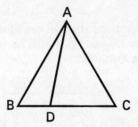

You can't be sure of the exact length of $\overline{AD}$, but any line segment drawn within $\triangle ABC$ has to be shorter than a side of the triangle. Therefore, it must be true that AC is greater than AD.

32. (4)

When a parabola appears in the form $y = ax^2 + bx + c$, the equation of its axis of symmetry is:

$$x = -\frac{b}{2a}$$

For this parabola, $a = 2$, $b = 7$, and $c = -5$. Thus the axis of symmetry is:

$$x = -\frac{-7}{2(2)} = -\frac{7}{4}$$

The equation for the line is $x = -\frac{7}{4}$.

33. (4)

It doesn't matter if the triangle is scalene or not. The answer will always be the same:

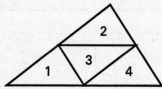

When you connect the midpoints of the sides of *any* triangle, you'll cut the triangle into four smaller congruent triangles.

34. (1)

No matter how hard you try, you can't factor the equation. (Cross off answer choices (3) and (4), which assume you can.) You have to use the Quadratic Formula:

$$x = \frac{-b \pm \sqrt{b^2 - 4ac}}{2a}$$

In the equation $2x^2 - 7x + 4 = 0$, $a = 2$, $b = -7$, and $c = 4$:

$$x = \frac{-(-7) \pm \sqrt{(-7)^2 - 4(2)(4)}}{2(2)} = \frac{7 \pm \sqrt{49 - 32}}{4} = \frac{7 \pm \sqrt{17}}{4}$$

35. (1)

The hint for this one is the information that $\overline{SR} \perp \overline{QR}$ and $\overline{ST} \perp \overline{QT}$·

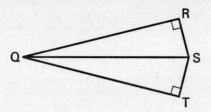

The fact that $\triangle QRS$ and $\triangle QTS$ are right triangles should get you thinking about Hypotenuse-Leg. $\overline{RS}$ and $\overline{ST}$ are congruent corresponding legs; $\overline{QS}$ is the hypotenuse of each triangle; and $QS = QS$ because of the Reflexive Property of Equality.

You can prove that the two triangles are congruent by using Hypotenuse-Leg.

Part II

36. *a* 101

Plug in 1.02 for x, and keep your calculator handy:

$$\frac{(1.02 + 1)^2}{(1.02)^2 - 1} = \frac{(2.02)^2}{(1.02)^2 - 1} = \frac{4.0804}{1.0404 - 1} = \frac{4.0804}{0.0404} = 101$$

Note: You can also make this problem a lot simpler by factoring the denominator to reduce

$$\frac{(x + 1)^2}{x^2 - 1} \quad \text{to} \quad \frac{x + 1}{x - 1}$$

***b*   0.618**

Whenever two fractions are equal to each other, you can cross-multiply:

$$\frac{1}{x} = \frac{x + 1}{1}$$
$$x(x + 1) = 1 \cdot 1$$
$$x^2 + x = 1$$
$$x^2 + x - 1 = 0$$

You can't factor the equation (the fact that your answer has to be rounded to nearest hundredth should be a clue), so you have to use the Quadratic Formula:

$$x = \frac{-b \pm \sqrt{b^2 - 4ac}}{2a}$$

In the equation $x^2 + x - 1 = 0$, $a = 1$, $b = 1$, and $c = -1$:

$$x = \frac{-1 \pm \sqrt{(1)^2 - 4(1)(-1)}}{2(1)} = \frac{-1 \pm \sqrt{1 + 4}}{2} = \frac{-1 + \sqrt{5}}{2}, \frac{-1 - \sqrt{5}}{2}$$

Use your calculator to determine that $\sqrt{5} = 2.2361$, and plug that into the two terms:

$$x = \frac{-1 + 2.2361}{2} \qquad\qquad x = \frac{-1 - 2.2361}{2}$$

$$= \frac{1.2361}{2} \qquad\qquad\qquad = \frac{-3.2361}{2}$$

$$= 0.61805 \qquad\qquad\qquad = -1.61805$$

The positive root is 0.61801, which rounds to 0.618.

c $x = \left\{ 2\sqrt{3}, -2\sqrt{3} \right\}$

Here are two more fractions to cross-multiply:

$$\frac{x + 2}{4} = \frac{2}{x - 2}$$
$$(x + 2)(x - 2) = 4 \bullet 2$$
$$x^2 - 4 = 8$$
$$x^2 = 12$$
$$x = \sqrt{12}, -\sqrt{12}$$

To reduce the radical, factor out a perfect square:

$$\sqrt{12} = \sqrt{4 \bullet 3} = \sqrt{4} \bullet \sqrt{3} = 2\sqrt{3}$$

They want *all* possible values of x, so don't forget to include the negative value.

37. *a*

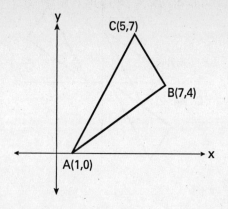

b **A′(−1,0), B′(−7,−4), C′(−5,−7)**

After a reflection in the origin, the *x*- and *y*-coordinates are both negated. In other words, $r_{(0,0)} (x,y) \rightarrow (-x,-y)$. Your diagram should look like this:

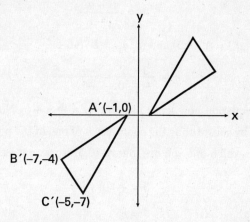

c **A″(0,5), B″(−6,1), C″(−4,−2)**

To find the images of the three points under the translation $(x + 1, y + 5)$, add 1 to each of the *x*-coordinates and add 5 to each of the *y*-coordinates. Now, your diagram should look like this:

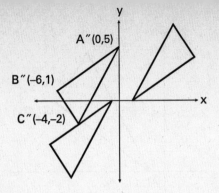

A″(0,5)

B″(−6,1)

C″(−4,−2)

y

x

d $y = \dfrac{2}{3}x + 5$

Your goal is to find the slope (represented by m) and the y-intercept (the b) and plug them into the form $y = mx + b$. Find the slope of $\overline{A''B''}$ using the slope formula:

$$m = \frac{y_2 - y_1}{x_2 - x_1}$$

Let $(x_1, y_1) = A''(0,5)$ and $(x_2, y_2) = B''(-6,1)$:

$$m = \frac{1 - 5}{-6 - 0} = \frac{-4}{-6} = \frac{2}{3}$$

Your equation now looks like this: $y = \dfrac{2}{3}x + b$. Now you have to find b by substituting the coordinates of one of the points. It doesn't matter which one you use, but $A''(0,5)$ works out easier:

$$5 = \frac{2}{3}(0) + b$$

$$5 = b$$

Note: If you realize that $(0,5)$ is the y-intercept of the line, you can recognize that $b = 5$.

The equation now reads: $y = \dfrac{2}{3}x + 5$.

38. **(2,–3) and (6,5)**

Algebraic Method

If you choose to do this algebraically, put the second equation into $y = mx + b$ form by subtracting 7 from both sides:

$$y + 7 = 2x$$
$$y = 2x - 7$$

Now you have two separate equations that are equal to y. Therefore, you can set them equal to each other:

$$x^2 - 6x + 5 = 2x - 7$$
$$x^2 - 8x + 5 = -7$$
$$x^2 - 8x + 12 = 0$$

Factor the trinomial and set each of the factors equal to zero:

$$(x - 6)(x - 2) = 0$$
$$x = \{6, 2\}$$

If $x = 6$, then $y = (6)^2 - 6(6) + 5$, or 5. One point of intersection is (6,5).

If $x = 2$, then $y = (2)^2 - 6(2) + 5$, or –3. The other point of intersection is (2,–3).

Graphing Method

If you choose to graph the two equations, you may want to find the axis of symmetry of the parabola before you make your T-chart. The formula for the axis of symmetry is:

$$x = -\frac{b}{2a}$$

In the parabola $y = x^2 - 6x + 5$, $a = 1$, $b = -6$, and $c = 5$:

$$x = -\frac{-6}{2(1)} = \frac{6}{2} = 3$$

The axis of symmetry is $x = 3$, so choose three x-coordinates to the left of 3 (0, 1, and 2) and three to the right of 3 (4, 5, and 6). Plug each one in for x in the equation to find the y-coordinate for each point. For example, if $x = 0$, then $y = (0)^2 - 6(0) + 5$, or 5. The coordinate pair is (0,5). The remaining points are below. Use some of the same x-coordinates when you graph the line $y = 2x - 7$ on the same set of axes. The graphs look like this:

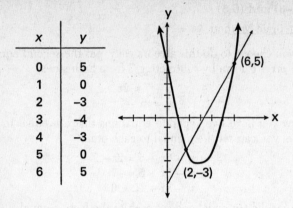

x	y
0	5
1	0
2	-3
3	-4
4	-3
5	0
6	5

The points of intersection are marked.

Note: Be sure to check the points by plugging them back into the system. Otherwise you'll lose 2 points.

39. *a* 39.7

Before you get started, it's important to note that the diagonals of a rhombus (*a*) bisect each other, and (*b*) are perpendicular.

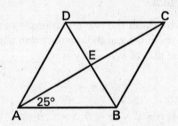

Therefore, $\triangle AED$ is a right triangle, and AE equals half the length of diagonal $\overline{AC}$ (or 9). To find the perimeter of the rhombus, you can find the length of one side and multiply it by 4 (because a rhombus has four equal sides). You know the length of the leg adjacent to $\angle EAB$, and you want to find the length of the hypotenuse $\overline{AB}$. Therefore, it's time to trig; use cosine (the CAH in SOHCAHTOA):

$$\text{cosine} = \frac{\text{adjacent}}{\text{hypotenuse}}$$

$$\cos \angle EAB = \frac{EA}{AB}$$

$$\cos 25° = \frac{9}{AB}$$

Since the cosine of 25° is 0.9063, enter that into the equation and cross-multiply:

$$0.9063 = \frac{9}{AB}$$

$$AB(0.9063) = 9$$

$$AB = \frac{9}{0.9063}$$

$$AB = 9.93$$

Multiply this value by 4 and you get 39.72, which becomes 39.7 when you round it off to the nearest tenth.

b   8.4

You could use trig here, but you don't have to. Instead, focus on right triangle ABE; you can find EB using the Pythagorean Theorem:

$$(AE)^2 + (EB)^2 = (AB)^2$$
$$9^2 + (EB)^2 = (9.93)^2$$
$$81 + (EB)^2 = 98.6$$
$$(EB)^2 = 17.6$$
$$EB = 4.19$$

Multiply this by 2 (because $\overline{BD}$ is twice as long as $\overline{EB}$), and you get 8.38. This rounds to 8.4.

40. a

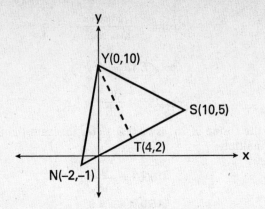

A median of a triangle is a line segment drawn from one vertex to the midpoint of the side opposite that vertex. To prove that $\overline{YT}$ is a median, you have to show that $T(4,2)$ is the midpoint of $\overline{NS}$ using the midpoint formula:

$$(\overline{x}, \overline{y}) = \left(\frac{x_1 + x_2}{2}, \frac{y_1 + y_2}{2} \right)$$

Let $(x_1, y_1) = N(-2, -1)$ and $(x_2, y_2) = S(10, 5)$:

$$(\overline{x}, \overline{y}) = \left(\frac{-2 + 10}{2}, \frac{-1 + 5}{2} \right) = \left(\frac{8}{2}, \frac{4}{2} \right) = (4, 2)$$

b

An altitude of a triangle is a line segment drawn from one vertex perpendicular to the side opposite that vertex. To prove that $\overline{YT}$ is an altitude, you have to find the slopes of $\overline{YT}$ and $\overline{NS}$ and show that the two slopes are negative reciprocals (that is, the product of their slopes equals -1). Use the slope formula:

$$m = \frac{y_2 - y_1}{x_2 - x_1}$$

To find the slope of $\overline{YT}$, let $(x_1, y_1) = Y(0,10)$ and $(x_2, y_2) = T(4,2)$. To find the slope of $\overline{NS}$, let $(x_1, y_1) = N(-2,-1)$ and $(x_2, y_2) = S(10,5)$:

Slope of $\overline{YT}$:

$$m = \frac{2 - 10}{4 - 0}$$

$$= \frac{-8}{4} = -2$$

Slope of $\overline{NS}$:

$$m = \frac{5 - (-1)}{10 - (-2)}$$

$$= \frac{6}{12} = \frac{1}{2}$$

Since $-2 \cdot \dfrac{1}{2} = -1$, the two segments are perpendicular, and $\overline{YT}$ is an altitude.

c   60

The best way to determine the area of $\triangle NYS$ is to work indirectly. First, circumscribe a rectangle on the triangle in the diagram, like so:

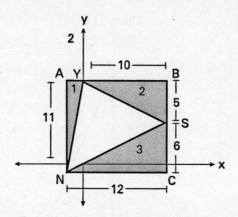

Triangle NYS is now surrounded by three other triangles within the rectangle. If you subtract their combined area from the area of the rectangle, the result will be the area of $\triangle NYS$.

The area of rectangle $ABCN$ is $12 \cdot 11$, or 132 square units. Now, calculate the area of the three outer triangles, using the formula $A = \frac{1}{2}bh$:

Triangle 1: $A = \frac{1}{2}(11)(2) = 11$

Triangle 2: $A = \frac{1}{2}(10)(5) = 25$

Triangle 3: $A = \frac{1}{2}(6)(12) = 36$

Total area of three triangles: $11 + 25 + 36 = 72$.

Subtract 72 from the rectangle's area (132), and you're left with 60 square units.

Part III

41.

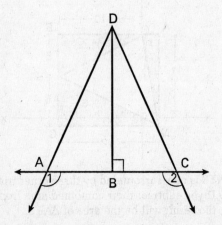

Prove: $\triangle ABD \cong \triangle CBD$

The plan: They've given you information about two angles, and the two triangles share a side. Use AAS.

Statements	Reasons
1. $m\angle 1 = m\angle 2$	1. Given
2. $\angle 1$ is supplementary to $\angle DAB$; $\angle 2$ is supplementary to $\angle DCB$.	2. Definition of supplementary angles
3. $\angle DAB \cong \angle DCB$	3. Angles that are supplementary to congruent angles are congruent.
4. $\overline{DB} \perp \overline{AC}$	4. Given
5. $\angle ABD$ and $\angle CBD$ are right angles.	5. Definition of perpendicular lines
6. $\angle ABD \cong \angle CBD$	6. All right angles are congruent.
7. $\overline{DB} \cong \overline{DB}$	7. Reflexive Property of Congruence
8. $\triangle ABD \cong \triangle CBD$	8. AAS $\cong$ AAS

42.

Here's the proof. Notice that the letters in the statements proceed alphabetically (more or less).

Statements	Reasons
1. $A \rightarrow (B \wedge C)$; $(B \wedge C) \rightarrow D$	1. Given
2. $A \rightarrow D$	2. Chain Rule (1)
3. A	3. Given
4. D	4. Law of Detachment (2, 3)
5. $\sim E \rightarrow \sim D$	5. Given
6. E	6. Law of *Modus Tollens* (4, 5)
7. $\sim(E \wedge F)$	7. Given
8. $\sim E \vee \sim F$	8. De Morgan's Laws
9. $\sim F$	9. Law of Disjunctive Inference (6, 8)
10. $\sim G \rightarrow F$	10. Given
11. G	11. Law of *Modus Tollens* (9, 10)

EXAMINATION
AUGUST 1996

Part I

Answer 30 questions from this part. Each correct answer will receive 2 credits. No partial credit will be allowed. Write your answers in the spaces provided on the separate answer sheet. Where applicable, answers may be left in terms of π or in radical form. [60]

1 The table below defines the operation • for the set $F = \{1, -1, y, -y\}$. What is the value of $(-1) \cdot y$?

×	1	−1	y	$-y$
1	1	−1	y	$-y$
−1	−1	1	$-y$	y
y	y	$-y$	−1	1
$-y$	$-y$	y	1	−1

2 In the accompanying diagram, $\overline{OA} \perp \overline{OB}$ and $\overline{OD} \perp \overline{OC}$. If m$\angle 3 = 39$, what is m$\angle 1$?

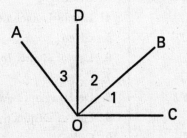

3 Solve for x: $\dfrac{x-2}{2} = \dfrac{x-1}{3}$

4 In rectangle $ABCD$, diagonal $AC = 20$ and segment $\overline{EF}$ joins the midpoints of $\overline{AB}$ and $\overline{BC}$, respectively. Find the length of $\overline{EF}$.

5 What is the total number of points equidistant from two intersecting lines and two centimeters from the point of intersection?

6 In $\triangle ABC$, $m\angle A = 40$ and the measure of an exterior angle B is $120°$. Which side is the longest in $\triangle ABC$?

7 What is the negative root of the equation $x^2 - x - 2 = 0$?

8 In the accompanying diagram of $\triangle ABC$, $\overline{DE} \parallel \overline{BC}$, $AD = 3$, $AB = 9$, and $AE = 5$. Find EC.

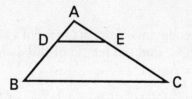

9 What is the image of $(-2,5)$ after a reflection in the x-axis?

10 In rhombus $ABCD$, $AB = 2x - 2$ and $BC = x + 8$. Find the length of $\overline{BC}$.

11 Express $\dfrac{x+2}{3} + \dfrac{x-3}{4}$ as a single fraction in simplest form.

12 In the accompanying diagram, $\overleftrightarrow{AB}$ is parallel to $\overleftrightarrow{CD}$, AED is a transversal, and $\overline{CE}$ is drawn. If $m\angle CED = 60$, $m\angle DAB = 2x$, and $m\angle DCE = 3x$, find x.

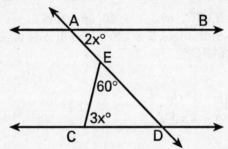

13 Find the area of a triangle whose vertices are $(-2,0)$, $(-2,6)$, and $(5,0)$.

14 If the endpoints of the diameter of a circle are $(3,1)$ and $(6,5)$, find the length of the diameter.

15 The coordinates of the midpoint of line segment $\overline{AB}$ are $(-2,4)$. If the coordinates of point A are $(7,10)$, find the coordinates of point B.

16 The sides of a triangle measure 5, 9, and 10. Find the perimeter of a similar triangle whose longest side measures 15.

Directions (17–34): For *each* question chosen, write the *numeral* preceding the word or expression that best completes the statement or answers the question.

17 The coordinates of point (x,y) after a reflection in the origin can be represented by

(1) (x,y) (3) $(x,-y)$
(2) $(-x,y)$ (4) $(-x,-y)$

18 If the length of the hypotenuse of a right triangle is 4 and the length of one leg is 2, what is the length of the other leg?

(1) 12   (3) $\sqrt{12}$
(2) 20   (4) $\sqrt{20}$

19 Which equation represents the line whose slope is –2 and that passes through point (0,3)?

(1) $y = -2x + 3$ (3) $y = 3x - 2$
(2) $y = -2x - 3$ (4) $y = 2x + 3$

20 If the lengths of two sides of a triangle are 4 and 8, the length of the third side may *not* be

(1) 5   (3) 7
(2) 6   (4) 4

21 What is the length of an altitude of an equilateral triangle whose side measures 6?

(1) $3\sqrt{2}$ (3) 3
(2) $3\sqrt{3}$ (4) $6\sqrt{3}$

22 What is the slope of a line parallel to the line whose equation is $y = 5x + 4$?

(1) $-\dfrac{4}{5}$ (3) 5

(2) $-\dfrac{5}{4}$ (4) 4

23 What is the contrapositive of $c \rightarrow (d \vee e)$?

(1) $\sim c \rightarrow \sim(d \vee e)$ (3) $\sim(d \vee e) \rightarrow \sim c$

(2) $c \rightarrow \sim(d \vee e)$ (4) $(d \vee e) \rightarrow c$

24 What is an equation of the circle whose center is $(-3,1)$ and whose radius is 10?

(1) $(x + 3)^2 + (y - 1)^2 = 10$
(2) $(x + 3)^2 + (y - 1)^2 = 100$
(3) $(x - 3)^2 + (y + 1)^2 = 10$
(4) $(x - 3)^2 + (y + 1)^2 = 100$

25 Given three premises: $A \rightarrow \sim C$, $\sim C \rightarrow R$, and $\sim R$. Which conclusion *must* be true?

(1) R (3) $A \wedge C$

(2) $\sim C$ (4) $\sim A$

26 In $\triangle ABC$, $m\angle A = 41$ and $m\angle B = 48$. What kind of triangle is $\triangle ABC$?

(1) right   (3) isosceles

(2) obtuse   (4) acute

27 If the altitude is drawn to the hypotenuse of a right triangle, then the two triangles formed are *always*

(1) congruent   (3) isosceles

(2) equal   (4) similar

28 The number of sides of a regular polygon whose interior angles each measure 108° is
(1) 5   (3) 7
(2) 6   (4) 4

29 Two triangles have altitudes of equal length. If the areas of these triangles have the ratio 3:4, then the bases of these triangles have the ratio

(1) 3:4   (3) $\sqrt{3}$:2

(2) 9:16   (4) $\dfrac{3}{2}$:2

30 In isosceles triangle ABC, $AC = BC = 20$, $m\angle A = 68$, and $\overline{CD}$ is the altitude to side $\overline{AB}$. What is the length of $\overline{CD}$ to the *nearest tenth*?
(1) 49.5   (3) 10.6
(2) 18.5   (4) 7.5

31 If quadrilateral $ABCD$ is a parallelogram, which statement must be true?

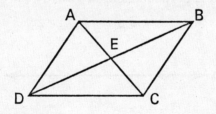

(1) $\overline{AC} \perp \overline{BD}$

(2) $\overline{AC} \cong \overline{BD}$

(3) $\overline{AC}$ bisects $\angle DAB$ and $\angle BCD$.

(4) $\overline{AC}$ and $\overline{BD}$ bisect each other.

32 How many different seven-letter arrangements can be formed from the letters in the word "GENESIS"?

(1) 210   (3) 1260

(2) 840   (4) 5040

33 What is the turning point of the graph of the function $y = x^2 - 6x + 2$?

(1) (3,−7)   (3) (3,11)

(2) (−3,−7)   (4) (−3,11)

34 A biology class has eight students. How many different lab groups may be formed that will consist of three students?

(1) 56   (3) 33

(2) 366   (4) 67

Directions (35): Leave all construction lines on the answer sheet.

35 *On the answer sheet*, construct a line through point P that is perpendicular to $\overline{AB}$.

• P

A ◄────────────────────► B

Part II

Answer *three* questions from this part. Clearly indicate the necessary steps, including appropriate formula substitutions, diagrams, graphs, charts, etc. Calculations that may be obtained by mental arithmetic or the calculator do not need to be shown.   [30]

36 *a* On graph paper, draw the graph of the equation $y = 2x^2 - 4x - 3$ for all values of x in the interval $-2 \leq x \leq 4$.   [6]

   b On the same set of axes, draw the reflection of the graph of the equation $y = 2x^2 - 4x - 3$ in the y-axis.   [2]

   c What is the equation of the axis of symmetry of the graph in part *b*?   [2]

37 Solve the following system of equations algebraically and check.

$$x^2 + y^2 + 4x = 0$$
$$x^2 + y^2 + 4x$$
$$x + y = 0 \quad [8,2]$$

38 Given: $M \rightarrow N$

   $\sim M \rightarrow P$
   $(L \wedge N) \rightarrow R$
   $\sim R$
   L

Using the laws of inference, prove P.   [10]

39 Answer both *a* and *b* for all values of *x* for which these expressions are defined.

  a Solve for *x* to the nearest hundredth:

$$\frac{1}{x-1} = \frac{x+4}{5}$$ [6]

  b Simplify:

$$\frac{x^2-4}{x^2+4x+4} \bullet \frac{x^2+2x}{x^2}$$ [4]

40 In the accompanying diagram of rectangle *ABCD*, diagonal $\overline{AC}$ is drawn, *DE* = 8, $\overline{DE} \perp \overline{AC}$ and m∠*DAC* = 55. Find the area of rectangle *ABCD* to the *nearest integer*. [10]

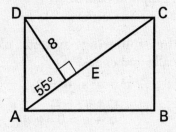

Part III

Answer *one* question from this part. Clearly indicate the necessary steps, including appropriate formula substitutions, diagrams, graphs, charts, etc. Calculations that may be obtained by mental arithmetic or the calculator do not need to be shown. [10]

41 Given parallelogram *DEBK*, $\overline{BC} \cong \overline{DA}$ and $\overline{DJ} \cong \overline{BL}$.

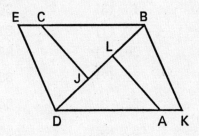

Prove: $\overline{CJ} \cong \overline{AL}$ [10]

42 Quadrilateral *ABCD* has coordinates *A*(0,−6), *B*(5,−1), *C*(3,3), and *D*(−1,1).

Using coordinate geometry, prove that

a at least two consecutive sides are not congruent. [5]

b the diagonals, $\overline{AC}$ and $\overline{BD}$, are perpendicular. [5]

ANSWERS AND EXPLANATIONS
AUGUST 1996
ANSWER KEY

Part I

1. $-y$
2. 39
3. 4
4. 10
5. 4
6. $\overline{AB}$
7. -1
8. 10
9. $(-2,-5)$
10. 18
11. $\dfrac{7x-1}{12}$
12. 24

13. 21
14. 5
15. $(-11,-2)$
16. 36
17. (4)
18. (3)
19. (1)
20. (4)
21. (2)
22. (3)
23. (3)
24. (2)

25. (4)
26. (2)
27. (4)
28. (1)
29. (1)
30. (2)
31. (4)
32. (3)
33. (1)
34. (1)
35. construction

Part II

36. a see explanations

   b see explanations

   c $x = -1$

37. $(0,0)$, $(-2,2)$

38. see explanations

39. a 1.85, -4.85

   b $\dfrac{x-2}{x}$

40. 136

Part III

41. see explanations

42. see explanations

EXPLANATIONS
Part I

1. $-y$

Find "−1" in the far left column, and run your finger along that row until you get to the column headed by "$-y$":

x	1	−1	y	−y
1	1	−1	y	−y
−1	−1	1	−y	y
y	y	−y	−1	1
−y	−y	y	1	−1

At this point of intersection, you'll find "$-y$." Therefore, the value of $(-1) \bullet y$ is $-y$.

2. **39**

Since $\overline{OA} \perp \overline{OB}$, $m\angle AOB = 90$ and $\angle 3$ is complementary to $\angle 2$. Using the same line of reasoning, you also know that $m\angle DOC = 90$ because $\overline{OD} \perp \overline{OC}$. Therefore, $\angle 1$ is complementary to $\angle 2$. If two angles are complementary to the same angle, they are congruent. Therefore, $m\angle 1 = m\angle 3 = 39°$.

3. **4**

Whenever two fractions are equal to each other, you can cross-multiply:

$$\frac{x-2}{2} = \frac{x-1}{3}$$
$$3(x-2) = 2(x-1)$$
$$3x - 6 = 2x - 2$$
$$3x = 2x + 4$$
$$x = 4$$

To check your math, plug 4 back into the equation and make sure it works.

4. 10

Draw your diagram first:

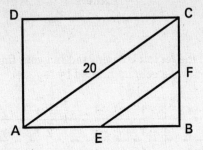

Focus your attention on △*ABC*. A segment that connects the midpoints of two sides of a triangle is half the length of the third side. *E* is the midpoint of $\overline{AB}$ and *F* is the midpoint of $\overline{BC}$, so *EF* must be half of *AC*. Since *AC* = 20, *EF* = 10.

5. 4

This problem can appear rather difficult at first glance. It requires a lot of visualization. Look at the intersecting lines first. These lines form two sets of vertical angles, and the locus of points equidistant from the two lines are the lines that bisect those vertical angles:

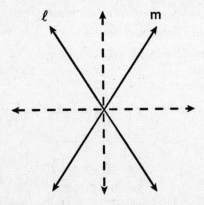

Now look at the point of intersection. The locus of points that are two centimeters from that point is a circle with a 2-centimeter radius:

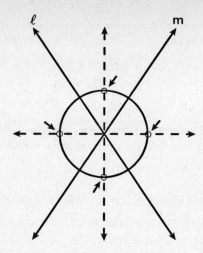

There are four points of intersection.

6. $\overline{AB}$

The triangle looks like this:

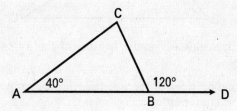

Since $\angle CBD$ is an exterior angle, it's supplementary to $\angle ABC$. Therefore, m$\angle ABC = 60$. Use the Rule of 180 to determine the measure of $\angle C$:

$$\text{m}\angle A + \text{m}\angle ABC + \text{m}\angle C = 180$$
$$40 + 60 + \text{m}\angle C = 180$$
$$\text{m}\angle C = 80$$

Since $\angle C$ is the largest angle in the triangle, the side opposite $\angle C$, or $\overline{AB}$, is the largest side.

7. –1

To find the roots of this trinomial, you have to factor it and set each factor equal to zero:

$$x^2 - x - 2 = 0$$
$$(x - 2)(x + 1) = 0$$
$$x = \{2, -1\}$$

They want the *negative* root, so get rid of the 2. To check your math, plug –1 back into the equation and make sure it works.

8. 10

The first thing to realize is that $\triangle ABC$ and $\triangle ADE$ are similar. This is true because $\overline{DE}$ is parallel to $\overline{BC}$; there are two pairs of corresponding angles: $\angle ADE$ and $\angle ABC$, and $\angle AED$ and $\angle ACB$:

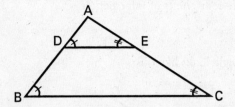

The two triangles are similar because of the Angle-Angle Rule of Similarity.

Corresponding sides of the two triangles are proportional. Set up the following proportion:

$$\frac{AD}{AB} = \frac{AE}{AC}$$
$$\frac{3}{9} = \frac{5}{AC}$$

Now cross-multiply:

$$3 \bullet (AC) = 9 \bullet 5$$
$$3(AC) = 45$$
$$AC = 15$$

Hold it. There's still a bit more work to do. You know that $AE = 5$ and $AC = 15$. Since $AC = AE + EC$, the length of $\overline{EC}$ is 10.

9. (–2,–5)

After a reflection in the x-axis, the x-coordinate remains the same and the y-coordinate is negated. In other words, $r_{x\text{-axis}}\ (x,y) \to (x,-y)$. The image of point (–2,5) is (–2,–5). To check your work, you can plot both points:

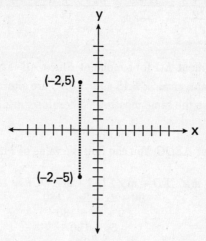

10. 18

A rhombus is a quadrilateral with four equal sides; therefore, $AB = BC$. Set the two equal to each other and solve for x:

$$2x - 2 = x + 8$$
$$2x = x + 10$$
$$x = 10$$

To find the length of $\overline{BC}$, substitute 10 for x and solve:

$$BC = x + 8 = 10 + 8 = 18$$

11. $\dfrac{7x-1}{12}$

You can't do anything until the two fractions have the same denominator. This number is the lowest common denominator (LCD) of 4 and 3, which is 12. To make the two fractions compatible, multiply the top and bottom of the first fraction by 4:

$$\frac{4}{4} \bullet \frac{(x + 2)}{3} = \frac{4x + 8}{12}$$

Multiply the top and bottom of the second fraction by 3:

$$\frac{3}{3} \bullet \frac{(x-3)}{4} = \frac{3x-9}{12}$$

Now you can add the fractions:

$$\frac{4x+8}{12} + \frac{3x-9}{12} = \frac{4x+8+3x-9}{12} = \frac{7x-1}{12}$$

12. 24

Ignore segment $\overline{EC}$ for a moment. Since $\overline{AB}$ is parallel to $\overline{CD}$, and $\overline{AD}$ is a transversal, $\angle BAE$ and $\angle EDC$ are alternate interior angles (which have the same measure). Therefore, m$\angle BAE$ = m$\angle EDC$ = $2x$.

Now look at $\triangle EDC$. You can find the value of x by using the Rule of 180:

$$\text{m}\angle CED + \text{m}\angle EDC + \text{m}\angle DCE = 180.$$
$$60 + 2x + 3x = 180$$
$$60 + 5x = 180$$
$$5x = 120$$
$$x = 24$$

13. 21

Plot the three points like this:

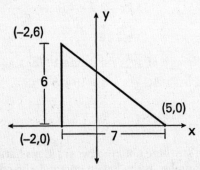

This triangle is a right triangle with a base of length 7 and a height of length 6. Use the formula for the area of a triangle (in which b represents the length of the base and h represents the height):

$$A = \frac{1}{2} bh = \frac{1}{2} (7)(6) = \frac{1}{2} (42) = 21$$

14. 5

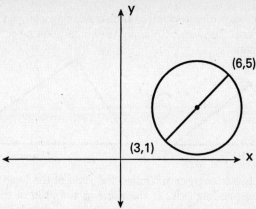

To find the distance between the two points, use the distance formula:

$$d = \sqrt{(x_2 - x_1)^2 + (y_2 - y_1)^2}$$

Let $(x_1, y_1) = (3,1)$ and $(x_2, y_2) = (6,5)$:

$$d = \sqrt{(6-3)^2 + (5-1)^2} = \sqrt{3^2 + 4^2} = \sqrt{9+16} = \sqrt{25} = 5$$

15. (−11,−2)

The formula for the midpoint of a line segment is:

$$(\overline{x}, \overline{y}) = \left(\frac{x_1 + x_2}{2}, \frac{y_1 + y_2}{2} \right)$$

You'll have to use this formula a little differently by solving for each coordinate individually. Let $(\overline{x}, \overline{y}) = (-2,4), (x_1, y_1) = A(7,10)$ and $(x_2, y_2) = B(x,y)$:

$$\overline{x} = \frac{x_1 + x_2}{2}$$
$$-2 = \frac{7 + x}{2}$$
$$-4 = 7 + x$$
$$-11 = x$$

$$\overline{y} = \frac{y_1 + y_2}{2}$$
$$4 = \frac{10 + y}{2}$$
$$8 = 10 + y$$
$$-2 = y$$

The coordinates of point B are $(-11,-2)$.

16. 36

Any time a problem involves similar triangles, all you do is set up a proportion. The key is lining up the corresponding sides. First draw a diagram:

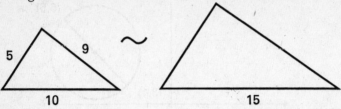

When two triangles are similar, the ratio of the lengths of any pair of corresponding sides is the same as the ratio of the perimeters. The longest side of the smaller triangle is 10 units long, and its counterpart of the larger triangle is 15 units long. The perimeter of the small triangle is 5 + 9 + 10, or 24, and you want to find the perimeter of the larger triangle (call it P). Your proportion should look like this:

$$\frac{10}{15} = \frac{24}{P}$$

Cross-multiply and solve:

$$10P = 360$$
$$x = 36$$

Multiple Choice

17. (4)

After a reflection in the origin, both the x- and y-coordinates are negated. In other words, $r_{(0.0)}(x,y) \rightarrow (-x,-y)$.

Process Of Elimination is a great help as well. Answer choice (1) is out right away, because the only point that remains unchanged after a reflection in the origin is the origin itself. Answer choice (2) represents a reflection in the y-axis, and answer choice (3) represents a reflection in the x-axis.

18. (3)

Draw your right triangle like this:

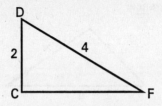

Use the Pythagorean Theorem to find the length of the other leg:

$$(DC)^2 + (CF)^2 = (DF)^2$$
$$2^2 + (CF)^2 = 4^2$$
$$4 + (CF)^2 = 16$$
$$(CF)^2 = 12$$
$$CF = \sqrt{12}$$

Note: If you know square roots well, you can do this problem without doing any math at all. The other leg ($\overline{CF}$) has to be shorter than the hypotenuse, which is only 4 units long. You can cross off answer choices (1) and (2) right off the bat; since $\sqrt{20}$ is also greater than 4, you can eliminate answer choice (4) as well.

19. (1)

When a line is written in the $y = mx + b$ format (as all the answer choices are), the m represents the slope of the line and the b represents the y-intercept. Since the slope of the line in question is –2, get rid of answer choices (3) and (4). Also, (0,3) is the y-intercept of the line because the x-coordinate is 0; b must equal 3. The correct equation is $y = -2x + 3$.

20. (4)

Given the lengths of two sides of a triangle, the length of the third side has to be smaller than the sum of the other two sides and larger than their difference:

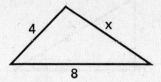

In this case, the length of the third side must be:

$$(8 - 4) < x < (8 + 4)$$
$$4 < x < 12$$

Answer choice (4) is not within this range. Remember that x must be *greater than* 4. It can't be equal to 4.

21. (2)

Draw an equilateral triangle and an altitude from the top vertex, like this:

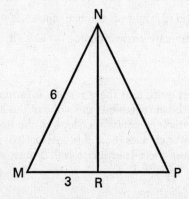

Look at $\triangle MNR$. An altitude of an equilateral triangle bisects the vertex angle and is perpendicular to the opposite side. Therefore, $\triangle MNR$ is a 30:60:90 triangle. In a 30:60:90 triangle, the short leg is half as long as the hypotenuse. Therefore, $MR = 3$. The length of the long leg of a 30:60:90 triangle equals the length of the short leg times $\sqrt{3}$. The length of $\overline{NR}$ (the altitude of the triangle) is $3\sqrt{3}$.

Note: If you never learned the special relationship between the sides of a 30:60:90 triangle, you can always use the Pythagorean Theorem. The key is realizing that $MR = 3$.

22. (3)

When a line is written in the $y = mx + b$ form, the m represents the slope of the line and the b represents the y-intercept. Therefore, the slope of the line $y = 5x + 4$ is 5. All parallel lines have the same slope, so any line parallel to this line will also have a slope of 5.

23. (3)

The contrapositive is an abbreviated reference to the Law of Contrapositive Inference (what we like to call the Flip-and-Negate Rule). To find the contrapositive of and "if-then" statement, flip the two terms to the opposite side of the arrow and negate them both, (For example, $a \rightarrow b$ becomes $\sim b \rightarrow \sim a$.) In this case, the contrapositive of $c \rightarrow (d \vee e)$ is :

$$\sim(d \vee e) \rightarrow \sim c$$

24. (2)

Use the formula for a circle, and remember that (h, k) is the center and r is the radius:

$$(x - h)^2 + (y - k)^2 = r^2$$
$$[x - (-3)]^2 + (y - 1)^2 = 10^2$$
$$(x + 3)^2 + (y - 1)^2 = 100$$

Since the formula involves r^2 and not r, you should recognize that the formula will equal 100, not 10. Therefore, eliminate answer choices (1) and (3).

25. (4)

Using the Chain Rule, you can combine the first two statements: if $A \rightarrow \sim C$ and $\sim C \rightarrow R$, you can conclude that $A \rightarrow R$. The contrapositive of this statement is $\sim R \rightarrow \sim A$ (if you're not sure why, see question 23). The statement $\sim R$ is given, so it must be true that $\sim A$.

26. (2)

Use the Rule of 180 to determine the measure of $\angle C$:

$$m\angle A + m\angle B + m\angle C = 180$$
$$41 + 48 + m\angle C = 180$$
$$m\angle C = 91$$

The measure of $\angle C$ is greater than 90, so it's an obtuse angle. Therefore, the triangle is also obtuse.

27. (4)

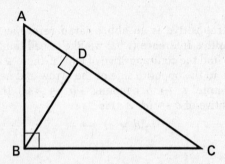

You've probably encountered this type of diagram before. When you draw the altitude of a right triangle, you cut the triangle into two smaller right triangles. All three of the triangles (the original one, $\triangle ABC$, and the two smaller ones, $\triangle BDC$ and $\triangle BAD$) are similar; all their corresponding sides and angles are proportional to each other.

Process of Elimination is also very helpful here. The two smaller triangles aren't the same size (so they can't be congruent); eliminate answer choices (1) and (2). None of the triangles is isosceles either.

28. (1)

Here's the formula for the number of degrees x in each angle of a regular polygon (n represents the number of sides in that polygon):

$$x = \frac{180(n-2)}{n}$$

Rather than plug in 108 for x, you might find it easier to plug each of the answer choices in for n. (**Note:** You don't have to bother with answer choice (4), because a regular polygon with four sides is a square, and you know each of those angles measures 90°.) Try plugging in $n = 5$:

$$x = \frac{180(5-2)}{5} = \frac{180(3)}{5} = \frac{540}{5} = 108$$

29. (1)

Create a diagram for each triangle and plug in some numbers. Let each altitude equal 5. The areas are in a ratio of 3:4, so let the area of triangle A equal 30 and the area of triangle B equal 40:

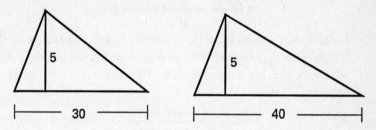

Using the formula for the area of a triangle $\left(A = \frac{1}{2}bh\right)$, find the length of each base:

$$A = \frac{1}{2}bh \qquad\qquad A = \frac{1}{2}bh$$

$$30 = \frac{1}{2}b(5) \qquad\qquad 40 = \frac{1}{2}b(5)$$

$$60 = 5b \qquad\qquad 80 = 5b$$

$$12 = b \qquad\qquad 16 = b$$

The two bases are 12 and 16, and the ratio 12:16 reduces to 3:4. Therefore, the two bases are in a 3:4 ratio.

30. (2)

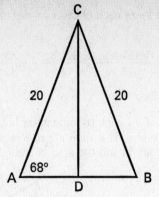

Look at $\triangle ACD$; you know the measure of $\angle A$. You also know the length of its hypotenuse, and you want to know the length of $\overline{CD}$, which is the leg opposite $\angle A$. Use the sine (the SOH in SOHCAHTOA):

$$\sin \angle A = \frac{\text{opposite}}{\text{hypotenuse}}$$

$$\sin 68° = \frac{CD}{20}$$

$$20(0.9272) = CD$$

$$18.544 = CD$$

When you round this off to the nearest *tenth*, your answer becomes 18.5.

31. (4)

The diagonals of a parallelogram bisect each other, so answer choice (4) is the correct response.

32. (3)

The formula to follow is a variation of the permutations rule. To find the number of possible arrangements of the letters in a word with n letters, in which one letter appears p times and another letter appears q times (remember that p and q are greater than 1), the formula looks like this:

$$\frac{n!}{p!\,q!}$$

GENESIS has seven letters, but there are two E's and two S's. Therefore, you can express the number of arrangements as:

$$\frac{7!}{2!\,2!} = \frac{7 \bullet 6 \bullet 5 \bullet 4 \bullet 3 \bullet 2 \bullet 1}{2 \bullet 1 \bullet (2 \bullet 1)} = \frac{7 \bullet 6 \bullet 5 \bullet 3 \bullet 2}{2} = 1,260$$

33. (1)

To find the turning point, or vertex, of a parabola, find the x-coordinate of the turning point by using the formula for the axis of symmetry. When a parabola appears in the form $y + ax^2 + bx + c$ as this one does, the equation of its axis of symmetry is:

$$x = -\frac{b}{2a}$$

For this parabola, $a = 1$, $b = -6$, and $c = 2$. Thus the axis of symmetry is:

$$x = -\frac{-6}{2(1)} = \frac{6}{2} = 3$$

The x-coordinate of the vertex is 3, so you can eliminate answer choices (2) and (4). Now plug 3 into the equation of the parabola to determine the vertex's y-coordinate:

$$y = (3)^2 - 6(3) + 2 = 9 - 18 + 2 = -7$$

The coordinates of the turning point are $(3,-7)$.

34. (1)

This is a combinations problem (because the order of the students in the lab group doesn't matter), so use the combinations formula:

$$_nC_r = \frac{n!}{r!(n-r)!}$$

There are eight students ($n = 8$), and you want to choose three of them ($r = 3$):

$$_8C_3 = \frac{8!}{3!\,5!} = \frac{8 \bullet 7 \bullet 6 \bullet 5 \bullet 4 \bullet 3 \bullet 2 \bullet 1}{(3 \bullet 2 \bullet 1) \bullet (5 \bullet 4 \bullet 3 \bullet 2 \bullet 1)}$$

$$= \frac{8 \bullet 7 \bullet 6}{3 \bullet 2 \bullet 1} = \frac{336}{6} = 56$$

35.

With the point of your compass on P, draw an arc (#1) that intersects $\overline{AB}$ in two places:

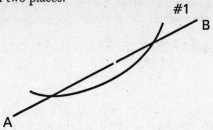

Without altering the width of your compass, place its point on A and draw an arc (#2) on the side opposite P. Then put the point of your compass on B and draw another arc (#3) that intersects arc #2:

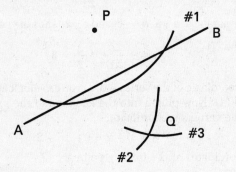

Draw the line defined by P and Q:

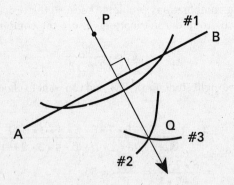

Part II

36. *a*

Start the graphing process by plugging the integers between –2 and 4, inclusive, into the equation for the parabola and determine its coordinates. For example, if $x = -2$, then $y = 2(-2)^2 - 4(-2) - 3$, or 13. Your first ordered pair is (–2,13). Here is the rest of your T-chart and the accompanying sketch:

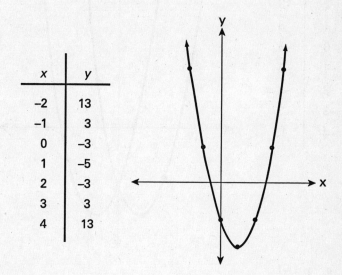

x	y
–2	13
–1	3
0	–3
1	–5
2	–3
3	3
4	13

b

After a reflection in the *y*-axis, the *x*-coordinate of each point is negated and the *y*-coordinate of each point remains unchanged. In other words, $r_{y\text{-axis}}\ (x,y) \to (-x,y)$. Use this formula to determine the new points; your graph should look like this:

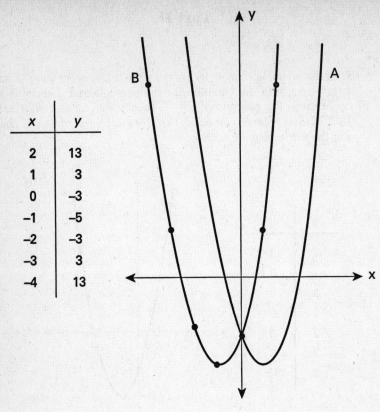

x	y
2	13
1	3
0	-3
-1	-5
-2	-3
-3	3
-4	13

c $x = -1$

When a parabola appears in the form $y = ax^2 + bx + c$ as this one does, the equation of its axis of symmetry is:

$$x = -\frac{b}{2a}$$

Don't bother trying to determine the equation of the parabola in Part B. You know the equation for the original parabola, so find its axis of symmetry and reflect it in the y-axis.

The original parabola appears in the standard $y = ax^2 + bx + c$ format; $a = 2$, $b = -4$, and $c = -3$. The axis of symmetry is:

$$x = -\frac{-4}{2(2)} = \frac{4}{4} = 1$$

Since the axis of symmetry of the original parabola is $x = 1$, the axis of symmetry of the parabola in Part B must be $x = -1$. (**Note:** You can always check the axis of symmetry by drawing it on the graph and making sure it cuts the second parabola in half.)

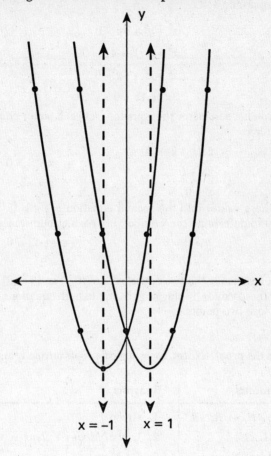

$x = -1$ $x = 1$

37. (0,0), (-2,2)

Look at the second equation first. If you subtract x from both sides, the equation $y + x = 0$ becomes $y = -x$. Substitute $-x$ for y in the first equation:

$$x^2 + y^2 + 4x = 0$$
$$x^2 + (-x)^2 + 4x = 0$$
$$x^2 + x^2 + 4x = 0$$
$$2x^2 + 4x = 0$$

Now you have to factor the equation, set each factor equal to 0, and solve for x:

$$2x(x + 2) = 0$$

$$2x = 0 \qquad\qquad x + 2 = 0$$

$$x = 0 \qquad\qquad x = -2$$

Plug these values into the second equation $y + x = 0$ (because it's easier) to determine the value of y in each circumstance:

$$y + 0 = 0 \qquad\qquad y + (-2) = 0$$

$$y = 0 \qquad\qquad y = 2$$

The solutions for the two equations are (0,0) and (-2,2). Be sure to check these values by plugging them into both equations. Otherwise, you'll lose two points.

38.

Here's the proof. (**Note:** These logical proofs normally appear in Part III.)

Statements	Reasons
1. $(L \wedge N) \to R$; $\sim R$	1. Given
2. $\sim(L \wedge N)$	2. Law of *Modus Tollens*
3. $\sim L \vee \sim N$	3. De Morgan's Laws
4. L	4. Given
5. $\sim N$	5. Law of Disjunctive Inference (3, 4)
6. $M \to N$	6. Given
7. $\sim M$	7. Law of *Modus Tollens* (5, 6)
8. $\sim M \to P$	8. Given
9. P	9. Law of Detachment (7, 8)

(**Note:** If your class didn't cover the Law of *Modus Tollens*, you can use a combination of the Law of Contrapositive Inference and the Law of Detachment.)

39. *a*   **1.85, –4.85**

Whenever two fractions are equal to each other, you can cross-multiply:

Try as you might, you can't factor this equation. (That would be too easy!) The fact that you have to solve for x to the nearest hundredth should be a clue that you have to use the Quadratic Formula:

$$\frac{1}{x-1} = \frac{x+4}{5}$$
$$(x-1)(x+4) = 1 \cdot 5$$
$$x^2 + 3x - 9 = 0$$

In the equation, $a = 1$, $b = 3$, and $c = -9$:

$$x = \frac{-3 - \sqrt{(3)^2 - 4(1)(-9)}}{2(1)} = \frac{-3 - \sqrt{9 + 36}}{2} = \frac{-3 + \sqrt{45}}{2}, \frac{-3 - \sqrt{45}}{2}$$

Use your calculator to determine that $\sqrt{45} = 6.708$, and plug that into the two terms:

$$x = \frac{-3 + 6.708}{2} \qquad\qquad x = \frac{-3 - 6.708}{2}$$
$$= \frac{3.708}{2} \qquad\qquad\qquad = \frac{-9.708}{2}$$
$$= 1.854 \qquad\qquad\qquad = -4.854$$

When you round each of these off to the nearest *hundredth*, your answers become 1.85 and –4.85. Check your math by plugging each of these values back into the original equation and making sure they work.

b $\dfrac{x-2}{x}$

Factor all the complex terms like this:

$$x^2 - 4 = (x + 2)(x - 2)$$

$$x^2 + 4x + 4 = (x + 2)(x + 2)$$

$$x^2 + 2x = x(x + 2)$$

Once you've factored these three terms, the problem looks like this:

$$\frac{(x + 2)(x - 2)}{(x + 2)(x + 2)} \cdot \frac{x(x + 2)}{x^2}$$

Cancel out all the factors that appear both on the top and on the bottom, and you're left with:

$$\frac{\cancel{(x + 2)}(x - 2)}{\cancel{(x + 2)}\cancel{(x + 2)}} \cdot \frac{\cancel{x}\cancel{(x + 2)}}{x^{\cancel{2}}} = \frac{x - 2}{x}$$

40. 136

To find the area of rectangle $ABCD$, you want to find AD and AB; once you find these lengths, you can use the formula for the area of a rectangle, $A = l \cdot w$.

To find AD, focus on right triangle EAD. You know the length of the leg opposite $\triangle EAD$, and $\overline{AD}$ is the hypotenuse. It's time for more trig; use the sine (the SOH in SOHCAHTOA):

$$\sin \angle EAD = \frac{\text{opposite}}{\text{hypotenuse}}$$

$$\sin 55° = \frac{8}{AD}$$

$$0.8192 = \frac{8}{AD}$$

$$AD\,(0.8192) = 8$$

$$AD = \frac{8}{0.8192}$$

$$AD = 9.77$$

So far, so good. Now look at $\triangle ABC$. Since $ABCD$ is a rectangle, opposite sides $\overline{AD}$ and $\overline{BC}$ are parallel. Therefore, $\angle EAD$ and $\angle BCA$ are alternate interior angles, which have the same measure; $m\angle BCA = 55$.

Furthermore, opposite sides of a rectangle are congruent, so *BC* also equals 9.77.

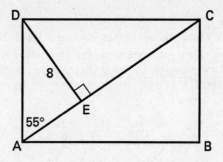

In △*ABC*, you know the length of the adjacent leg, and you want to find the length of the opposite leg, $\overline{AB}$ are parallel. Use the tangent (the TOA in SOHCAHTOA):

$$\tan - BCA = \frac{\text{opposite}}{\text{adjacent}}$$

$$\tan 55 = \frac{AB}{9.77}$$

$$1.4281 = \frac{AB}{9.77}$$

$$(1.4281)(9.77) = AB$$

$$AB = 13.95$$

Now you've found the rectangle's dimensions. When you multiply them together, you get:

$$13.95 \bullet 9.77 = 136.29$$

When you round this off to the nearest *integer*, your answer becomes 136.

Part III

41.

The plan: $\overline{CJ}$ and $\overline{AL}$ are corresponding sides of $\triangle JCB$ and $\triangle LAD$, respectively. They gave you some information to work with involving those two triangles, so prove that they're congruent using SAS, then use CPCTC.

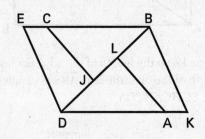

Statements	Reasons
1. $\overline{BC} \cong \overline{DA}$; $DEBK$ is a parallelogram	1. Given
2. $\overline{EB}$ is parallel to $\overline{DK}$	2. Definition of a parallelogram
3. $\angle CBL \cong \angle JDA$	3. Alternate interior angles are congruent.
4. $\overline{DJ} \cong \overline{BL}$	4. Given
5. $DJ = BL$	5. Definition of congruence
6. $JL = JL$	6. Reflexive Property of Equality
7. $DJ + JL = BL + JL$	7. Additive Property of Equality
8. $DL = BJ$	8. Segment Addition Postulate
9. $\overline{DC} \cong \overline{BJ}$	9. Definition of congruence
10. $\triangle JCB \cong \triangle LAD$	10. SAS $\cong$ SAS
11. $\overline{CJ} \cong \overline{AL}$	11. Corresponding Parts of Congruent Triangles are Congruent (CPCTC)

42. *a*

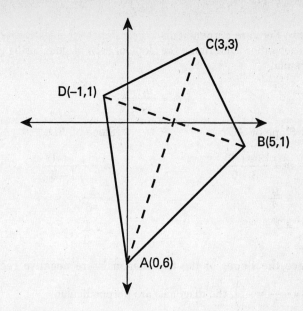

All you have to do is find one pair of consecutive sides that are not the same length. Use the distance formula to determine the lengths of the sides of *ABCD*; try $\overline{AB}$ and $\overline{BC}$ first:

$$d = \sqrt{(x_2 - x_1)^2 + (y_2 - y_1)^2}$$

$$AB = \sqrt{(5 - 0)^2 + [-1 - (-6)]^2} \qquad BC = \sqrt{(3 - 5)^2 + [3 - (-1)]^2}$$
$$= \sqrt{5^2 + 5^2} \qquad\qquad\qquad = \sqrt{(-2)^2 + 4^2}$$
$$= \sqrt{25 + 25} \qquad\qquad\qquad = \sqrt{4 + 16}$$
$$= \sqrt{50} \qquad\qquad\qquad\qquad = \sqrt{20}$$
$$= 5\sqrt{2} \qquad\qquad\qquad\qquad = 2\sqrt{5}$$

You've found a pair of consecutive sides that are not congruent.

b

If two lines are perpendicular, their slopes are negative reciprocals of each other. Determine the slope of each diagonal using the slope formula:

$$m = \frac{y_2 - y_1}{x_2 - x_1}$$

Slope of $\overline{AC}$:

$$m = \frac{3 - (-6)}{3 - 0}$$

$$= \frac{9}{3}$$

$$= 3$$

Slope of $\overline{BD}$:

$$m = \frac{1 - (-1)}{-1 - 5}$$

$$= \frac{2}{-6}$$

$$= -\frac{1}{3}$$

Since the slopes of the two diagonals are negative reciprocals $\left(3 \cdot -\frac{1}{3} = -1\right)$, the diagonals are perpendicular.

EXAMINATION
JANUARY 1997

Part I

Answer 30 questions from this part. Each correct answer will receive 2 credits. No partial credit will be allowed. Write your answers in the spaces provided on the separate answer sheet. Where applicable, answers may be left in terms of π or in radical form. [60]

1 Using the accompanying table, solve for x if $x \, \circledcirc \, b = a$.

$\circledcirc$	a	b	c
a	a	b	c
b	b	a	c
c	c	c	b

2 In the accompanying diagram, $\triangle ABC$ is similar to $\triangle A'B'C'$, $AB = 14.4$, $BC = 8$, $CA = 12$, $A'B' = x$, and $B'C' = 4$. Find the value of x.

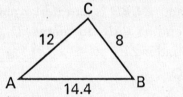 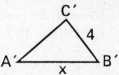

3 In the accompanying diagram, parallel lines $\overleftrightarrow{AB}$ and $\overrightarrow{CD}$ are intersected by $\overrightarrow{GH}$ at E and F, respectively. If $m\angle BEF = 5x - 10$ and $m\angle CFE = 4x + 20$, find x.

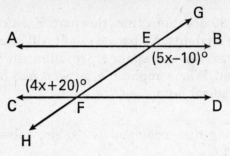

4 If $\tan A = 0.5400$, find the measure of $\angle A$ to the *nearest degree*.

5 Find the length of a side of a square if two consecutive vertices have coordinates $(-2,6)$ and $(6,6)$.

6 In the accompanying diagram of isosceles triangle ABC, $CA = CB$ and $\angle CBD$ is an exterior angle formed by extending $\overline{AB}$ to point D. If $m\angle CBD = 130$, find $m\angle C$.

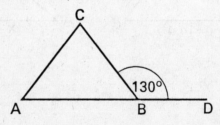

7 If $\overleftrightarrow{AB}$ intersects $\overleftrightarrow{CD}$ at E, m∠AEC = 3x, and m∠AED = 5x − 60, find the value of x.

8 Point (x,y) is the image of (2,4) after a reflection in point (5,6). In which quadrant does (x,y) lie?

9 In the accompanying diagram, ABCD is a parallelogram, $\overline{EC} \perp \overline{DC}$, ∠B ≅ ∠E, and m∠A = 100. Find m∠CDE.

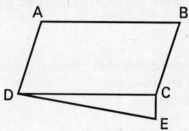

10 The lengths of the sides of △DEF are 6, 8, and 10. Find the perimeter of the triangle formed by connecting the midpoints of the sides of △DEF.

11 The coordinates of the midpoint of line segment $\overline{AB}$ are (1,2). If the coordinates of point A are (1,0), find the coordinates of point B.

12 In △PQR, ∠Q ≅ ∠R. If PQ = 10x − 14, PR = 2x + 50, and RQ = 4x − 30, find the value of x.

13 What is the image of (−2,4) after a reflection in the x-axis?

14 In rectangle $ABCD$, $\overline{AC}$ and $\overline{BD}$ are diagonals. If m∠1 = 55, find m∠ABD.

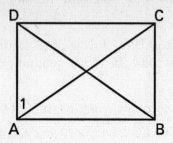

15 What is the slope of the line that passes through points $(-1,5)$ and $(2,3)$?

16 The coordinates of the turning point of the graph of the equation $y = x^2 - 2x - 8$ are $(1,k)$. What is the value of k?

Directions (17–35): For *each* question chosen, write the *numeral* preceding the word or expression that best completes the statement or answers the question.

17 Which equation represents the line that has a slope of $\frac{1}{2}$ and contains the point $(0,3)$?

(1) $y = \frac{1}{3}x + \frac{1}{2}$ (3) $y = \frac{3}{2}x$

(2) $y = 3x + \frac{1}{2}$ (4) $y = \frac{1}{2}x + 3$

18 If the measures of the angles in a triangle are in the ratio 3:4:5, the measure of an exterior angle of the triangle can *not* be

(1) 165°   (3) 120°
(2) 135°   (4) 105°

19 According to De Morgan's laws, which statement is logically equivalent to ~(p ∧ q)?

(1) ~p ∨ ~q   (3) ~p ∧ q
(2) ~p ∨ q   (4) ~p ∧ ~q

20 One angle of the triangle measures 30°. If the measures of the other two angles are in the ratio 3:7, the measure of the largest angle of the triangle is

(1) 15°   (3) 126°
(2) 105°   (4) 147°

21 In the accompanying diagram, *ABCD* is a rectangle, *E* is a point on $\overline{CD}$, m∠*DAE* = 30, and m∠*CBE* = 20.

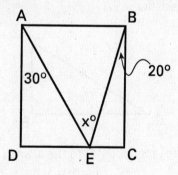

What is m∠x?

(1) 25   (3) 60
(2) 50   (4) 70

22 The graph of the equation $y = ax^2 + bx + c$, $a \neq 0$, forms

(1) a circle   (3) a straight line
(2) a parabola   (4) an ellipse

23 Which set of numbers can represent the lengths of the sides of a triangle?

(1) {4,4,8}   (3) {3,5,7}
(2) {3,9,14}   (4) {1,2,3}

24 Which is an equation of the line that passes through point (3,5) and is parallel to the x-axis?

(1) $x = 3$ (3) $y = 5$
(2) $x = 5$ (4) $y = 3$

25 What are the factors of $y^3 - 4y$?

(1) $y(y - 2)(y - 2)$ (3) $y(y^2 + 1)(y - 4)$
(2) $y(y + 4)(y - 4)$ (4) $y(y + 2)(y - 2)$

26 In the accompanying diagram of right triangle ABC, $AB = 4$ and $BC = 7$.

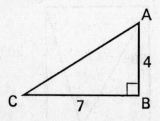

What is the length of $\overline{AC}$ to the *nearest hundredth*?

(1) 5.74   (3) 8.06
(2) 5.75   (4) 8.08

27 Which is the converse of the statement "If today is President's Day, then there is no school"?

(1) If there is school, then today is not Presidents' Day.

(2) If there is no school, then today is Presidents' Day.

(3) If today is Presidents' Day, then there is school.

(4) If today is not Presidents' Day, then there is school.

28 How many different eight-letter permutations can be formed from the letters in the word "PARALLEL"?

(1) $\dfrac{8!}{3!\,2!}$

(3) 360

(2) 8!

(4) $\dfrac{8!}{3!}$

29 Which equation describes the locus of points equidistant from $A(-3,2)$ and $B(-3,8)$?

(1) $x = -3$

(3) $x = 5$

(2) $y = -3$

(4) $y = 5$

30 A translation maps $A(1,2)$ onto $A'(-1,3)$. What are the coordinates of the image of the origin under the same translation?

(1) $(0,0)$

(3) $(-2,1)$

(2) $(2,-1)$

(4) $(-1,2)$

31 The solution set of the equation $x^2 + 5x = 0$ is

(1) $\{0\}$

(3) $\{-5\}$

(2) $\{5\}$

(4) $\{0, -5\}$

32 In the accompanying diagram of parallelogram *MATH*, m∠*T* = 100 and $\overline{SH}$ bisects ∠*MHT*.

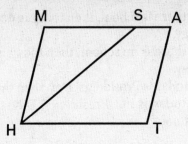

What is m∠*HSA*?

(1) 80   (3) 120
(2) 100   (4) 140

33 What are the roots of the equation $x^2 + 9x + 12 = 0$?

(1) $\dfrac{-9 \pm \sqrt{33}}{2}$ (3) $\dfrac{-9 \pm \sqrt{129}}{2}$

(2) $\dfrac{9 \pm \sqrt{33}}{2}$ (4) $\dfrac{9 \pm \sqrt{129}}{2}$

34 The vertices of trapezoid *ABCD* are *A*(−3,0), *B*(−3,4), *C*(2,4), and *D*(4,0). What is the area of trapezoid *ABCD*?

(1) 6   (3) 28
(2) 24   (4) 48

35 The accompanying diagram shows how $\triangle A'B'C'$ is constructed similar to $\triangle ABC$.

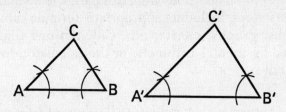

Which statement proves the construction?

(1) If two triangles are congruent, they are similar.

(2) If two triangles are similar, the angles of one triangle are congruent to the corresponding angles of the other triangle.

(3) Two triangles are similar if two angles of one triangle are congruent to two angles of the other triangle.

(4) The corresponding sides of two similar triangles are proportional.

Part II

Answer *three* questions from this part. Clearly indicate the necessary steps, including appropriate formula substitutions, diagrams, graphs, charts, etc. Calculations that may be obtained by mental arithmetic or the calculator do not need to be shown. [30]

36 Answer both *a* and *b* for all values of y for which these expressions are defined.

  a Express as a single fraction in lowest terms:

$$\frac{y-4}{2y} + \frac{3y-5}{5y} \quad \text{[4]}$$

  b Simplify:

$$\frac{y^2 - 7y + 10}{5y - y^2} \div \frac{y^2 - 4}{25y^3} \quad \text{[6]}$$

37 In the accompanying diagram of isosceles triangle KLC, $\overline{LK} \cong \overline{LC}$, m$\angle K = 53$, altiutde $\overline{CA}$ is drawn to leg $\overline{LK}$, and $LA = 3$. Find the perimeter of $\triangle KLC$ to the *nearest integer*. [10]

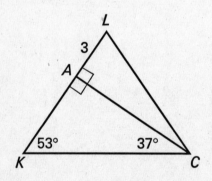

38 *a* On graph paper, draw the graph of the equation $y = -x^2 + 6x - 8$ for all values of x in the interval $0 \le x \le 6$.   [6]

 b What is the maximum value of y in the equation $y = -x^2 + 6x - 8$?   [2]

 c Write an equation of the line that passes through the turning point and is parallel to the x-axis.   [2]

39 At a video rental store, Elyssa has only enough money to rent three videos. She has chosen four comedies, six dramas, and one mystery movie to consider.

 a How many different selections of three videos may she rent from the movies she has chosen?   [2]

 b How many selections of three videos will consist of one comedy and two dramas?   [3]

 c What is the probability that a selection of three videos will consist of one of each type of video?   [3]

 d Elyssa decides to rent one comedy, one drama, and one mystery movie. In how many different orders may she view these videos?   [2]

40 In the accompanying diagram of right triangle ABC, altitude is drawn to hypotenuse $\overline{BD}$, $AC = 20$, $AD < DC$, and $BD = 6$.

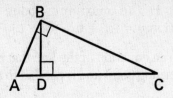

a If $AD = x$, express DC in terms of x.   [1]

b Solve for x.   [6]

c Find AB in simplest radical form.   [3]

Part III

Answer *one* question from this part. Clearly indicate the necessary steps, including appropriate formula substitutions, diagrams, graphs, charts, etc. Calculations that may be obtained by mental arithmetic or the calculator do not need to be shown. [10]

41 Given: $\triangle ABC$; $\overline{BD}$ is both the median and the altitude to $\overline{AC}$.

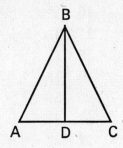

Prove: $\overline{BA} \cong \overline{BC}$ [10]

42 Quadrilateral $ABCD$ has vertices $A(-6,3)$, $B(-3,6)$, $C(9,6)$, and $D(-5,-8)$. Prove that quadrilateral $ABCD$ is

a a trapezoid [6]

b *not* an isosceles trapezoid [4]

ANSWERS AND EXPLANATIONS
JANUARY 1997
ANSWER KEY

Part I

1. b
2. 7.2
3. 30
4. 28
5. 8
6. 80
7. 30
8. I
9. 10
10. 12
11. (1,4)

12. 8
13. (−2,−4)
14. 35
15. $-\dfrac{2}{3}$
16. −9
17. (4)
18. (1)
19. (1)
20. (2)
21. (2)
22. (2)
23. (3)

24. (3)
25. (4)
26. (3)
27. (2)
28. (1)
29. (4)
30. (3)
31. (4)
32. (4)
33. (1)
34. (2)
35. (3)

Part II

36. a $\dfrac{11y - 30}{10y}$

b $\dfrac{-25y^2}{y + 2}$

37. 35

38. a see explanations

b 1

c $y = 1$

39. a 165

b 60

c $\dfrac{24}{165}$

d 6

40. a $20 - x$

b 2

c $2\sqrt{10}$

Part III

41. see explanations
42. see explanations

EXPLANATIONS
Part I

1. ***b***

Look along the top row for the column headed by b, and run your finger down that column until you find a in row b:

❂	a	b	c
a	a	b	c
b	b	a	c
c	c	c	b

Since row b and column b intersect at point a, it must be true that $b \circledast b = a$. Therefore, $x = b$.

2. 7.2

Any time a problem involves similar triangles, all you do is set up a proportion. The key is lining up the corresponding sides:

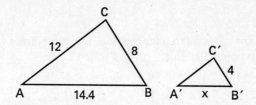

This problem is a little easier because the sides are labeled. Set up a proportion involving corresponding sides:

$$\frac{AB}{A'B'} = \frac{BC}{B'C'}$$

$$\frac{14.4}{x} = \frac{8}{4}$$

Cross-multiply and solve:

$$8x = 57.6$$
$$x = 7.2$$

Note: An even quicker way to solve this is to realize that since $BC = 8$ and $B'C' = 4$, each side of $\triangle ABC$ is twice as long as its counterpart of $\triangle A'B'C'$. Therefore, $A'B'$ must be half as long as AB, or 7.2.

3. 30

Since $\overleftrightarrow{AB} \parallel \overleftrightarrow{CD}$, $\angle BEF$ and $\angle CFE$ are alternate interior angles, which must have the same measure. Set them equal to each other and solve for x:

$$m\angle BEF = m\angle CFE$$
$$5x - 10 = 4x + 20$$
$$5x = 4x + 30$$
$$x = 30$$

4. 28

Use the "inverse tangent" button on your calculator. (It usually says "tan^{-1}" and involves the "second function" button.) Once you're sure your calculator is in "degree mode," type in 0.54 and press "tan^{-1}." You should get 28.369. When you round this off to the nearest degree, as instructed, you get 28°.

5. 8

There are two ways to solve this one. The most direct way is to graph the two points like this:

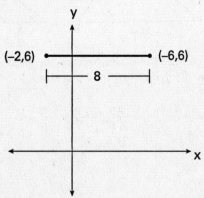

Since the segment between the points is horizontal, you can count the units between them; the segment is 8 units long.

Otherwise, you can use the distance formula.

6. 80

Since $\angle CBD$ is an exterior angle, it's supplemental to $\angle ABC$. Therefore, m$\angle ABC = 50°$. It's also given that $\triangle ABC$ is isosceles. Since $CA = CB$, the angles opposite those sides, $\angle ABC$ and $\angle A$, respectively, are also equal in measure. Therefore, m$\angle A = 50°$.

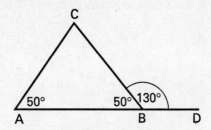

Now it's just a matter of using the Rule of 180:

$$m\angle A + m\angle ABC + m\angle C = 180$$
$$50 + 50 + m\angle C = 180$$
$$m\angle C = 80$$

7. 30

Always draw a diagram if you're not given one

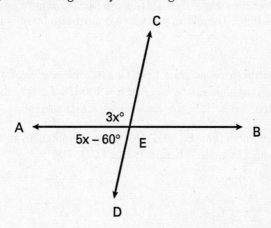

The diagram illustrates that ∠AEC and ∠AED are supplemental. Therefore, their sum is 180:

$$m\angle AEC + m\angle AED = 180$$
$$3x + (5x - 60) = 180$$
$$8x - 60 = 180$$
$$8x = 240$$
$$x = 30$$

8. **Quadrant I**

You might be tempted to find the exact coordinates of the image of (2,4), but you don't have to. Both (2,4) and (5,6) are in the first Quadrant:

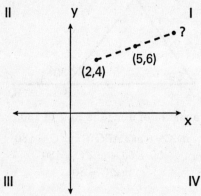

Whatever the image of (2,4) is, it will be somewhere up and to the right of (5,6). Therefore, you know it must also be in Quadrant I.

9. **10**

Look at the parallelogram first. Consecutive angles of a parallelogram are supplementary, and $m\angle A = 100$. That means that $m\angle B = 80$. Since $\angle B \cong \angle E$, the measure of $\angle E$ is also 80.

You also know that $\overline{EC}$ and $\overline{DC}$ are perpendicular, so they intersect in a right angle Therefore, $m\angle ECD = 90$

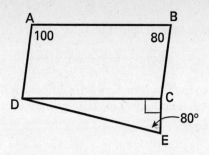

Now use the Rule of 180 in $\triangle CDE$:

$$m\angle CDE + m\angle ECD + m\angle E = 180$$
$$m\angle CDE + 90 + 80 = 180$$
$$m\angle CDE = 10$$

10. 12

Draw a diagram, and let points X, Y, and Z be the midpoints of the three sides:

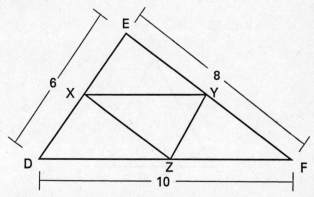

Look first at segment $\overline{XY}$. A segment that connects the midpoints of two sides of a triangle is half the length of the third side. Since X is the midpoint of $\overline{DE}$ and Y is the midpoint of $\overline{EF}$, $XY = 5$. Similarly, $XZ = 4$ and $YZ = 3$ Add these lengths up, and you'll have the perimeter of smaller triangle XYZ:

$$3 + 4 + 5 = 12$$

11. (1,4)

The formula for the midpoint of a line segment is:

$$(\bar{x}, \bar{y}) = \left(\frac{x_1 + x_2}{2}, \frac{y_1 + y_2}{2} \right)$$

You'll have to use this formula a little differently by solving for each coordinate individually. Let $(\bar{x}, \bar{y}) = (1, 2)$, $(x_1, y_1) = A(1,0)$ and $(x_2, y_2) = B(x,y)$:

$$\bar{x} = \frac{x_1 + x_2}{2}$$

$$1 = \frac{1 + x}{2}$$

$$2 = 1 + x$$

$$1 = x$$

$$\bar{y} = \frac{y_1 + y_2}{2}$$

$$2 = \frac{0 + y}{2}$$

$$4 = 0 + y$$

$$4 = y$$

The coordinates of point B are (1,4).

12. 8

The triangle looks like this:

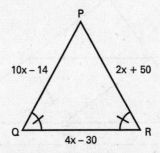

Since $\angle Q \cong \angle R$, the sides opposite those two angles ($\overline{PR}$ and $\overline{PQ}$, respectively) are equal in length. Therefore, you can set PR equal to PQ and solve for x:

$$PR = PQ$$
$$2x + 50 = 10x - 14$$
$$64 = 8x$$
$$8 = x$$

To check your math, plug 8 back into the original equation and make sure it works.

13. (–2,–4)

After a reflection in the x-axis, the x-coordinate remains the same and the y-coordinate is negated. In other words, $r_{x\text{-axis}}(x, y) \rightarrow (x, -y)$. The image of point (–2,4) is (–2,–4).

14. 35

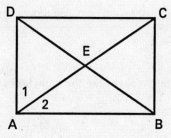

Since a rectangle has four right angles, m$\angle 1$ + m$\angle 2$ = 90. Therefore, m$\angle 2$ = 35. Now look at the point at which the diagonals intersect (labeled E). The diagonals of a rectangle are congruent, so $AC = BD$. The diagonals also bisect each other, so $AE = EB$. Now you know that $\triangle AEB$ is isosceles, which means that m$\angle 2$ = m$\angle ABD$. Thus, m$\angle ABD$ = 35.

15. $-\dfrac{2}{3}$

Determine the slope of the line using the slope formula:

$$m = \frac{y_2 - y_1}{x_2 - x_1}$$

Let (x_1, y_1) = (–1,5) and (x_2, y_2) = (2,3):

$$m = \frac{3 - 5}{2 - (-1)} = \frac{-2}{3} = -\frac{2}{3}$$

16. –9

The x-coordinate of the turning point is 1. To find the value of k, plug 1 in for x in the equation of the parabola:

$$y = (1)^2 - 2(1) - 8 = 1 - 2 - 8 = -9$$

Multiple Choice

17. (4)

Each of the answer choices is in the slope-intercept form $y = mx + b$, so m must be $\dfrac{1}{2}$ in the correct answer. This is true only in answer choice (4), so it must be correct. You don't even have to worry about (0,3)!

18. (1)

First, find the measures of the three angles in the triangle using the Rule of 180:

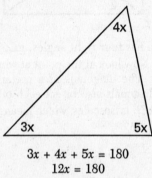

$$3x + 4x + 5x = 180$$
$$12x = 180$$
$$x = 15$$

The smallest angle measures 3 • 15, or 45. The other two angles must therefore measure 60 and 75. (The total of these three is 180—it's always good to check as you go.) An exterior angle must be supplemental to any of these angles. Therefore, the only possible measures of an exterior angle are 135, 120, and 105. The only answer not among these three is answer choice (1).

19. (1)

De Morgan's Laws state that when you negate a parenthetical statement with a " $\wedge$ " or " $\vee$ " in it, negate each symbol and turn the symbol upside down:

$$\sim (p \wedge q) \rightarrow \sim p \vee \sim q$$

Note: Since De Morgan's Laws always flip the symbol, you could have crossed off answer choices (3) and (4) right away.

20. (2)

If one angle of a triangle measures 30°, the sum of the other two must be 150°. Since the ratio of the two unknown angles is 3:7, you can set up an equation like this:

$$3x + 7x = 150$$
$$10x = 150$$
$$x = 15$$

Hold it. Don't get careless and pick answer choice (1). The measure of the largest angle is 7 • 15, or 105°.

21. (2)

Since *ABCD* is a rectangle, ∠*DAB* and ∠*ABC* are right angles; that is, m∠*DAB* = m∠*ABC* = 90. Therefore, m∠*EAB* = 60, and m∠*ABE* = 70:

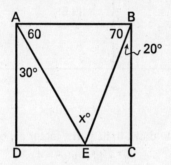

Now use the Rule of 180 within Δ*ABE*:

$$m∠EAB + m∠ABE + m∠BEA = 180$$
$$60 + 70 + x = 180$$
$$x = 50$$

22. (2)

The equation $y = ax^2 + bx + c$ is the standard form of a parabola. The reason they bother to include that $a \neq 0$ is that if $a = 0$, the x^2 term would drop out of the equation. The resulting equation, $y = bx + c$, is a line.

Note: POE works well here. For a graph to be a circle or an ellipse, both x and y must be squared. Eliminate answer choices (1) and (4). Further, the equation for a straight line has no squared terms, so you can get rid of answer choice (3).

23. (3)

Given the lengths of two sides of a triangle, the length of the third side has to be smaller than the sum of the other two sides. Since $4 + 4 = 8$ and $1 + 2 = 3$, answer choices (1) and (4) can't be correct. Answer choice (2) is also impossible, because $3 + 9$ is less than 14. The only choice left is answer choice (3).

24. (3)

Any line that is parallel to the x-axis is horizontal. The lines $x = 3$ and $x = 5$ are vertical, so you can eliminate answer choices (1) and (2). The y-coordinate of (3,5) is 5; the equation of the line that passes through the point (3,5) must be $y = 5$.

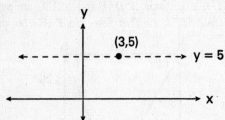

25. (4)

To break $y^3 - 4y$ down to its parts, factor a y out of each term first:
$$y^3 - 4y = y(y^2 - 4)$$
The term in parentheses is a difference of squares, so it breaks down like this:
$$y(y^2 - 4) = y(y - 2)(y + 2)$$

26. (3)

Use the Pythagorean Theorem:

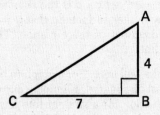

$$(AC)^2 = (AB)^2 + (CB)^2$$
$$(AC)^2 = 4^2 + 7^2$$
$$(AC)^2 = 16 + 49$$
$$(AC)^2 = 65$$
$$AC = \sqrt{65}$$

Use your calculator to find the square root of 65, which is 8.0622. Rounded to the nearest *hundredth*, your answer is 8.06.

Note: Use POE to eliminate answer choices (1) and (2); since the hypotenuse of a right triangle is always the largest of the three sides, AC must be greater than 7.

27. (2)

To find the converse of a conditional statement (otherwise known as an "if-then" statement), just switch the order of the statement. In other words, the converse of $p \rightarrow q$ is $q \rightarrow p$.

Therefore, the converse of "If today is Presidents' Day, then there is no school" is "If there is no school, then today is Presidents' Day."

28. (1)

The formula to follow is a variation of the permutations rule. To find the number of possible arrangements of the letters in a word with n letters, in which one letter appears p times and another letter appears q times (remember that p and q are greater than 1), the formula looks like this:

$$\frac{n!}{p!\,q!}$$

PARALLEL has 8 letters, but there are three L's and two A's. Therefore, you can express the number of arrangements as:

$$\frac{8!}{3!\,2!}$$

29. (4)

To help you out, plot the two points like this:

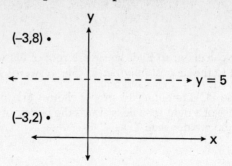

The locus of points between A and B is a horizontal line, so eliminate the vertical lines in answer choices (1) and (3). You have two lines left, but the line $y = -3$ is below both points. All you have left is the line $y = 5$, which runs right between the points.

30. (3)

The translation that maps the point $A(1,2)$ onto $A'(-1,3)$ subtracts 2 from the x-coordinate (because $1 - 2 = -1$) and adds 1 to the y-coordinate (because $2 + 1 = 3$). You can write the translation like this: $(x,y) \rightarrow (x - 2, y + 1)$.

Under this same translation, the origin $(0,0)$ is mapped onto $(0 - 2, 0 + 1)$, or $(-2,1)$.

31. (4)

Solve for x by factoring x out of each term on the left side of the equation:

$$x(x + 5) = 0$$

When the product of two numbers is zero, one of those numbers must be zero. Set each term in the equation to find the solution set:

$$x = 0$$
$$x + 5 = 0; x = -5$$

The solution set is $\{0, -5\}$.

32. (4)

The sum of any two adjacent angles in a parallelogram is 180. Since m$\angle T$ = 100, the measure of $\angle MHT$ is 80. Since $\overline{SH}$ bisects $\angle MHT$, it must be true that m$\angle MHS$ = m$\angle SHT$ = 40:

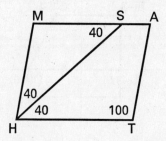

MATH is a parallelogram, so $\overline{MA}$ is parallel to $\overline{HT}$. Since $\overline{SH}$ is a transversal, $\angle MSH$ and $\angle SHT$ are alternate interior angles (which have the same measure). Therefore, m$\angle MSH$ = 40. Angles *MSH* and *HSA* are supplementary, so their sum is 180. Thus, m$\angle HSA$ = 140.

33. (1)

As the answer choices suggest, you can't factor the equation; you have to use the Quadratic Formula:

$$x = \frac{-b \pm \sqrt{b^2 - 4ac}}{2a}$$

In the equation $x^2 + 9x + 12 = 0$, $a = 1$, $b = 9$, and $c = 12$:

$$x = \frac{-9 \pm \sqrt{(9)^2 - 4(1)(12)}}{2(1)} = \frac{-9 \pm \sqrt{81 - 48}}{2} = \frac{-9 \pm \sqrt{33}}{2}$$

34. (2)

When you plot the four points, trapezoid *ABCD* looks like this:

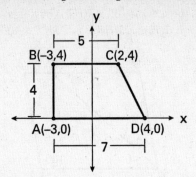

The formula for the area of a trapezoid is:

$$A = \frac{1}{2}(b_1 + b_2)h$$

Use the graph paper to determine the lengths of the two bases: *AD* = 7 and *BC* = 5. The height of the trapezoid can be represented by the length *AB*, which is 4. Plug these numbers into the formula:

$$A = \frac{1}{2}(7 + 5)(4) = \frac{1}{2}(12)(4) = 24$$

35. (3)

Look at the construction; ∠*A*′ has been constructed to be congruent to ∠*A*, and ∠*B*′ has been constructed to be congruent to ∠*B*. The two triangles are therefore similar because of the Angle-Angle Theorem of Similarity. Answer choice (3) restates this rule.

Note: POE is a great help here. Since Δ*ABC* and Δ*A*′*B*′*C*′ are clearly not the same size, they're not congruent. Eliminate answer choice (1). Get rid of answer choice (4), because the construction only involves angles, not sides. Be careful of answer choice (2), which is backwards. The triangles are similar because the angles are congruent, not the other way around.

Part II

36. *a* $\dfrac{11y - 30}{10y}$

You can't do anything until the two fractions have the same denominator. Multiply the top and bottom of the first fraction by 5:

$$\frac{5}{5} \cdot \frac{y - 4}{2y} = \frac{5(y - 4)}{5(2y)} = \frac{5y - 20}{10y}$$

Similarly, multiply the top and bottom of the second fraction by 2:

$$\frac{2}{2} \cdot \frac{3y - 5}{5y} = \frac{2(3y - 5)}{2(5y)} = \frac{6y - 10}{10y}$$

Now add them:

$$\frac{5y - 20}{10y} + \frac{6y - 10}{10y} = \frac{11y - 30}{10y}$$

b $\dfrac{-25y^2}{y + 2}$

First, turn the division problem into a multiplication problem by flipping the second term:

$$\frac{y^2 - 7y + 10}{5y - y^2} \cdot \frac{25y^3}{y^2 - 4}$$

Now, factor all the complex terms like this:

$$y^2 - 7y + 10 = (y - 2)(y - 5)$$
$$5y - y^2 = y(5 - y)$$
$$y^2 - 4 = (y - 2)(y + 2)$$

Once you've factored these three terms, the problem looks like this:

$$\frac{(y - 2)(y - 5)}{y(5 - y)} \cdot \frac{25y^3}{(y - 2)(y + 2)}$$

Cancel out all the factors that appear both on the top and on the bottom, you're left with:

$$\frac{(y - 2)(y - 5)}{y(5 - y)} \cdot \frac{25y^3}{(y - 2)(y + 2)} = \frac{25y^2(y - 5)}{(y + 2)(5 - y)}$$

You're not done yet. Since $y - 5 = (-1)(5 - y)$, make the substitution:

$$\frac{25y^2(y-5)}{(y+2)(5-y)} = \frac{25y^2(-1)(5-y)}{(y+2)(5-y)} = \frac{-25y^2}{y+2}$$

37. 35

This problem is going to involve a lot of trigonometry, so you should find the measure of some angles. Since $\overline{LK} \cong \overline{LC}$, the angles opposite them, LCK and $\angle K$, are also equal in measure. Therefore, $m\angle LCK = 53$. Use the Rule of 180 on $\triangle AKC$:

$$m\angle KAC + m\angle K + m\angle ACK = 180$$
$$90 + 53 + m\angle ACK = 180$$
$$m\angle ACK = 37$$

Since $m\angle ACK + m\angle LCA = m\angle LCK$, you can calculate that $m\angle LCA = 16$:

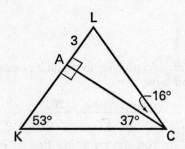

Now do the trig in $\triangle LCA$. You want to find the length LC, which is the hypotenuse of the triangle. You know the length of the opposite leg, $\overline{LA}$. Thus, use the sine (the SOH in SOHCAHTOA):

$$\sin 16° = \frac{LA}{LC}$$

$$0.2756 = \frac{3}{LC}$$

$$0.2756(LC) = 3$$

$$LC = \frac{3}{0.2756}$$

$$LC = 10.88$$

Now you have the lengths of two sides (since $\overline{LK} \cong \overline{LC}$, $LK = 10.88$). There's one more calculation to make, and then you'll be done: you have to find KC. Look at $\triangle ACK$. Since $AL = 3$, $AK = 10.88 - 3$, or 7.88. $\overline{AK}$ is the side adjacent to $\angle K$, and you want to find the hypotenuse KC. Use cosine (the CAH in SOHCAHTOA):

$$\cos 53° = \frac{AK}{KC}$$

$$0.6018 = \frac{7.88}{KC}$$

$$0.6018(KC) = 7.88$$

$$KC = \frac{7.88}{0.6018}$$

$$KC = 13.09$$

Add up all three sides of $\triangle KLC$, and you'll have the perimeter:

$$P = LK + LC + KC = 10.88 + 10.88 + 13.09 = 34.85$$

When you round this off to the nearest meter, as instructed, your answer becomes 35.

38. *a*

Start the graphing process by plugging the integers between 0 and 6, inclusive, into the equation for the parabola and determine its coordinates. For example, if $x = 0$, then $y = -(0)^2 + 6(0) - 8$, or -8. Your first ordered pair is $(0,-8)$. Here is the rest of your T-chart and the accompanying sketch:

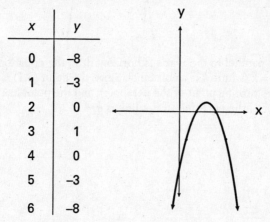

x	y
0	-8
1	-3
2	0
3	1
4	0
5	-3
6	-8

b **1**

From the graph, you can see that the parabola reaches its peak at $x = 3$. Substitute 3 for x in the equation to find the value of y:

$$y = -(3)^2 + 6(3) - 8 = -9 + 18 - 8 = 1$$

Note: If you're not sure where the maximum value of y is, you can determine the axis of symmetry of the parabola using the formula:

$$x = -\frac{b}{2a}$$

In the parabola $y = -x^2 + 6x - 8$, $a = -1$ and $b = 6$:

$$x = -\frac{6}{2(-1)} = \frac{-6}{-2} = 3$$

c $y = 1$

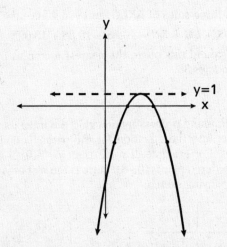

A line parallel to the x-axis is horizontal, so the equation must look like $y = k$ (where k is a constant). Since the point $(3,1)$ is on the line (it's the turning point of the parabola), and the point has a y-coordinate of 1, the equation of the line is $y = 1$.

39. *a* 165

Since the order in which Elyssa chooses the videos doesn't matter, use the combinations rule:

$$_nC_r = \frac{n!}{r!\,(n-r)!}$$

Elyssa has 11 videos to choose from ($n = 11$), and she wants to choose three ($r = 3$):

$$_{11}C_3 = \frac{11!}{3!\,8!} = \frac{11 \cdot 10 \cdot 9 \cdot 8 \cdot 7 \cdot 6 \cdot 5 \cdot 4 \cdot 3 \cdot 2 \cdot 1}{3 \cdot 2 \cdot 1 \cdot (8 \cdot 7 \cdot 6 \cdot 5 \cdot 4 \cdot 3 \cdot 2 \cdot 1)}$$

$$= \frac{990}{6} = 165$$

b 60

There are four comedies, and Elyssa wants to choose one of them. The number of combinations is $_4C_1$, or 4. There are also six dramas, and Elyssa chooses two of them. Using the same technique, you know that the number of combinations of dramas is $_6C_2$, or 15. The number of three-video combinations consisting of one comedy and two dramas is 4 × 15, or 60.

c $\dfrac{24}{165}$

First, calculate the number of combinations consisting of one of each type of video. Elyssa can choose one of four comedies ($_4C_1 = 4$), one of six dramas ($_6C_1 = 6$), and only one mystery ($_1C_1 = 1$). The number of combinations is $4 \cdot 6 \cdot 1$, or 24. From part A, you know there are 165 possible combinations of three videos, so the probability that a combination will contain one of each type of video is $\dfrac{24}{165}$.

d 6

In this case, the order of the films does matter, so you have to use the permutations rule:

$$_nP_r = \frac{n!}{r!}$$

There are three videos ($n = 3$), and Elyssa watches one at a time ($r = 1$):

$$_3P_1 = \frac{3!}{1!} = 3 \cdot 2 \cdot 1 = 6$$

40. a $20 - x$

From the Segment Addition Postulate, $AD + DC = AC$. Since $AC = 20$ and $AD = x$, you can rewrite the equation as:

$$x + DC = 20$$
$$DC = 20 - x$$

b 2

When you draw the altitude of a right triangle, you cut the triangle into two smaller right triangles. All three of the triangles (the original one, $\triangle ABC$, and the two smaller ones, $\triangle BDC$ and $\triangle ADB$) are similar; all their corresponding sides and angles are proportional to each other.

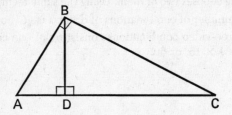

$\overline{AD}$ is the short side of $\triangle ADB$, and $\overline{BD}$ is the long side. In $\triangle BDC$, $\overline{BD}$ is the short side and $\overline{DC}$ is the long side. Set up the proportion:

$$\frac{AD}{BD} = \frac{BD}{DC}$$
$$\frac{x}{6} = \frac{6}{20 - x}$$

Cross-multiply and solve for x:

$$x(20 - x) = 36$$
$$20x - x^2 = 36$$
$$20x - x^2 - 36 = 0$$

Multiply the equation by –1 and rearrange the expression until it's a quadratic in standard form:

$$x^2 - 20x + 36 = 0$$
$$(x - 2)(x - 18) = 0$$
$$x = \{2, 18\}$$

There are two possible values, but the problem specifies that $AD < DC$. Therefore, $x = 2$.

c $2\sqrt{10}$

Use the Pythagorean Theorem on $\triangle ADB$:

$$(AB)^2 = (AD)^2 + (BD)^2$$
$$(AB)^2 = 2^2 + 6^2$$
$$(AB)^2 = 4 + 36$$
$$(AB)^2 = 40$$
$$AB = \sqrt{40}$$

Since the question specifies "simplest radical form," this answer is not sufficient. You have to reduce the radical by factoring out a perfect square:

$$\sqrt{40} = \sqrt{4 \cdot 10} = \sqrt{4} \cdot \sqrt{10} = 2\sqrt{10}$$

Part III

41.

The plan: $\overline{BD}$ is an altitude, so it's perpendicular to $\overline{AC}$. Thus, $\angle ADB$ and $\angle CDB$ are right angles. $\overline{BD}$ is also a median, so $\overline{AD} = \overline{DC}$ Prove that $\triangle ADB$ and $\triangle CDB$ are congruent using SAS, then use CPCTC.

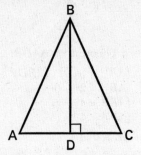

Statements	Reasons
1. $\overline{BD}$ is the median to $\overline{AC}$	1. Given
2. D is the midpoint of $\overline{AC}$	2. Definition of a median
3. $\overline{AD} \cong \overline{DC}$	3. Definition of midpoint
4. $\overline{BD}$ is the altitude to $\overline{AC}$	4. Given
5. $\overline{BD}$ is perpendicular to $\overline{AC}$	5. Definition of an altitude
6. $\angle ADB$ and $\angle CDB$ are right angles	6. Definition of perpendicular
7. $\angle ADB \cong \angle CDB$	7. All right angles are congruent.
8. $\overline{BD} \cong \overline{BD}$	8. Reflexive Property of Congruence
9. $\triangle ADB \cong \triangle CDB$	9. SAS $\cong$ SAS
10. $\overline{BA} \cong \overline{BC}$	10. CPCTC

42. *a*

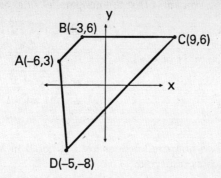

A trapezoid has exactly one pair of opposite parallel sides. To prove that *ABCD* is a trapezoid, you have to show that two of the sides are parallel and the other two are not. To do this, find the slope of each of the sides using the slope formula:

$$m = \frac{y_2 - y_1}{x_2 - x_1}$$

Slope of $\overline{AB}$:   Slope of $\overline{BC}$:   Slope of $\overline{CD}$:   Slope of $\overline{AD}$:

$m = \dfrac{6 - 3}{-3 - (-6)}$ $m = \dfrac{6 - 6}{9 - (-3)}$ $m = \dfrac{-8 - 6}{-5 - 9}$ $m = \dfrac{-8 - 3}{-5 - (-6)}$

$= \dfrac{3}{3}$ $= \dfrac{0}{12}$ $= \dfrac{-14}{-14}$ $= \dfrac{-11}{1}$

$= 1$ $= 0$ $= 1$ $= -11$

Since $\overline{AB}$ and $\overline{CD}$ have the same slope, those two sides are parallel. The other two have different slopes, so they are not parallel. Thus, quadrilateral *ABCD* is a trapezoid.

b

In an isosceles trapezoid, the two non-parallel sides have the same length. To prove that *ABCD* is NOT an isosceles trapezoid, find the length of the nonparallel sides using the distance formula:

$$d = \sqrt{(x_2 - x_1)^2 + (y_2 - y_1)^2}$$

From part A, you know that the nonparallel sides are $\overline{BC}$ and $\overline{AD}$:

Length of $\overline{BC}$:

$$d = \sqrt{(6-6)^2 + [9-(-3)]^2}$$
$$= \sqrt{0^2 + 12^2}$$
$$= \sqrt{144}$$
$$= 12$$

Length of $\overline{AD}$:

$$d = \sqrt{(-8-3)^2 + [-5-(-6)]^2}$$
$$= \sqrt{(-11)^2 + 1^2}$$
$$= \sqrt{121+1}$$
$$= \sqrt{122}$$

Since the two nonparallel sides are not equal in length, $ABCD$ is not an isosceles trapezoid.

EXAMINATION
JUNE 1997

Part I

Answer 30 questions from this part. Each correct answer will receive 2 credits. No partial credit will be allowed. Write your answers in the spaces provided on the separate answer sheet. Where applicable, answers may be left in terms of π or in radical form. [60]

1 Using the table below, compute $(1 \star 5) \star (2 \star 7)$.

$\star$	1	2	5	7
1	2	7	1	5
2	7	5	2	1
5	1	2	5	7
7	5	1	7	2

2 In the accompanying diagram, line l is parallel to line k, line $m \perp$ line k, and m$\angle x$ = m$\angle y$. Find m$\angle x$.

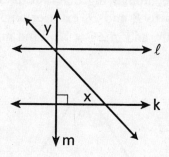

3 If ♥ is a binary operation defined as $a ♥ b = \sqrt{a^2 + b^2}$, find the value of 12 ♥ 5.

4 In the accompanying diagram of similar triangles ABE and ACD, $\overline{ABC}$, $\overline{AED}$, $AB = 6$, $BC = 3$, and $ED = 4$. Find the length of $\overline{AE}$.

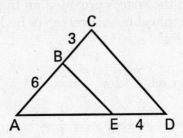

5 How many different 5-letter arrangements can be formed from the letters in the word "DANNY"?

6 Evaluate: $\dfrac{9!}{3! \, 5!}$

7 In the accompanying diagram of $\triangle ABC$, $\overline{AB}$ is extended to E and D, exterior angle CBD measures 130°, and m$\angle C = 75$. Find m$\angle CAE$.

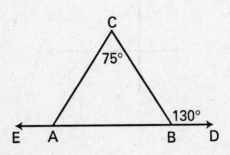

8 In right triangle ABC, $\angle C$ is a right triangle and m$\angle B$ = 60. What is the ratio of m$\angle A$ to m$\angle B$?

9 In $\triangle ABC$, m$\angle A$ = 3x + 40, m$\angle B$ = 8x + 35, and m$\angle C$ = 10x. Which is the longest side of the triangle?

10 A bookshelf contains seven math textbooks and three science textbooks. If two textbooks are drawn at random without replacement, what is the probability both books are science textbooks?

11 Express the product in lowest terms:

$$\frac{x^2 - x - 6}{3x - 9} \bullet \frac{2}{x + 2}$$

12 In rhombus $ABCD$, the measure of $\angle A$ is 30° more than twice the measure of $\angle B$. Find m$\angle B$.

13 The endpoints of the diameter of a circle are (−6,2) and (10,−2). What are the coordinates of the center of the circle?

14 Find the area of a triangle whose vertices are (1,2), (8,2), and (1,6).

15 Find the distance between points (−1,−1) and (2,−5).

16 In the accompanying diagram, the bisectors of ∠A and ∠B in acute triangle ABC meet at D, and m∠ADB = 130. Find m∠C.

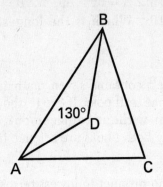

17 Point P is on line m. What is the total number of points 3 centimeters from line m and 5 centimeters from point P?

18 The diagonals of a rhombus are 8 and 10. Find the measure of a side of the rhombus to the *nearest tenth*.

Directions (19–34): For *each* question chosen, write on the separate answer sheet the *numeral* preceding the word or expression that best completes the statement or answers the question.

19 In isosceles triangle ABC, $\overline{AB} \cong \overline{BC}$, point D lies on $\overline{AC}$, and $\overline{BD}$ is drawn. Which inequality is true?
   (1) m∠A > m∠ADB   (3) BD > AB
   (2) m∠C > m∠CDB   (4) AB > BD

20 If the statements m, $m \rightarrow p$, and $r \rightarrow {\sim}p$ are true, which statement must also be true?

(1) ~r   (3) $r \wedge {\sim}p$

(2) ~p   (4) ${\sim}p \vee {\sim}m$

21 If a point in Quadrant IV is reflected in the y-axis, its image will lie in Quadrant

(1) I   (3) III

(2) II   (4) IV

22 In right triangle ABC, m$\angle C$ = 90, m$\angle A$ = 63, and AB = 10. If BC is represented by a, then which equation can be used to find a?

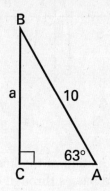

(1) $\sin 63° = \dfrac{a}{10}$ (3) $\tan 63° = \dfrac{a}{10}$

(2) $a = 10 \cos 63°$ (4) $a = \tan 27°$

23 If point $R'(6,3)$ is the image of point $R(2,1)$ under a dilation with respect to the origin, what is the constant of the dilation?

(1) 1   (3) 3

(2) 2   (4) 6

24 What is an equation of a line that passes through the point $(0,3)$ and is perpendicular to the line whose equation is $y = 2x - 1$?

(1) $y = -2x + 3$ (3) $y = -\dfrac{1}{2}x + 3$

(2) $y = 2x + 3$ (4) $y = \dfrac{1}{2}x + 3$

25 What is an equation of the function shown in the accompanying diagram?

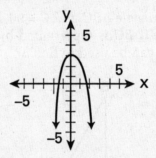

(1) $y = x^2 + 3$ (3) $y = -x^2 - 3$
(2) $y = -x^2 + 3$ (4) $y = (x - 3)^2$

26 What is an equation of the line that is parallel to the y-axis and passes through the point $(2,4)$?

(1) $x = 2$ (3) $x = 4$
(2) $y = 2$ (4) $y = 4$

27 In the accompanying diagram, the altitude to the hypotenuse of right triangle *ABC* is 8.

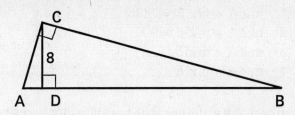

The altitude divides the hypotenuse into segments whose measures may be

(1) 8 and 12   (3) 6 and 10
(2) 3 and 24   (4) 2 and 32

28 If the coordinates of the center of a circle are (−3,1) and the radius is 4, what is an equation of the circle?

(1) $(x - 3)^2 + (y + 1)^2 = 4$
(2) $(x + 3)^2 + (y - 1)^2 = 16$
(3) $(x + 3)^2 + (y - 1)^2 = 4$
(4) $(x - 3)^2 + (y + 1)^2 = 16$

29 Which expression is a solution for the equation $2x^2 - x = 7$?

(1) $\dfrac{-1 \pm \sqrt{57}}{2}$ (3) $\dfrac{-1 \pm \sqrt{57}}{4}$

(2) $\dfrac{1 \pm \sqrt{57}}{2}$ (4) $\dfrac{1 \pm \sqrt{57}}{4}$

30 If the complement of $\angle A$ is greater than the supplement of $\angle B$, which statement *must* be true?
   (1) $m\angle A + m\angle B = 180$
   (2) $m\angle A + m\angle B = 90$
   (3) $m\angle A < m\angle B$
   (4) $m\angle A > m\angle B$

31 How many different four-person committees can be formed from a group of six boys and four girls?

   (1) $\dfrac{10!}{4!}$ (3) $_6C_2 \cdot {}_4C_2$

   (2) $_{10}P_4$ (4) $_{10}C_4$

32 Which equation represents the axis of symmetry of the graph of the equation $y = x^2 - 4x - 12$?
   (1) $y = 4$ (3) $y = -2$
   (2) $x = 2$ (4) $x = -4$

33 What is $\dfrac{1}{x} + \dfrac{1}{1-x}$, $x \neq 1, 0$, expressed as a single fraction?

   (1) $\dfrac{1}{x(1-x)}$ (3) $\dfrac{2}{-x}$

   (2) $\dfrac{-1}{x(x+1)}$ (4) $\dfrac{1}{x(x-1)}$

34 In the accompanying diagram, $\overline{RL} \perp \overline{LP}$, $\overline{LR} \perp \overline{RT}$, and M is the midpoint of $\overline{TP}$.

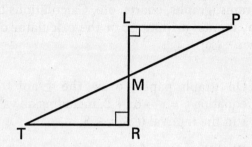

Which method could be used to prove $\triangle TMR \cong \triangle PML$?

(1) SAS ≅ SAS   (3) HL ≅ HL
(2) AAS ≅ AAS   (4) SSS ≅ SSS

Directions (35): Leave all construction lines on the answer sheet.

35 *On the answer sheet*, construct an equilateral triangle in which $\overline{AB}$ is one of the sides.

Part II

Answer *three* questions from this part. Clearly indicate the necessary steps, including appropriate formula substitutions, diagrams, graphs, charts, etc. Calculations that may be obtained by mental arithmetic or the calculator do not need to be shown. [30]

36 *a* On graph paper, draw the graph of the equation $y = x^2 - 8x + 2$, including all values of x in the interval $0 \le x \le 8$. [6]

b Find the roots of the equation $x^2 - 8x + 2 = 0$ to the *nearest hundredth*. [*Only an algebraic solution will be accepted.*] [4]

37 The coordinates of the endpoints of $\overline{AB}$ are $A(-2,4)$ and $B(4,1)$.

a On a set of axes, graph $\overline{AB}$. [1]

b On the same set of axes, graph and state the coordinates of

(1) $\overline{A'B'}$, the image of $\overline{AB}$ after a reflection in the x-axis [2]

(2) $\overline{A''B''}$, the image of $\overline{A'B'}$ after a translation that shifts (x,y) to $(x + 2,y)$ [2]

c Using coordinate geometry, determine if $\overline{A'B'} \cong \overline{A''B''}$. Justify your answer. [5]

38 Answer both *a* and *b* for all values for which these expressions are defined.

  a Solve for x: $-\dfrac{2}{5} + \dfrac{x+4}{x} = 1$ [4]

  b Express the difference in simplest form:

$$\frac{3y}{y^2 - 4} - \frac{2}{y + 2} \quad \text{[6]}$$

39 Solve the following system of equations algebraically and check:

$$y = 2x^2 - 4x - 5$$
$$2x + y + 1 = 0 \quad \text{[8,2]}$$

40 In the accompanying diagram of $\triangle ABC$, altitude $AD = 13$, $\overline{AB} \cong \overline{AC}$, and m$\angle BAC$ = 70.

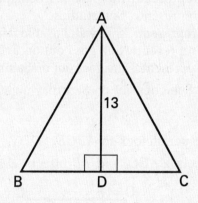

  a Find BC to the *nearest tenth*. [4]

  b Using the answer from part *a*, find, to the *nearest tenth*, the

  (1) area of $\triangle ABC$ [2]
  (2) perimeter of $\triangle ABC$ [4]

Part III

Answer *one* question from this part. Clearly indicate the necessary steps, including appropriate formula substitutions, diagrams, graphs, charts, etc. Calculations that may be obtained by mental arithmetic or the calculator do not need to be shown. [10]

41 Given: If Sue goes out on Friday night and not on Saturday night, then she does not study.

If Sue does not fail mathematics, then she studies.

Sue does not fail mathematics.

If Sue does not go out on Friday night, then she watches a movie.

Sue does not watch a movie.

Let *A* represent: "Sue fails mathematics."

Let *B* represent: "Sue studies."

Let *C* represent: "Sue watches a movie."

Let *D* represent: "Sue goes out on Friday night."

Let *E* represent: "Sue goes out on Saturday night."

Prove: Sue goes out on Saturday night. [10]

42 Given: parallelogram $ABCD$, $\overline{DFC}$, $\overline{AEB}$, $\overline{ED}$ bisects $\angle ADC$, and $\overline{FB}$ bisects $\angle ABC$.

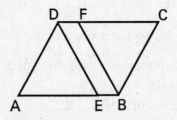

Prove: $\overline{EB} \cong \overline{DF}$ [10]

ANSWERS AND EXPLANATIONS
JUNE 1997
ANSWER KEY

Part I

1. 2	13. (2,0)	25. (2)
2. 45	14. 14	26. (1)
3. 13	15. 5	27. (4)
4. 8	16. 80	28. (2)
5. 60	17. 4	29. (4)
6. 504	18. 6.4	30. (3)
7. 125	19. (4)	31. (4)
8. $\frac{1}{2}$	20. (1)	32. (2)
9. $\overline{AC}$	21. (3)	33. (1)
10. $\frac{1}{15}$	22. (1)	34. (2)
11. $\frac{2}{3}$	23. (3)	35. construction
12. 50	24. (3)	

Part II

36. *a* see explanations

    b 0.26 and 7.74

37. *a* see explanations

    b (1) $A'(-2,-4), B'(4,-1)$

       (2) $A''(0,-4), B''(6,-1)$

    c see explanations

38. *a* 10

    b $\dfrac{y+4}{y^2-4}$

39. $(2,-5)$ and $(-1,1)$
   Check

40. *a* 18.2

    b (1) 118.3

       (2) 49.9

Part III

41. see explanations
42. see explanations

EXPLANATIONS
Part I

1. 2

Figure out the terms in parentheses first. To calculate 1 ★ 5, find
the 1 in the leftmost column and run your finger along that row until
you reach the column headed by the 5. You'll find that 1 ★ 5 = 1:

★	1	2	5	7
1	2	7	1	5
2	7	5	2	1
5	1	2	5	7
7	5	1	7	2

Similarly find the other term in parentheses: 2 H 7 = 1. The problem now looks like this:

$$(1 \star 5) \star (2 \star 7) = 1 \star 1$$

Similarly, $1 \star 1 = 2$

2. 45

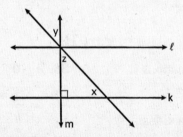

Look at the triangle in the center of the diagram. The sum of the
three angles is 180°. Since one of the angles is a right angle, the
sum of the other two angles, $\angle x$ and $\angle z$ is 90. Now look at the angles.
The problem states that m $\angle x$ = m $\angle y$. Since $\angle y$ and $\angle z$ are vertical angles, m $\angle y$ = m $\angle z$. Therefore, m $\angle x$ = m $\angle z$.

Since angles x and z are equal to each other and have a sum of 90,
each angle must measure 45°. Therefore, m $\angle x$ = 45.

3. 13

Don't let the symbols freak you out. This function question defines what the " ♥ " means, so all you have to do is plug in $a = 12$ and $b = 5$·

$$a \heartsuit b = \sqrt{a^2 + b^2}$$

$$12 \heartsuit 5 = \sqrt{12^2 + 5^2} = \sqrt{144 + 25} = \sqrt{169} = 13$$

4. 8

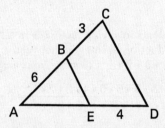

Corresponding sides of the two triangles are proportional. Since $AC = AB + BC$, you can infer that $AC = 9$. Let $AE = x$ and set up the following proportion:

$$\frac{AB}{AC} = \frac{AE}{AD}$$

$$\frac{6}{9} = \frac{x}{x + 4}$$

Now cross-multiply:

$$9x = 6(x + 4)$$
$$9x = 6x + 24$$
$$3x = 24$$
$$x = 8$$

5. 60

The formula to follow is a variation of the permutations rule. To find the number of possible arrangements of the letter in a word with n letters, in which one letter appears p times (when that p is greater than 1), the formula looks like this:

$$\frac{n!}{p!}$$

DANNY has 5 letters, but there are two N's. Therefore, you can express the number of arrangements as:

$$\frac{5!}{2!} = \frac{5 \cdot 4 \cdot 3 \cdot 2 \cdot 1}{2 \cdot 1} = 60$$

If your name is Danny, think of how you can impress your friends at parties!

6. 504

Wow. Two problems involving factorials in a row. The term $n!$ represents the product of all integers between 1 and n, inclusive. For example, $4! = 4 \cdot 3 \cdot 2 \cdot 1$. Calculate your answer like this:

$$\frac{9!}{3!\,5!} = \frac{9 \cdot 8 \cdot 7 \cdot 6 \cdot 5 \cdot 4 \cdot 3 \cdot 2 \cdot 1}{3 \cdot 2 \cdot 1 \cdot (5 \cdot 4 \cdot 3 \cdot 2 \cdot 1)} = 9 \cdot 8 \cdot 7 = 504$$

7. 125

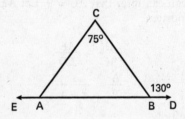

The measure of an exterior angle of a triangle equals the sum of the two non-adjacent interior angles, and $\angle CBD$ is an exterior angle:

$$m\angle CAB + m\angle C = m\angle CBD$$
$$m\angle CAB + 75 = 130$$
$$m\angle CAB = 55$$

Since $\angle CAE$ and $\angle CAB$ are supplementary, $m\angle CAE = 125$.

8. $\dfrac{1}{2}$

Given that $\angle C$ is a right angle, m$\angle C$ = 90. Since m$\angle B$ = 60, the Rule of 180 dictates that m$\angle A$ = 30.

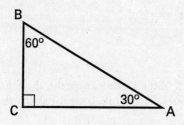

The ratio of m$\angle A$ to m$\angle B$ is $\dfrac{30}{60}$, or $\dfrac{1}{2}$.

9. $\overline{AC}$

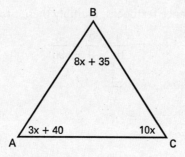

Solve for x first, using the Rule of 180:

$$m\angle A + m\angle B + m\angle C = 180$$
$$(3x + 40) + (8x + 35) + 10x = 180$$
$$21x + 75 = 180$$
$$21x = 105$$
$$x = 5$$

Now find the size of each angle:

$$m\angle A = 3(5) + 40 = 55$$
$$m\angle B = 8(5) + 35 = 75$$
$$m\angle C = 10(5) = 50$$

Since $\angle B$ is the largest angle of $\triangle ABC$, the side opposite $\angle B$, side $\overline{AC}$, is the largest side.

10. $\dfrac{1}{15}$

There is a total of ten textbooks on the shelf, and three of them are science textbooks. Therefore, the probability that you'll select a science textbook the first time is $\dfrac{3}{10}$.

After one book is selected, there are nine books left and only two of them are science textbooks. The probability that a second book is selected is $\dfrac{2}{9}$. To find the probability that the first two books selected are science textbooks, multiply these two fractions together:

$$\frac{3}{10} \cdot \frac{2}{9} = \frac{6}{90}$$

This fraction reduces to $\dfrac{1}{15}$.

11. $\dfrac{2}{3}$

If you do a little factoring, you'll see how nicely this thing reduces:

$$x^2 - x - 6 = (x - 3)(x + 2)$$
$$3x - 9 = 3(x - 3)$$

The product now looks like this:

$$\frac{(x-3)(x+2)}{3(x-3)} \cdot \frac{2}{x+2}$$

Cross off the terms that appear both on the top and bottom, and you're left with:

$$\frac{\cancel{(x-3)}\cancel{(x+2)}}{3\cancel{(x-3)}} \cdot \frac{2}{\cancel{x+2}} = \frac{2}{3}$$

12. 50

If $m\angle B = x$, then $m\angle A = 2x + 30$:

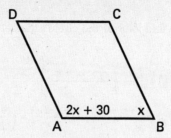

All rhombi are parallelograms, and the sum of any two consecutive angles in a parallelogram is 180°. Since $\angle A$ and $\angle B$ are consecutive angles, $m\angle A + m\angle B = 180$:

$$x + (2x + 30) = 180$$
$$3x + 30 = 180$$
$$3x = 150$$
$$x = 50$$

Check your work when you're done: if $m\angle B = 50$, then $m\angle A = 2(50) + 30$, or 130. Since $50 + 130 = 180$, the two angles are supplementary.

13. (2,0)

If the endpoints of the diameter of a circle are $(-6,2)$ and $(10,-2)$, then the center of the circle must be the midpoint of the segment between those two points:

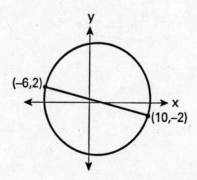

The formula for the midpoint of a segment is:

$$(\bar{x}, \bar{y}) = \left(\frac{x_1 + x_2}{2}, \frac{y_1 + y_2}{2} \right)$$

Therefore, the midpoint of the circle's diameter is:

$$(\bar{x}, \bar{y}) = \left(\frac{x_1 + x_2}{2}, \frac{y_1 + y_2}{2} \right)$$

$$(\bar{x}, \bar{y}) = \left(\frac{-6 + 10}{2}, \frac{2 + (-2)}{2} \right) = \left(\frac{4}{2}, \frac{0}{2} \right) = (2, 0)$$

14. 14

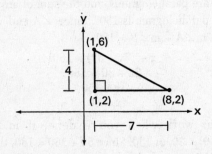

From the diagram, you can discern that the triangle is a right triangle. The base of the triangle is 7 units long ($b = 7$), and the triangle's height is 4 units ($h = 4$). Use the formula for the area of a triangle to find the triangle's area:

$$area = \frac{1}{2} \cdot base \cdot altitude$$

$$= \frac{1}{2} \cdot 7 \cdot 4 = 14$$

15. 5

Use the distance formula to find the distance between two points:

$$d = \sqrt{(y_2 - y_1) + (x_2 - x_1)}$$

Let (x_1, y_1) equal $(-1,-1)$, and (x_2, y_2) equal $(2,-5)$:

$$d = \sqrt{\left[-5 - (-1)\right]^2 + \left[2 - (-1)\right]^2} = \sqrt{(-4)^2 + 3^2} = \sqrt{16 + 9} = \sqrt{25} = 5$$

16. 80

This one's tricky because it requires a little imagination. Look at $\triangle ADB$. The sum of all three angles in $\triangle ADB$ equals 180, so $m\angle BAD + m\angle DBA = 50$.

Here's where the imagination kicks in. There's no way you can know the exact measures of $\angle BAD$ and $\angle DBA$, but you don't have to. Their sum is 50, so let $m\angle BAD = 30$ and $m\angle DBA = 20$:

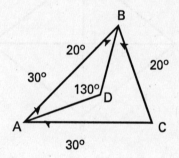

Since $\overline{AD}$ bisects $\angle BAC$, $m\angle BAC = 60$. Similarly, $m\angle CBA = 40$. Now you can use the Rule of 180 to find $m\angle C$:

$$m\angle BAC + m\angle CBA + m\angle C = 180$$
$$60 + 40 + m\angle C = 180$$
$$m\angle C = 80$$

17. 4

The locus of points 5 centimeters from point P is a circle with a radius of 5. The locus of points that are 3 centimeters from line m is two lines. The diagram looks like this:

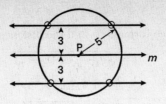

There are four points of intersection

18. 6.4

The diagonals of a rhombus bisect each other. Since the length of diagonal $\overline{AC}$ is 10, then $AE = 5$. Using this same logic, you can figure out that $BE = 4$.

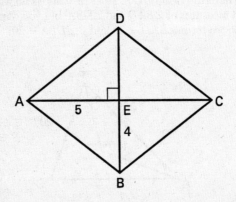

The diagonals of a rhombus are also perpendicular to each other, so $\triangle ABE$ is a right triangle. Therefore, you can use the Pythagorean Theorem to find the length of $\overline{AB}$:

$$(AB)^2 = (AE)^2 + (BE)^2$$
$$(AB)^2 = 5^2 + 4^2$$
$$(AB)^2 = 25 + 16$$
$$(AB)^2 = 41$$
$$AB = \sqrt{41}$$

Use your calculator to find $\sqrt{41}$, which equals 6.403. When you round this to the nearest tenth, as instructed, you get 6.4.

Multiple Choice

19. (4)

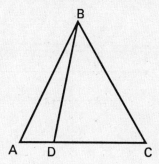

Since $AB = BC$, any line segment drawn from B to $\overline{AC}$ has to be shorter than either side of the triangle. Therefore, AB has to be bigger than BD.

20. (1)

Here's a little mini-proof. Given that m and $m \to p$, the Law of Detachment dictates that the result is p. It looks like this in symbolic form:

$$[(m \to p) \wedge m] \to p$$

The second rule to use is the Rule of *Modus Tollens*, which combines the Law of Detachment and the Law of Contrapositive Inference:

$$[(r \to \sim p) \wedge m] \to \sim r$$

The statement $\sim r$ must be true

21. (3)

The quadrants look like this.

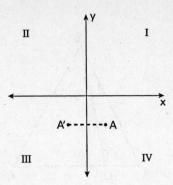

If point A in Quadrant IV is reflected in the y-axis, the image of the point, A', will appear in Quadrant III

22. (1)

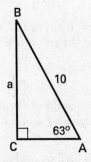

Side a is the leg opposite $\angle A$, and $\overline{AB}$ is the hypotenuse, which is 10 units long. Since you know the opposite and the hypotenuse, use the sine (the SOH in SOHCAHTOA):

$$\sin A = \frac{\text{opposite}}{\text{hypoteneuse}}$$

$$\sin 63° = \frac{a}{10}$$

Since no other answer choice mentions the sine, you can cross them all off.

23. (3)

When a point undergoes a dilation, each coordinate of that point is multiplied by a constant. The image of (x,y), for example, is (kx,ky).

Each coordinate of point $R(2,1)$ is multiplied by 3 in order to map it onto its image, $R(6,3)$. Therefore, the constant of the dilation is 3.

24. (3)

Because the equation $y = 2x - 1$ is in slope-intercept form ($y = mx + b$), you know that the slope of the line is 2. The slopes of perpendicular lines are negative reciprocals (their product is -1), so the slope of the line you're looking for is $-\dfrac{1}{2}$.

Each of the answer choices is also in slope-intercept form, and the only one with a slope of $-\dfrac{1}{2}$ is answer choice (3).

25. (2)

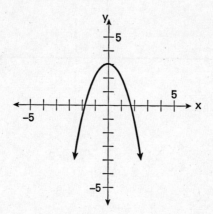

The parabola in this question opens down, so the coefficient of the x^2 term, otherwise known as a, is negative. (The rule is: if $a > 0$, the parabola "smiles"; if $a < 0$, it "frowns.") Eliminate answer choices (1) and (4), because a is positive in each of them.

The only bit of information left is the y-intercept. The parabola intercepts the y-axis at the point $(0,3)$, so its y-intercept is 3. Therefore, the proper equation is $y = -x^2 + 3$.

Note: Even though there are only two terms in the equation, the equation of this parabola is still in standard form. It just happens that $b = 0$.

26. (1)

Lines that are parallel to the y-axis are vertical and have the equation $x = h$, in which h is a constant. You can eliminate answer choices (2) and (4), because they have y's in them.

Now look at the point in the question. The x-coordinate of $(2,4)$ is 2, so the equation of the line must be $x = 2$.

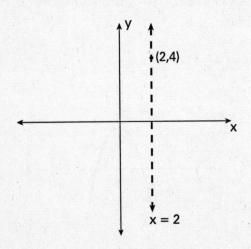

27. (4)

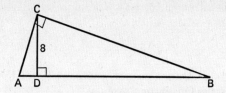

When you draw the altitude of a right triangle, you cut the triangle into two smaller right triangles. All three of the triangles (the original one, $\triangle ABC$, and the two smaller ones, $\triangle ACD$ and $\triangle CBD$) are similar; all their corresponding sides are proportional to each other. In $\triangle ACD$, AD is the short leg and CD is the long leg. In $\triangle CBD$, CD is the short leg and DB is the long leg. Therefore:

$$\frac{AD}{CD} = \frac{CD}{DB}$$

Since $CD = 8$, you can substitute and cross-multiply:

$$\frac{AD}{8} = \frac{8}{DB}$$
$$AD \cdot DB = 64$$

The product of the lengths AD and DB must be 64, and only answer choice (4) fulfills this requirement. To be sure, you can check the proportion:

$$\frac{2}{8} = \frac{8}{32}$$
$$\frac{1}{4} = \frac{1}{4}$$

28. (2)

Use the formula for a circle, and remember that (h,k) is the center and r is the radius:

$$(x - h) + (y - k) = r^2$$
$$[x - (-3)]^2 + (y - 1) = 4^2$$
$$(x + 3)^2 + (y - 1)^2 = 16$$

Since the formula involves r^2 and not r, you should recognize that the formula will equal 16, not 4. Therefore, eliminate answer choices (1) and (3).

29. (4)

As the answer choices suggest, you can't factor the equation; you have to use the Quadratic Formula:

$$x = \frac{-b \pm \sqrt{b^2 - 4ac}}{2a}$$

Before you do that, though, you have to put the equation in standard form by subtracting 7 from both sides:

$$2x^2 - x = 7$$
$$2x^2 - x - 7 = 0$$

In the equation $2x^2 - x - 7 = 0$, $a = 2$, $b = -1$, and $c = -7$:

$$x = \frac{-(-1) \pm \sqrt{(-1)^2 - 4(2)(-7)}}{2(2)} = \frac{1 \pm \sqrt{1 + 56}}{4} = \frac{1 \pm \sqrt{57}}{4}$$

30. (3)

To get a grip on this problem, plug in some numbers (and make sure the numbers you choose fit the requirements). If $m\angle A = 40$, then the complement of $\angle A$ is 50. If $m\angle B = 160$, then the supplement of $\angle B$ is 20. At this point, you can tell that $m\angle A < m\angle B$, and that the rest of the answer choices can't be correct.

31. (4)

Don't be distracted by the fact that there are six boys and four girls. It doesn't matter how many boys and girls there are in the four-person group, so you only have to note that there are ten kids to choose from.

To find the number of ways you can choose four of ten people, use the combinations rule:

$$_{10}C_4$$

You don't even have to solve it.

32. (2)

When a parabola appears in the form $y = ax^2 + bx + c$ as this one does, the equation of its axis of symmetry is:

$$x = -\frac{b}{2a}$$

For this parabola, $a = 1$, $b = -4$, and $c = -12$. Thus the axis of symmetry is:

$$x = -\frac{-4}{2(1)} = \frac{4}{2} = 2$$

The equation of the axis of symmetry is $x = 2$.

Note: When the equation of a parabola is in standard form, its axis of symmetry is vertical and its equation is $x = k$, in which k is a constant. Therefore, you can eliminate answer choices (1) and (3).

33. (1)

You can't do anything until the two fractions have the same denominator. To make two fractions compatible, multiply the top and bottom of the first fraction by $(1 - x)$:

$$\frac{(1-x)}{(1-x)} \cdot \frac{1}{x} = \frac{1-x}{x(1-x)}$$

Multiply the top and bottom of the second fraction by x:

$$\frac{x}{x} \cdot \frac{1}{1-x} = \frac{x}{x(1-x)}$$

Now you can add the fractions:

$$\frac{1-x}{x(1-x)} + \frac{x}{x(1-x)} = \frac{1-x+x}{x(1-x)} = \frac{1}{x(1-x)}$$

34. (2)

Be careful here; don't be suckered into choosing Hy-Leg just because the triangles in the diagram are right triangles. You know that the hypotenuses are congruent because M is the midpoint of $\overline{TP}$, but you don't know anything about either of the legs.

All right angles are congruent, so ∠L ≅ ∠R. Further, ∠LMP and ∠TMR are vertical angles, so they're congruent. Since you know of two congruent angles, the applicable congruency theorem involves 2 angles. The only one that does is answer choice (2).

35.

This is one of the easiest constructions to do (if you remember it, that is). Make your compass exactly as wide as $\overline{AB}$; put the pointy end on A and make an arc above the segment, like this:

A   B

Without changing the width of your compass, put the point on B and make another arc above the segment. Identify the point of intersection as point C.

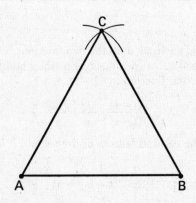

Once you draw $\overline{AC}$ and $\overline{BC}$, you've constructed equilateral triangle ABC.

Part II

36. *a*

Start the graphing process by plugging the integers between 0 and 8, inclusive, into the equation for the parabola and determine its coordinates. For example, if $x = 0$, then $y = (0)^2 - 8(0) + 2$, or 2. Your first ordered pair is (0,2). Here's the rest of your T-chart and the accompanying sketch:

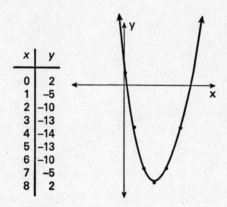

x	y
0	2
1	-5
2	-10
3	-13
4	-14
5	-13
6	-10
7	-5
8	2

b $x = \{7.74, 0.26\}$

You can't factor the equation (the fact that you have to solve for x to the nearest hundredth should give you a hint), so you have to use the Quadratic Formula:

$$x = \frac{-b \pm \sqrt{b^2 - 4ac}}{2a}$$

In the equation $x^2 - 8x + 2 = 0$, $a = 1$, $b = -8$, and $c = 2$:

$$x = \frac{-(-8) - \sqrt{(-8^2) - 4(1)(2)}}{2(1)} = \frac{8 - \sqrt{64 - 8}}{2} = \frac{8 + \sqrt{56}}{2}, \frac{8 - \sqrt{56}}{2}$$

Use your calculator to find that $\sqrt{56} = 7.48$ and substitute:

$$x = \frac{8 + 7.48}{2} \qquad\qquad x = \frac{8 - 7.48}{2}$$

$$= \frac{15.48}{2} \qquad\qquad\qquad = \frac{.52}{2}$$

$$= 7.74 \qquad\qquad\qquad\quad = 0.26$$

37. *a*

The graph is the easy part:

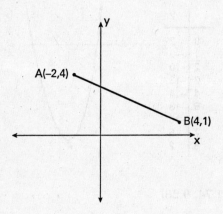

b   (1)   *A′*(–2,–4), *B′*(4,–1)

After a reflection in the *x*-axis, the *y*-coordinate of each point is negated and the *x*-coordinate of each point remains unchanged. In other words, $r_{x\text{-axis}}\ (x,y) \to (x,-y)$.

Therefore, the image of *A*(–2,4) is *A′*(–2,–4), and the image of *B*(4,1) is *B′*(4,–1).

    (2)   *A″*(0,–4), *B″*(6,–1)

Under a translation $(x + 2,y)$, each *x*-coordinate increases by 2 and each *y*-coordinate remains the same. The image of *A′*(–2,4) is *A″*(–2 + 2,4), or *A″*(0,4); the image of *B′*(4,–1) is *B″*(4 + 2,1), or *B″*(6,1).

Your graph should now look like this:

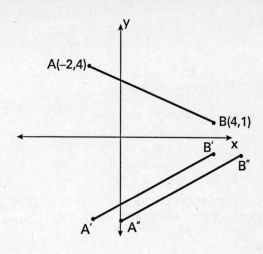

c

It should be obvious that $\overline{A'B'} = \overline{A''B''}$, because a translation doesn't change the size of an object. The Regents folks want you to prove it using algebra, so use the distance formula to find the length of each segment:

$$d = \sqrt{(x_2 - x_1)^2 + (y_2 - y_1)^2}$$

$$A'B' = \sqrt{\left[4 - (-2)\right]^2 + \left[-1 - (-4)\right]^2} \qquad A''B'' = \sqrt{(6 - 0)^2 + \left[-1 - (-4)\right]^2}$$

$$= \sqrt{6^2 + 3^2} \qquad\qquad\qquad = \sqrt{6^2 + 3^2}$$

$$= \sqrt{36 + 9} \qquad\qquad\qquad = \sqrt{36 + 9}$$

$$= \sqrt{45} \qquad\qquad\qquad\qquad = \sqrt{45}$$

$$= 3\sqrt{5} \qquad\qquad\qquad\qquad = 3\sqrt{5}$$

The two segments have the same length.

38. *a* **10**

The easiest way to start is to add $\dfrac{2}{5}$ to both sides:

$$-\frac{2}{5} + \frac{x+4}{x} + \frac{2}{5} = 1 + \frac{2}{5}$$

$$\frac{x+4}{x} = \frac{7}{5}$$

Now you can cross-multiply and solve:

$$7x = 5(x+4)$$
$$7x = 5x + 20$$
$$2x = 20$$
$$x = 10$$

As always, remember to check your work by plugging 10 in for x in the original equation and making sure it works.

b $\dfrac{y+4}{y^2-4}$

You can't do anything until the two fractions have the same denominator. Since $y^2 - 4 = (y+2)(y-2)$, you don't have to do anything to the first fraction. Multiply the top and bottom of the second fraction by $(y-2)$:

$$\frac{(y-2)}{(y-2)} \cdot \frac{2}{y+2} = \frac{2(y-2)}{(y+2)(y-2)} = \frac{2y-4}{y^2-4}$$

Now subtract them:

$$\frac{3y}{y^2-4} - \frac{2y-4}{y^2-4} = \frac{3y - (2y-4))}{y^2-4} = \frac{y+4}{y^2-4}$$

Be careful with the minus signs. You're subtracting $2y - 4$ from $3y$, so be sure to use parentheses. Otherwise, your numerator will be $y - 4$, and you'll lose points.

39. **(2,–5) and (–1,1)**

Look at the second equation first, and rearrange it until only y appears on the left side of the equation:

$$2x + y + 1 = 0$$
$$2x + y = -1$$
$$y = -2x - 1$$

Set the two equations equal to each other like this:

$$y = 2x^2 - 4x - 5$$
$$y = -2x - 1$$
$$2x^2 - 4x - 5 = -2x - 1$$
$$2x^2 - 2x - 5 = -1$$
$$2x^2 - 2x - 4 = 0$$

Since each coefficient is divisible by 2, divide each term to make the quadratic easier to factor:

$$x^2 - x - 2 = 0$$

Factor and solve for x:

$$(x - 2)(x + 1) = 0$$
$$x = \{2, -1\}$$

You have the two x-values, so you have to find each corresponding y-values:

If $x = 2$, then $y = 2(2)^2 - 4(2) - 5$, or –5. The first solution is (2,–5).

If $x = -1$, then $y = 2(-1)^2 - 4(-1) - 5$, or 1. The second solution is (–1,1).

Be sure to check your work by substituting back into the equations, or you'll lose two points.

40. ***a*** **18.2**

Since $\overline{AB} \cong \overline{AC}$, $\triangle ABC$ is isosceles. The altitude from the vertex of an isosceles triangle bisects the vertex angle, so m$\angle BAD$ = m$\angle DAC$ = 35.

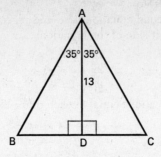

Use trigonometry in $\triangle ABD$ to find BD. You know the adjacent leg ($AD = 13$), and you want to find the opposite leg. Use tangent (the TOA in SOHCAHTOA):

$$\tan \angle BAD = \frac{BD}{AD}$$

$$\tan 35° = \frac{BD}{13}$$
$$13(0.7002) = BD$$
$$9.1 = BD$$

The altitude of an isosceles triangle is also a median of that triangle. Therefore, D is the midpoint of $\overline{AC}$ and $BD = DC$. Thus, BC is twice as long as BD, or 18.2.

b **(1)** **118.3**

The area is a piece of cake. You know the length of $\overline{AB}$ the base ($BC = 18.2$) and the height ($AD = 13$), so use the formula for the area of a triangle:

$$A = \frac{1}{2} bh = \frac{1}{2} (18.2)(13) = 118.3$$

(2) 49.9

You know that $AB = AC$, so find the length of $\overline{AB}$ using the Pythagorean Theorem. From part A, you know that $BD = 9.1$:

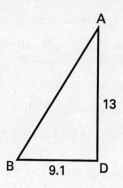

$$(AB)^2 = (AD)^2 + (BD)^2$$
$$(AB)^2 = 13^2 + (9.1)^2$$
$$(AB)^2 = 169 + 82.81$$
$$(AB)^2 = 251.81$$
$$AB = \sqrt{251.81} \ = 15.87$$

Add up all three sides of ABC, and you'll have the perimeter:

$$P = AB + BC + AC = 15.87 + 18.2 + 15.87 = 49.94$$

When you round this off to the nearest *tenth* of a meter, as instructed, your answer becomes 49.9.

Part III

41.

In this proof, they've already given you the symbols.

Step One: Turn all the givens into symbolic terms:

"If Sue goes out on Friday night and not on Saturday night, then she does not study." $(D \wedge \sim E) \rightarrow \sim B$

"If Sue does not fail mathematics, then she studies." $\sim A \rightarrow B$

"Sue does not fail mathematics." $\sim A$

"If Sue does not go out on Friday night, then she watches a movie." $\sim D \rightarrow C$

"Sue does not watch a movie." $\sim C$

Step Two: Decide what you want to prove:

"Sue goes out on Saturday night." $\sim E$

Step Three: Write the proof.

Statements	Reasons
1. $\sim A \rightarrow B$ $\sim A$	1. Given
2. B	2. Law of Detachment
3. $(D \wedge \sim E) \rightarrow \sim B$	3. Given
4. $\sim(D \wedge \sim E)$	4. Law of *Modus Tollens* (2,3)
5. $\sim D \vee E$	5. De Morgan's Law
6. $\sim D \rightarrow C$ $\sim C$	6. Given
7. D	7. Law of *Modus Tollens*
8. E	8. Law of Disjunctive Inference (5,7)

42.

The plan: Prove that *DFBE* is a parallelogram, then prove that because opposite sides of a parallelogram are congruent.

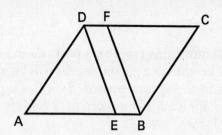

Statements	Reasons
1. *ABCD* is a parallelogram	1. Given
2. $\overline{DC}$ is parallel to $\overline{AC}$	2. Definition of a parallelogram
3. ∠CFB ≅ ∠ABF	3. Alternate interior angles are congruent.
4. m∠ADC = m∠ABC	4. Opposite angles of a parallelogram are equal in measure.
5. $\overline{DE}$ bisects ∠ADC; $\overline{FB}$ bisects ∠ABC	5. Given
6. m∠CDE = m∠ADC m∠ABF = m∠ABC	6. Definition of angle bisector
7. m∠CDE = m∠ABF	7. Halves of equal quantities are equal
8. m∠CDE = m∠CFB	8. Transitive Property of Equality
9. $\overline{DE}$ is parallel to $\overline{FE}$	9. If two lines are cut by a transversal and corresponding angles are congruent, then the lines are parallel.
10. *DFBE* is a parallelogram	10. Definition of a parallelogram
11 $\overline{EB}$ ≅ $\overline{DF}$	11 Opposite sides of a parallelogram are congruent

EXAMINATION
AUGUST 1997

Part 1

Answer 30 questions from this part. Each correct answer will receive 2 credits. No partial credit will be allowed. Write your answers in the spaces provided on the separate answer sheet. Where applicable, answers may be left in terms of π or in radical form. [60]

1 If $\blacklozenge$ is a binary operation defined by $m \blacklozenge n = (2m - n)^2$, find the value of $7 \blacklozenge 4$.

2 In the accompanying diagram, $\angle 1$ and $\angle 2$ are supplementary. What is $m\angle 3$?

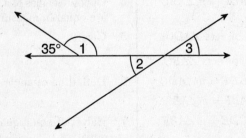

3 Perform the indicated operation and express in lowest terms:

$$\frac{x^2 - 25}{14} \div \frac{x - 5}{28}$$

4 The altitudes of two similar triangles are in the ratio 2:3. If the perimeter of the smaller triangle is 18, find the perimeter of the larger triangle.

5 The lengths of the sides of a triangle are 5, 7, and 8. What is the perimeter of the triangle that is formed by joining the midpoints of these sides?

6 If the measure of an exterior angle of one of the base angles in an isosceles triangle is 110°, find the number of degrees in the measure of the vertex angle.

7 What are the coordinates of the image of point $(-1,8)$ after a reflection in the origin?

8 What is the positive root of the equation $3x^2 + 5x = 8$?

9 In the accompanying diagram of isosceles trapezoid $ABCD$, $AB = 18$, $CD = 10$, and $AD = BC = 5$. Find the height of the trapezoid.

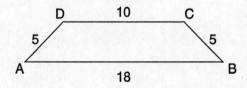

10 Solve the following system of equations for the positive value of x:

$$y = x$$
$$y = x^2$$

11 In the accompanying diagram of △ABC, $\overline{AFB}$, $\overline{AEC}$, $\overline{AC} \perp \overline{CB}$, $\overline{AE} \perp \overline{EF}$, BF = 8, FA = 12, FE = 9, and BC = x. What is the value of x?

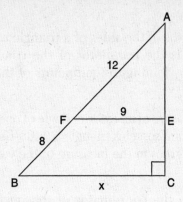

12 The coordinates of A are (4,5) and the coordinates of B are (10,y). If the midpoint of $\overline{AB}$ is (7,–2), find the value of y.

13 A parabola whose equation is $y = x^2 - 2x + k$ has a turning point with coordinates (1,–5). Find the value of k.

Directions (14–35): For *each* question chosen, write on the separate answer sheet the *numeral* preceding the word or expression that best completes the statement or answers the question.

14 What is the negation of the statement "The Sun is shining and it is warm"?

   (1) The Sun is not shining or it is not warm.
   (2) The Sun is shining and it is not warm.
   (3) The Sun is shining or it is not warm.
   (4) The Sun is not shining or it is warm.

15 What is the sum of $\dfrac{x-2}{3}$ and $\dfrac{x-3}{2}$?

   (1) $\dfrac{2x-5}{2}$ (3) $\dfrac{3x-5}{3}$

   (2) $\dfrac{3x-5}{2}$ (4) $\dfrac{5x-13}{6}$

16 Which equation represents the locus of points equidistant from points (1,1) and (7,1)?

   (1) $x = 4$ (3) $x = -4$
   (2) $y = 4$ (4) $y = -4$

17 In the accompanying diagram, $\overleftrightarrow{AGB} \parallel \overleftrightarrow{CED}$, m∠AGF = 30, and m∠CEF = 45.

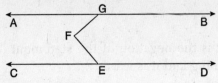

What is m∠GFE?

(1) 45   (3) 60
(2) 52   (4) 75

18 After the translation that shifts (x,y) to $(x + 2, y-2)$, the image of point $B(-3,0)$ lies in Quadrant

(1) I   (3) III
(2) II   (4) IV

19 If the statements $a \rightarrow {\sim}b$ and ${\sim}c \rightarrow b$ are true, which statement is a logically valid conclusion?

(1) $a \rightarrow c$ (3) $b \rightarrow a$
(2) $a \rightarrow {\sim}c$ (4) ${\sim}b \rightarrow a$

20 Which statement about a parallelogram is *not* always true?

(1) Diagonals are perpendicular.
(2) Opposite sides are congruent.
(3) Opposite angles are congruent.
(4) Consecutive angles are supplementary.

21 Which equation represents the line that passes through the point (0,1) and is parallel to the line whose equation is $3x + y = 5$?

(1) $3x + y = 3$ (3) $3x + y = 0$

(2) $3x + y = 1$ (4) $3x + y = -1$

22 If the lengths of the diagonals of a rhombus are 6 and 8, the perimeter of the rhombus is

(1) 5   (3) 20

(2) 10   (4) 40

23 Which equation represents a line perpendicular to the line whose equation is $y = -3x + 2$?

(1) $y = -3x - 4$ (3) $y = \dfrac{1}{3}x - 6$

(2) $y = 3x + 4$ (4) $y = -\dfrac{1}{3}x - 6$

24 The vertices of $\triangle ABC$ are $A(9,0)$, $B(-3,0)$, and $C(0,5)$. What is the area of $\triangle ABC$ in square units?

(1) 22.5   (3) 45

(2) 30   (4) 60

25 Which statement is the converse of "If two sides of a triangle are congruent, then the triangle is isosceles"?

(1) If a triangle is not isosceles, then two sides of the triangle are not congruent.
(2) If two sides of a triangle are not congruent, then the triangle is not isosceles.
(3) If a triangle is isosceles, then two sides of the triangle are congruent.
(4) If two sides of a triangle are not congruent, then the triangle is isosceles.

26 If the measure of an exterior angle of a regular polygon is 45°, then the polygon is

(1) a decagon   (3) a pentagon
(2) an octagon   (4) a square

27 What are the coordinates of A', the image of $A(1,2)$ after the reflection in the line $y = x$?

(1) $(1,-2)$ (3) $(-2,-1)$
(2) $(-1,2)$ (4) $(2,1)$

28 The solution of the quadratic equation $x^2 + 3x - 5 = 0$ is

(1) $\dfrac{3 \pm \sqrt{11}}{2}$ (3) $\dfrac{3 \pm \sqrt{29}}{2}$

(2) $\dfrac{-3 \pm \sqrt{11}}{2}$ (4) $\dfrac{-3 \pm \sqrt{29}}{2}$

29 Expressed as a fraction in lowest terms,
$\dfrac{x^2 - x - 2}{x^2 - 4}, x \neq \pm 2$, is equivalent to

(1) $\dfrac{-x - 2}{-4}$

(3) $\dfrac{x - 1}{x - 2}$

(2) $\dfrac{x}{x + 2}$

(4) $\dfrac{x + 1}{x + 2}$

30 If the lengths of two sides of a triangle measure 7 and 12, the length of the third side could measure

(1) 16

(3) 3

(2) 19

(4) 5

31 If the graphs of the equations $x^2 + y^2 = 25$ and $y = x$ are drawn on the same set of axes, what is the total number of points common to both graphs?

(1) 1

(3) 3

(2) 2

(4) 0

32 A 100-foot wire is extended from the ground to the top of a 60-foot pole, which is perpendicular to the level ground. To the *nearest degree*, what is the measure of the angle that the wire makes with the ground?

(1) 31

(3) 53

(2) 37

(4) 59

33 How many different six-letter arrangements can be made from the letters in the name "JENNIE"?

(1) 15

(3) 180

(2) 30

(4) 720

34 There are 5 blue pencils and 3 gold pencils in a container. If 2 pencils are drawn at random without replacement, what is the probability that both pencils drawn are gold?

(1) $\dfrac{1}{4}$

(3) $\dfrac{3}{28}$

(2) $\dfrac{5}{14}$

(4) $\dfrac{9}{64}$

35 Which statement is illustrated in the construction sketched below?

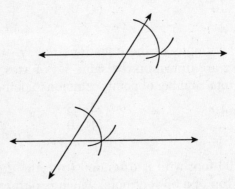

(1) Through a point not on a given line, exactly one line can be drawn perpendicular to the given line.
(2) If two lines cut by a transversal form congruent alternate interior angles, then the two lines are parallel.
(3) If two lines cut by a transversal form congruent corresponding angles, then the two lines are parallel.
(4) If two lines cut by a transversal form same side interior angles that are supplementary, then the two lines are parallel

Part II

Answer three questions from this part. Clearly indicate the necessary steps, including appropriate formula substitutions, diagrams, graphs, charts, etc. Calculations that may be obtained by mental arithmetic or the calculator do not need to be shown. [30]

36 *a* On graph paper, draw the graph of the equation $y = x^2 + 4x + 4$ for all values of x in the interval $-5 \leq x \leq 1$.   [6]

    b Describe fully the locus of points 3 units from the turning point of the graph of the equation. [2]

    c Describe fully the locus of points 5 units from the axis of symmetry of the graph of the equation. [2]

37 In the accompanying table, the operation ♠ is commutative.

♠	a	–b	–a	b
a	–b		b	
–b	–a	b		–b
–a		a	–b	
b	a		–a	b

    a On your answer paper, copy and complete the table.   [2]

    b What is the identity element for the operation ♠?   [2]

c What is the inverse of $-a$ under the operation ♠? [2]

d Evaluate: $a ♠ a ♠ a$ [2]

e Solve for x: $(-a ♠ a) ♠ x = -b$ [2]

38 Answer *a* and *b* for all values of x for which these expressions are defined.

a Find the values of x to the *nearest hundredth*:

$$\frac{1}{x} = \frac{x+2}{2x+3}$$ [4]

b Solve for x in simplest radical form:

$$\frac{x^2 + 2x + 4}{x} = \frac{2x}{1}$$ [6]

39 *a* Given: $(D \wedge \sim L) \rightarrow R$
$\sim R$
D

Prove: L [5]

b Three sophomores, four juniors, and two seniors are trying out for the mathematics team. The coach must select three students from this group for the team.

(1) How many selections of three students can be made from this group? [2]

(2) What is the probability that one sophomore and two juniors are selected for the team? [3]

40 In the accompanying diagram of right triangle *LPG*,
    $\overline{GNP} \perp \overline{PL}$, *LG* = 52, *LP* = 20, and m∠*NLP* = 35.

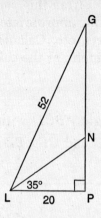

a Find, to the *nearest integer*, the length of $\overline{PN}$.

[2]

b Find, to the *nearest integer*, the length of $\overline{GN}$.

[4]

c Find, to the *nearest degree*, the measure of angle
    GLN.

[4]

Part III

Answer one question from this part. Clearly indicate the necessary steps, including appropriate formula substitutions, diagrams, graphs, charts, etc. Calculations that may be obtained by mental arithmetic or the calculator do not need to be shown.   [10]

41 Given: rectangle $ABCD$ with diagonal $\overline{BFED}$ drawn, $\overline{AE} \perp \overline{BD}$, and $\overline{CF} \perp \overline{BD}$.

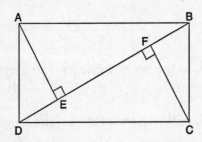

Prove: $\overline{AE} \cong \overline{CF}$ [10]

42 Quadrilateral $ABCD$ has coordinates $A(-2,0)$, $B(6,4)$, $C(2,8)$, and $D(-2,6)$.

Using coordinate geometry, prove that

a $ABCD$ is a trapezoid.   [7]

b $ABCD$ is *not* an isosceles trapezoid.   [3]

ANSWERS AND EXPLANATIONS
AUGUST 1997
ANSWER KEY

Part I

1. 100	13. −4	25. (3)
2. 35	14. (1)	26. (2)
3. $2(x + 5)$	15. (4)	27. (4)
4. 27	16. (1)	28. (4)
5. 10	17. (4)	29. (4)
6. 40	18. (3)	30. (1)
7. (1,−8)	19. (1)	31. (2)
8. 1	20. (1)	32. (2)
9. 3	21. (2)	33. (3)
10. 1	22. (3)	34. (3)
11. 15	23. (3)	35. (3)
12. −9	24. (2)	

Part II

36. *a* see explanations

   b $(x + 2)^2 + y^2 = 9$

     or

   A circle whose center is (−2,0) and radius is 3.

   c $x = 3$ and $x = −7$

     or

   Two lines parallel to the line $x = −2$ and 5 units from it.

37. *a* see explanations

   b *b*

   c *a*

   d −*a*

   e −*b*

38. *a* ±1.73

   b $1 ± \sqrt{5}$

39. *a* see explanations

   b (1) 84

     (2) $\dfrac{18}{84}$

40. *a* 14

   b 34

   c 32

Part III

41. see explanations

42. see explanations

EXPLANATIONS
Part I

1. **100**

   They've already defined the function for you, so just plug in $m = 7$ and $n = 4$:

   $$7 \blacklozenge 4 = \left[2(7) - 4\right]^2 = (14 - 4)^2 = (10)^2 = 100$$

2. **35**

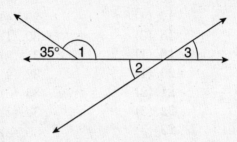

   Start from the left. The 35° angle and $\angle 1$ are supplementary, because they form a straight line. Therefore, $m\angle 1 = 180 - 35$, or 145. The question tells you that $\angle 1$ and $\angle 2$ are supplementary, so $m\angle 2 = 35$. Since $\angle 2$ and $\angle 3$ are vertical angles, they have the same measure. You now know that $\angle 3$ also measures 35°.

3. **$2(x + 5)$**

   When dividing fractions, don't ask why; just flip the second and multiply. When you flip the second fraction here, the problem becomes:

   $$\frac{x^2 - 25}{14} \cdot \frac{28}{x - 5}$$

   Factor $x^2 - 25$ into $(x + 5)(x - 5)$ and substitute:

   $$\frac{(x + 5)(x - 5)}{14} \cdot \frac{28}{x - 5}$$

   The $(x - 5)$ on the top and bottom cancel out, and 14 divides into 28 twice. Make the cancellations, and you're left with $2(x + 5)$.

4. 27

All parts of corresponding triangles are proportional. If the ratio of the altitudes of two similar triangles is 2:3, then the relationship between each of the corresponding sides is also 2:3:

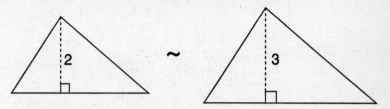

Therefore, the ratio of the perimeters is also 2:3. Set up the proportion (where x is the perimeter of the larger triangle):

$$\frac{2}{3} = \frac{18}{x}$$
$$2x = 54$$
$$x = 27$$

5. 10

Whenever the test doesn't give you a diagram, draw one

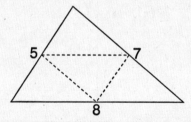

If you connect the midpoints of the three sides of a triangle, the perimeter of the smaller triangle is exactly half the perimeter of the original triangle. Since the perimeter of the original triangle is 5 + 7 + 8, or 20, then the perimeter of the smaller triangle is half of 20, or 10.

6. 40

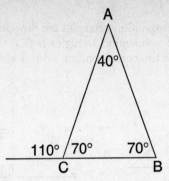

The exterior angle at C is supplementary to $\angle ACB$, so m$\angle ACB = 70$. The exterior angle is supplementary to one of the base angles, so the other base angle, $\angle B$, is also 70°. Now you have to find the measure of the vertex angle, $\angle A$. The sum of the three angles in a triangle is 180:

$$\text{m}\angle A + \text{m}\angle B + \text{m}\angle ACB = 180$$
$$\text{m}\angle A + 70 + 70 = 180$$
$$\text{m}\angle A = 40.$$

7. (1,–8)

Whenever a point is reflected in the origin, both coordinates of that point are negated. In other words, $r_{(0,0)}(x,y) \rightarrow (-x,-y)$:

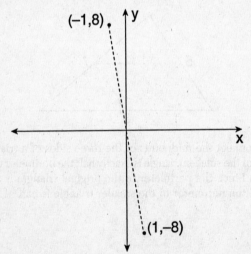

Thus, the image of (–1,8) after a reflection in the origin is (1,–8).

8. 1

Before you can factor anything, you have to subtract 8 from both sides of the equation to put the equation in standard form:

$$3x^2 + 5x - 8 = 0$$

Now factor the equation and solve for x:

$$(3x + 8)(x - 1) = 0$$

Set each factor equal to zero in order to find the roots:

$$3x + 8 = 0 \qquad\qquad x - 1 = 0$$
$$3x = -8 \qquad\qquad x = 1$$
$$x = -\frac{8}{3}$$

You want the positive root, so get rid of $-\frac{8}{3}$. Your answer is 1, and it pays to plug 1 back into your original equation to make sure it works:

$$3(1)^2 + 5(1) = 8$$
$$3 + 5 = 8. \text{ Check.}$$

Note: If you have trouble factoring the equation, there's always the Quadratic Formula.

9. 3

Add the altitudes $\overline{DX}$ and $\overline{CY}$ to the diagram like this:

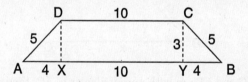

Since $ABCD$ is a trapezoid, $\overline{AB}$ is parallel to $\overline{CD}$. Thus $XYCD$ is a rectangle, and $XY = DC$ (because opposite sides of a rectangle are equal in length). Now look at the base. $AB = 18$, so $AX + YB = 8$. This is an isosceles trapezoid, so $AX = YB = 4$. From there, you can find the altitude by looking at right triangle AXD. You can use the Pythagorean Theorem to find that $DX = 3$, but it's faster if you realize that $\triangle AXD$ is a 3:4:5 right triangle.

10. 1

Since x^2 and x are both equal to y, you can set them equal to each other:

$$x^2 = x$$

Here's where most kids mess up. You can't divide both sides of the equation by x, because x might equal zero. You have to subtract x from both sides. The equation becomes:

$$x^2 - x = 0$$

Now factor x out of each term:

$$x(x - 1) = 0$$

Set each term equal to zero and solve for x:

$$x = \{0, 1\}$$

You want the positive value, so get rid of 0. (Remember that zero is neither positive nor negative!)

11. 15

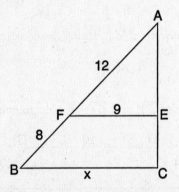

Since BC and FE are both perpendicular to AC, they are parallel to each other. Thus, $\triangle AFE$ and $\triangle ABC$ are similar (and corresponding parts are proportional). Set up the proportion:

$$\frac{AF}{FE} = \frac{AB}{BC}$$

Now, substitute all the values you know. (Since $AB = AF + FB$, you know that $AB = 20$.): $\dfrac{12}{9} = \dfrac{20}{x}$

Cross-multiply and solve for x:

$$12x = 180$$
$$x = 15$$

12. –9

Use the formula for the midpoint of a line segment:

$$(\overline{x}, \overline{y}) = \left(\frac{x_1 + x_2}{2}, \frac{y_1 + y_2}{2} \right)$$

For this problem, the midpoint $(\overline{x}, \overline{y})$ is $(7, -2)$, and you can let $(x_1, y_1) = A(4,5)$ and $(x_2, y_2) = (10, y)$. However, you only need to deal with the y-coordinate:

$$\overline{y} = \frac{y_1 + y_2}{2}$$
$$-2 = \frac{5 + y}{2}$$
$$-4 = 5 + y$$
$$-9 = y$$

13. –4

This looks like it requires more work than it actually does. It doesn't matter that $(1, -5)$ is the turning point of the parabola. All you need to know is that $(1, -5)$ is on the parabola. All you have to do is plug in $x = 1$ and $y = -5$ to the equation and solve for k:

$$y = x^2 - 2x + k$$
$$-5 = (1)^2 - 2(1) + k$$
$$-5 = 1 - 2 + k$$
$$-5 = -1 + k$$
$$-4 = k$$

Multiple Choice

Don't forget that one of the best techniques on these Multiple Choice questions is to use Process of Elimination to get rid of answer choices that aren't possible.

14. (1)

If you let S = "The Sun is shining" and let W = "The Sun is warm," you can express the statement symbolically like this:

$$S \wedge W$$

Remember that "$\wedge$" means "and" (the $\wedge$ looks sort of like a capital A, as in "And"). Now use De Morgan's Law to negate it:

$$\sim(S \wedge W) \rightarrow \sim S \vee \sim W$$

Since the symbol $\vee$ means "or," the translation of this statement is: "Either the Sun is *not* shining OR the Sun is *not* warm."

15. (4)

The lowest common denominator of the two fractions is 6, so you have to multiply both the top and bottom of the first fraction by 2 and the top and bottom of the second fraction by 3. From there, the algebra is rather basic:

$$\frac{x-2}{3} + \frac{x-3}{2} =$$

$$\frac{x-2}{3} \cdot \frac{(2)}{(2)} + \frac{x-3}{2} \cdot \frac{(3)}{(3)} =$$

$$\frac{2x-4}{6} + \frac{3x-9}{6} =$$

$$\frac{2x-4+3x-9}{6} = \frac{5x-13}{6}$$

16. (1)

The locus of points equidistant from any two points is the perpendicular bisector of the segment that connects the two points.

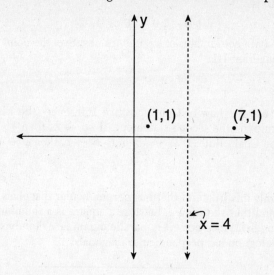

In this problem, the perpendicular bisector is vertical, so the equation must have the form $x = k$, where k is a constant. Eliminate (2) and (4). The constant k must also be halfway between 1 and 7. Thus, k can't be negative—eliminate (3).

17. (4)

This is a tricky one, and a lot of students probably skipped it. The key is drawing a third line that goes through point F (label it XY) and is parallel to lines $\overline{AB}$ and $\overline{CD}$, like this:

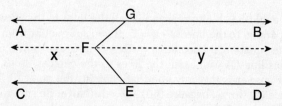

Now, FG becomes a transversal. Since alternate interior angles are congruent, m$\angle GFY = 30$. Similarly, m$\angle EFY = 45$. Since m$\angle GFE =$ m$\angle GFY +$ m$\angle EFY$, the measure of $\angle GFY$ is 75.

18. (3)

The translation $(x + 2, y - 2)$ shifts the x-coordinate 2 units to the right and the y-coordinate down 2 units. Therefore, the image of $B(-3,0)$ is:

$$(-3 + 2, 0 - 2) = (-1,-2).$$

When both coordinates of a point are negative, the point must be in the Quadrant III.

19. (1)

First, use the Law of Contrapositive Inference (the Flip-and-Negate rule) on the second statement: If $\sim c \rightarrow b$, then $\sim b \rightarrow c$. Now use the Chain Rule: If $a \rightarrow \sim b$ and $\sim b \rightarrow c$, then $a \rightarrow c$.

20. (1)

The only quadrilateral that has perpendicular diagonals is a rhombus (and thus the square, because a square is a rhombus with four 90° angles). Since not every parallelogram is a rhombus, not every parallelogram has perpendicular diagonals:

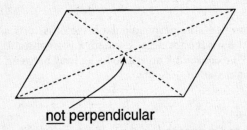

not perpendicular

Each of the other three answer choices is a property of a parallelogram.

21. (2)

You might be able to realize that all the lines in the answer choices are parallel to the line $3x + y = 5$. If you subtract $3x$ from both sides of the equation, it becomes $y = -3x + 5$; now you know that the slope of this line (as well as all the lines in the choices) is -3. Thus, the right answer is the only one that contains the point $(0, 1)$. Answer choice (2) works, because $3(0) + 1 = 1$. (**Note:** Be sure to substitute $x = 0$ and $y = 1$. If you get these reversed, you'll choose (1) instead.)

22. (3)

The rhombus is made up of four right triangles, each with legs measuring 6 and 8:

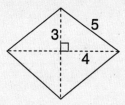

If you look carefully, you'll find that each triangle is a 3:4:5 triangle; thus, each hypotenuse equals 5. That makes the perimeter 4 • 5, or 20.

23. (3)

The line $y = -3x + 2$ is in standard form, so you know that the line's slope is -3. Since the slopes of any two lines are negative reciprocals (that is, their product is -1), any line that is perpendicular to $y = -3x + 2$ must have a slope of $\frac{1}{3}$. Each of the answer choices is also in standard $y = mx + b$ format, so (3) is the only line that has a slope of $\frac{1}{3}$.

24. (2)

Graph the points like this:

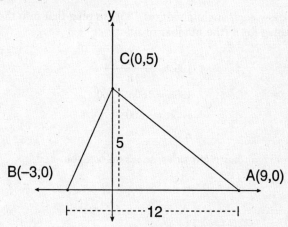

The length of the base (segment $\overline{AB}$) runs from $(-3,0)$ to $(9,0)$, so it's 12 units long. The triangle's altitude runs from the base to point C, so it's 5 units long. Now you can use the formula for the area of a triangle:

$$A = \frac{1}{2} bh$$

$$= \frac{1}{2}(12)(5)$$

$$= 30$$

25. (3)

To find the converse of any logical statement, just change the symbols around. (For example, the converse of $A \rightarrow B$ is $B \rightarrow A$.) In this problem, let A = "Two sides of a triangle are congruent" and B = "The triangle is isosceles." The statement given is $A \rightarrow B$, so the converse is "If the triangle is isosceles, then two sides of the triangle are congruent."

26. (2)

If the measure of an exterior angle of a regular polygon is 45°, then each interior angle measures 135°. The formula for finding the measure of an interior angle of a regular polygon is:

$$\text{angle} = \frac{180(n-2)}{n}$$

You know each angle measures 135°, so plug that into the formula and solve for n (the number of sides):

$$135 = \frac{180(n-2)}{n}$$

$$135n = 180n - 360$$

$$-45n = -360$$

$$n = 8.$$

The polygon has eight sides, so it's an octagon.

27. (4)

Whenever a point is reflected in the line $y = x$, the coordinates of that point are interchanged. In other words, $r_{y=x}(x,y) \rightarrow (y,x)$:

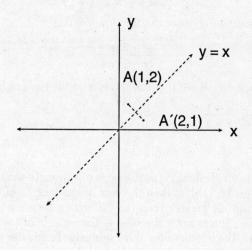

Thus, the image of $(1,2)$ after a reflection in the line $y = x$ is $(2,1)$.

28. (4)

Since the answer choices all contain square root signs, you should take the hint that you can't factor the equation—you need to use the Quadratic Formula:

$$x = \frac{-b \pm \sqrt{b^2 - 4ac}}{2a}$$

This equation is in standard $ax^2 + bx + c = 0$ format, and $a = 1$, $b = 3$, and $c = -5$:

$$x = \frac{-3 \pm \sqrt{(3)^2 - 4(1)(-5)}}{2(1)}$$

$$= \frac{-3 \pm \sqrt{9 + 20}}{2} = \frac{-3 \pm \sqrt{29}}{2}$$

29. (4)

You have to factor both the top and bottom of the fraction to simplify it:

$$x^2 - x - 2 = (x - 2)(x + 1)$$
$$x^2 - 4 = (x - 2)(x + 2)$$

Thus, you can re-write the fraction like this·

$$\frac{(x - 2)(x + 1)}{(x - 2)(x + 2)}$$

Once you cancel out the $(x - 2)$ terms on the top and bottom, you're left with $\dfrac{x + 1}{x + 2}$.

30. (1)

The rule for the lengths of the sides of a triangle states that any one side must be (1) less than the sum of the lengths of the other two sides, and (2) greater than the difference between of those same two sides. Since two of the sides of the triangle in question measure 7 and 12, the length of the third side must be greater than $12 - 7$, or 5, and less than $12 + 7$, or 19. Now look at the answer choices: 16 is the only choice within that range.

31. (2)

The first graph is a circle of radius 5 centered at the origin, and you should recognize $y = x$ as a line that goes through the origin and has a slope of 1:

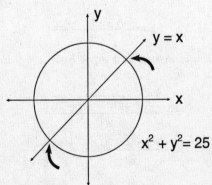

There are two points of intersection.

32. (2)

Draw the diagram like this:

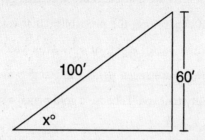

You want to find the value of x, so it's time for a little trigonometry. You know the length of the opposite side (60) and the length of the hypotenuse (60), so use sine (the SOH in SOHCAHTOA):

$$\sin x = \frac{60}{100}$$
$$\sin x = 0.6$$

Now hit the "sin^{-1}" button on your calculator. You should get $x = 36.87°$. When you round this to the nearest degree, as instructed, you get 37°.

33. (3)

To find the number of possible arrangements of the letters in a word with n letters, in which one letter appears p times and a different letter appears q times (remember that p and q are greater than 1), the formula looks like this:

$$\frac{n!}{p!\,q!}$$

JENNIE has six letters, but there are two E's and two N's. Therefore, you can express the number of arrangements as:

$$\frac{6!}{2!\,2!} = \frac{6 \cdot 5 \cdot 4 \cdot 3 \cdot 2 \cdot 1}{2 \cdot 1 \cdot (2 \cdot 1)} = \frac{720}{4} = 180$$

34. (3)

Before any pencils are chosen, there are three gold pencils out of a total of eight. Therefore, the probability that your first pencil will be gold is three out of eight, or $\frac{3}{8}$. After you've taken the gold pencil out, there are seven pencils left and two of them are gold. The probability that you'll choose a gold pencil a second time is two out of seven, or $\frac{2}{7}$.

To find the probability that you'll get two gold pencils, multiply the two individual probabilities together:

$$\frac{3}{8} \cdot \frac{2}{7} = \frac{6}{56}$$

This fraction reduces to $\frac{3}{28}$.

35. (3)

This construction illustrates the process whereby you construct a parallel line through a specific point. You use the compass to construct a second angle (the top one) that is congruent to and corresponds to the first one. The best answer choice that sums up this strategy is (3).

Part II

36. *a*

Create a chart by plugging in every number within the given range and finding the coordinates of the parabola.

x	$x^2 + 4x + 4$	y
–5	$(-5)^2 + 4(-5) + 4$	9
–4	$(-4)^2 + 4(-4) + 4$	4
–3	$(-3)^2 + 4(-3) + 4$	1
–2	$(-2)^2 + 4(-2) + 4$	0
–1	$(-1)^2 + 4(-1) + 4$	1
0	$(0)^2 + 4(0) + 4$	4
1	$(1)^2 + 4(1) + 4$	9

Now graph it like this:

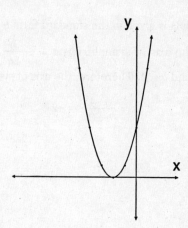

b

Using the chart in Part A, you can determine that the turning point of the parabola is (–2,0). The locus of points that are equidistant from a certain point is a circle, so the complete description of the locus is a circle with a radius of 3 and centered at (–2,0).

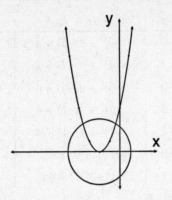

c

When a parabola is given in the standard form $y = ax^2 + bx + c$, the formula for the axis of symmetry is $x = -\dfrac{b}{2a}$. In this parabola, $a = 1$, $b = 4$, and $c = 4$. Therefore, the axis of symmetry is:

$$x = -\frac{4}{2(1)} = -2$$

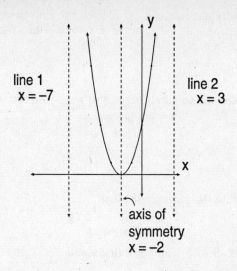

line 1
x = –7

line 2
x = 3

axis of
symmetry
x = –2

The locus of points equidistant from this line is two lines parallel to the line $x = -2$ and 5 units from it. One is five units to the left; subtract 5 from –2 and you get $x = -7$. The other line is five units to the right; add 5 to –2 and you get $x = 3$.

37. *a*

If a system is commutative, it's symmetrical over the central diagonal:

♠	*a*	*–b*	*–a*	*b*
a	*–b*	*–a*	*b*	*a*
–b	*–a*	*b*	*a*	*–b*
–a	*b*	*a*	*–b*	*–a*
b	*a*	*–b*	*–a*	*b*

b *b*

If you look at the bottom column (with the *b* character at the far left), you'll see that the letters along that column match the headings above them. Therefore, *b* is the identity element.

c **a**

The identity element is b, so you want to find the value that turns $-a$ into b. Look at the completed system: Since $(-a \spadesuit a) = b$, the inverse of $-a$ is $a \cdot$

d **$-a$**

Since there are no parentheses, just work your way left to right:

$$a \spadesuit a \spadesuit a =$$
$$-b \spadesuit a =$$
$$-a$$

e **$-b$**

Work within the parentheses first:

$$(-a \spadesuit a) \spadesuit x = -b$$
$$b \spadesuit x = -b$$

Since $b \spadesuit -b = -b$, you know that $x = -b$.

38. **a**   **± 1.73**

Whenever two fractions are equal to each other, you can cross-multiply:

$$\frac{1}{x} = \frac{x+2}{2x+3}$$
$$2x + 3 = x(x+2)$$
$$2x + 3 = x^2 + 2x$$

Since $2x$ cancels out on either side of the equation, the remaining equation is:

$$x^2 = 3$$

Thus, x must equal $\pm \sqrt{3}$, which is approximately equal to ± 1.73 (Use your calculator, and don't forget to include the "±". If you do forget, you'll lose 2 points.)

b $1 \pm \sqrt{5}$

Again, cross-multiply the two fractions:

$$\frac{x^2 + 2x + 4}{x} = \frac{2x}{1}$$

$$x^2 + 2x + 4 = 2x^2$$

$$-x^2 + 2x + 4 = 0$$

If you don't like the negative sign in front of the x^2, multiply every term in the equation by -1:

$$x^2 - 2x - 4 = 0$$

You can't factor this (you seldom can on a question in Part II), so you'll have to use the Quadratic Formula:

$$x = \frac{-b \pm \sqrt{b^2 - 4ac}}{2a}$$

In this equation, $a = 1$, $b = -2$, and $c = -4$:

$$x = \frac{-(-2) \pm \sqrt{(-2)^2 - 4(1)(-4)}}{2(1)}$$

$$= \frac{2 \pm \sqrt{4 + 16}}{2} = \frac{2 \pm \sqrt{20}}{2}$$

Unfortunately, you're not done yet. To find the *simplest radical form*, as instructed, you have to reduce the radical:

$$\sqrt{20} = \sqrt{4 \cdot 5} = \sqrt{4} \cdot \sqrt{5} = 2\sqrt{5}$$

Substitute the new term into the original fraction and reduce:

$$\frac{2 \pm 2\sqrt{5}}{2} = \frac{2(1 \pm \sqrt{5})}{2} = 1 \pm \sqrt{5}$$

39. *a*

Statements	Reasons
1. $(D \land \sim L) \rightarrow R$ $\sim R$	1. Given
2. $\sim(D \land \sim L)$	2. Law of *Modus Tollens* (1)
3. $\sim D \lor L$	3. De Morgan's Law (2)
4. D	4. Given
5. L	5. Law of Disjunctive Inference (3, 4)

Note: If you never learned the Law of *Modus Tollens*, you can use the Law of Contrapositive Inference first; $(D \land \sim L) \rightarrow R$ becomes $\sim R \rightarrow \sim(D \land \sim L)$. Now you can use the Law of Detachment.

b **(1) 84**

This is a basic combinations problem. There are nine students, and you have to choose three. Use the formula $_nC_r = \dfrac{n!}{r!(n-r)!}$ and plug in $n = 9$ and $r = 3$:

$$_9C_3 = \frac{9!}{3!6!} = \frac{9 \cdot 8 \cdot 7 \cdot 6 \cdot 5 \cdot 4 \cdot 3 \cdot 2 \cdot 1}{3 \cdot 2 \cdot 1 \cdot (6 \cdot 5 \cdot 4 \cdot 3 \cdot 2 \cdot 1)} = \frac{9 \cdot 8 \cdot 7}{3 \cdot 2 \cdot 1} = 84$$

(2) $\dfrac{18}{24}$

This is a bit more complicated, but not much. You have to choose one sophomore out of three:

$$_3C_1 = \frac{3!}{1!2!} = \frac{3 \cdot 2 \cdot 1}{1 \cdot (2 \cdot 1)} = 3$$

You have choose two juniors out of four:

$$_4C_2 = \frac{4!}{2!2!} = \frac{4 \cdot 3 \cdot 2 \cdot 1}{2 \cdot 1 \cdot (2 \cdot 1)} = 6$$

And you choose zero seniors out of two: $_2C_0 = 1$

(Remember that $_xC_0 = 1$. It might be easier to recognize that there's only one way to leave both seniors out.) Now multiply the three probabilities together: $3 \cdot 6 \cdot 1 = 18$.

There are eighteen groups that contain one sophomore and two juniors, and there are eighty-four possible combinations. Thus, the probability that a group will contain one sophomore and two juniors is $\dfrac{18}{24}$.

40. *a*   14

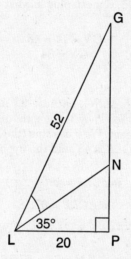

This first part requires trigonometry. In $\triangle LPN$, you know an angle (35°) and the length of the adjacent leg ($\overline{LP}$). You want to find the length of the opposite leg, so use tangent (the TOA in SOHCAHTOA):

$$\tan 35° = \frac{PN}{20}$$
$$PN = 20 \tan 35°$$
$$PN = 14.0042$$

When you round this off to the nearest integer, you get 14.

b 34

You might think this one requires trig as well, but it doesn't. Find GP using the Pythagorean Theorem:

$$(LG)^2 = (LP)^2 + (GP)^2$$
$$(52)^2 = (20)^2 + (GP)^2$$
$$2704 = 400 + (GP)^2$$
$$2304 = (GP)^2$$
$$48 = GP$$

Since $GN + NP = GP$, you can plug in what you know already to find the value of GN:

$$GN + 14 = 48$$
$$GN = 34$$

c 32

You can't work with $\triangle LNG$, because it's not a right triangle. Deal with $\triangle LPG$ instead. You know the lengths of all three sides, so choose sine, cosine, or tangent. We'll use sine (the SOH in SOHCAHTOA); the leg opposite $\angle GLP$ is 48, and the hypotenuse is 52:

$$m\angle GLP = \sin^{-1}\left(\frac{48}{52}\right)$$
$$m\angle GLP = 67.38$$

Since $m\angle GLN + m\angle NLP = m\angle GLP$, you can find the measure of $\angle GLN$ like this:

$$m\angle GLN + 35 = 67.38$$
$$m\angle GLN = 32.38$$

When you round this off to the nearest degree, as instructed, you get $32°$.

Part III

41. **The plan:** $\overline{AE}$ and $\overline{CF}$ are corresponding parts of $\triangle AEB$ and $\triangle DFC$, respectively, so you want to prove that the triangles are congruent using Angle-Angle-Side, then use CPCTC.

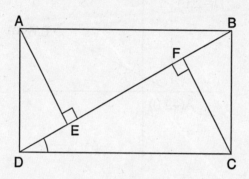

Statements	Reasons
1. $ABCD$ is a rectangle	1. Given
2. $\overline{AB} \cong \overline{DC}$	2. Opposite sides of a rectangle are congruent
3. $\overline{AB}$ is parallel to $\overline{DC}$	3. Opposite sides of a rectangle are parallel
4. $\angle EDC \cong \angle ABF$	4. When two parallel lines are cut by a transversal, alternate interior angles are congruent.
5. $\overline{AE} \perp \overline{BD}; \overline{CF} \perp \overline{BD}$	5. Given
6. $\angle AEF$ and $\angle EFC$ are right angles	6. Definition of right angles
7. $\angle AEF \cong \angle EFC$	7. All right angles are congruent.
8. $\triangle AEB \cong \triangle DFC$	8. AAS $\cong$ AAS
9. $\overline{AE} \cong \overline{CF}$	9. CPCTC

42. *a*

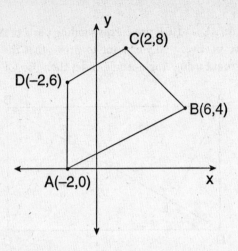

A trapezoid has exactly one pair of opposite parallel sides. To prove that *ABCD* is a trapezoid, you have to show that one pair of opposite sides are parallel and the other pair are not. To do this, find the slope of each of the sides using the slope formula:

$$m = \frac{y_2 - y_1}{x_2 - x_1}$$

Slope of $\overline{AB}$:   Slope of $\overline{BC}$:   Slope of $\overline{CD}$:   Slope of $\overline{AD}$:

$$m = \frac{4 - 0}{6 - (-2)} \qquad m = \frac{8 - 4}{2 - 6} \qquad m = \frac{6 - 8}{-2 - 2} \qquad m = \frac{0 - 6}{-2 - (-2)}$$

$$= \frac{4}{8} \qquad\qquad = \frac{4}{-4} \qquad\qquad = \frac{-2}{-4} \qquad\qquad = \frac{-6}{0}$$

$$= \frac{1}{2} \qquad\qquad = -1 \qquad\qquad = \frac{1}{2} \qquad\qquad = \infty$$

Since $\overline{AB}$ and $\overline{CD}$ have the same slope, those two sides are parallel.

The other two sides don't have the same slope (the slope of $\overline{AD}$ is undefined, so it's parallel to the *y*-axis), so they are not parallel. Thus, quadrilateral *ABCD* is a trapezoid.

b

The sides of a trapezoid that are not parallel are called legs, and the legs of an isosceles trapezoid are congruent. To prove that *ABCD* is NOT an isosceles trapezoid, find the length of each leg ($\overline{BC}$ and $\overline{AD}$) using the distance formula:

$$d = \sqrt{(x_2 - x_1)^2 + (y_2 - y_1)^2}$$

Length of $\overline{BC}$:

$d = \sqrt{(2 - 6)^2 + (8 - 4)^2}$

$= \sqrt{(-4)^2 + (4)^2}$

$= \sqrt{16 + 16}$

$= \sqrt{32} = 4\sqrt{2}$

Length of $\overline{AD}$:

$d = \sqrt{[-2 - (-2)]^2 + (0 - 6)^2}$

$= \sqrt{0^2 + (-6)^2}$

$= \sqrt{36}$

$= 6$

Since the two legs are not equal in length, *ABCD* is NOT an isosceles trapezoid.

EXAMINATION
JANUARY 1998

Part I

Answer 30 questions from this part. Each correct answer will receive 2 credits. No partial credit will be allowed. Write your answers in the spaces provided on the separate answer sheet. Where applicable, answers may be left in terms of π or in radical form. [60]

1 If a binary operation is defined as $a \star b = \dfrac{2a+b}{b}$, evaluate $6 \star 3$.

2 In the accompanying diagram, rectangle $ABCD$ is similar to rectangle $EFGH$, $AD = 3$, $AB = 5$, $EF = 8$, and $FG = x$. Find the value of x.

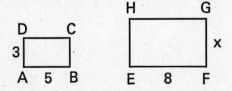

3 In the accompanying diagram, $\overleftrightarrow{ALB} \parallel \overleftrightarrow{CJD}$ and $\overleftrightarrow{LJ}$ is a transversal. If m$\angle JLB = 6x - 7$ and m$\angle LJD = 7x + 5$, find the value of x.

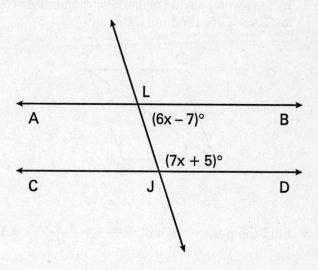

4 Factor completely: $2x^2 - 18$

5 In accompanying diagram, m$\angle ECB = 6x$, m$\angle ECD = 3x - 11$, and m$\angle DCB = 74$. What is the value of x?

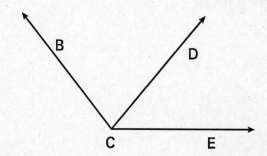

6 In $\triangle MEC$, an exterior angle at C measures 115°, and the measure of $\angle M$ is 60°. Which is the *shortest* side of $\triangle MEC$?

7 In the accompanying diagram of rhombus $ABCD$, $m\angle CAB = 35$. Find $m\angle CDA$.

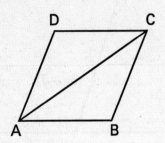

8 Find the positive root of $\dfrac{1}{x-1} = \dfrac{x+2}{4}, x \neq 1$.

9 The length of a side of a square is 5. In simplest radical form, find the length of a diagonal of the square.

10 In which quadrant does the image of $(4,-7)$ lie after the translation that shifts (x,y) to $(x-6, y+3)$?

11 If the endpoints of the diameter of a circle are $A(5,2)$ and $B(-3,4)$, find the coordinates of the center of the circle.

12 Solve for x: $\dfrac{2}{x} + \dfrac{4}{3} = \dfrac{14}{3x}$

13 In right triangle ABC, $m\angle C = 90$ and altitude $\overline{CD}$ is drawn to hypotenuse $\overline{AB}$. If $AD = 4$ and $DB = 5$, find AC.

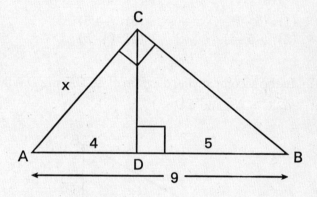

14 Find the slope of a line that passes through points $(-6,8)$ and $(2,-4)$.

Directions (15–34): For *each* question chosen, write on the separate answer sheet the *numeral* preceding the word or expression that best completes the statement or answers the question.

15 If the statements $s \rightarrow t$ and $t \rightarrow u$ are true, then what is a logically valid conclusion?

(1) $\sim u \rightarrow \sim s$ (3) $u \rightarrow \sim t$

(2) $\sim u \rightarrow t$ (4) $t \rightarrow \sim u$

16 What is the image of $(-4,-5)$ when reflected in the x-axis?

(1) $(5,-4)$ (3) $(-4,5)$

(2) $(-5,-4)$ (4) $(4,-5)$

17 In the accompanying diagram of $\triangle CDE$, $m\angle D = 90$, $m\angle C = 28$, and $ED = 15$.

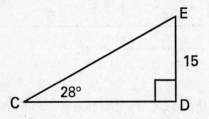

Which equation can be used to find CD?

(1) $\sin 28° = \dfrac{15}{CD}$ (3) $\tan 28° = \dfrac{15}{CD}$

(2) $\sin 28° = \dfrac{CD}{15}$ (4) $\tan 28° = \dfrac{CD}{15}$

18 The expression $\dfrac{12!}{8!\,4!}$ is equivalent to

(1) 1   (3) 2970

(2) 495   (4) 3960

19 What is the locus of points at a given distance from a line?

(1) 1 point   (3) 1 circle

(2) 2 points   (4) 2 parallel lines

20 Which statement is *false* about the line whose equation is $y = -2x - 5$?

(1) Its slope is −2.

(2) It is parallel to the line whose equation is $y = 2x + 5$.

(3) Its y-intercept is −5.

(4) It is perpendicular to the line whose equation is $y = \dfrac{1}{2}x - 5$.

21 What is the total number of different six-letter permutations that can be formed from the letters in the word "MUUMUU"?

(1) 6   (3) 120

(2) 15   (4) 180

22 In the accompanying diagram, $\overline{ACE}$, $\overline{BCD}$, $\overline{AB}$, and $\overline{DE}$, $\angle A \cong \angle E$, and C is the midpoint of $\overline{AE}$

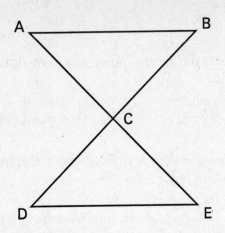

Which theorem justifies $\triangle ABC \cong \triangle EDC$?

(1) SSS $\cong$ SSS   (3) ASA $\cong$ ASA
(2) SAS $\cong$ SAS   (4) SSA $\cong$ SSA

23 What is the value of $(P \blacksquare S) \blacksquare (L \blacksquare U)$ in the system defined below?

$\blacksquare$	P	L	U	S
P	U	S	P	L
L	S	P	L	U
U	P	L	U	S
S	L	U	S	P

(1) P (3) U
(2) L (4) S

24 In right triangle *ABC*, angle *C* is the right angle. If the coordinates of *A* are (−1,1) and the coordinates of *B* are (4,−2), the coordinates of *C* may be

(1) (−1,−2)   (3) (1,2)
(2) (−1,2)   (4) (1,−2)

25 In the accompanying diagram, parallel lines $\overleftrightarrow{AB}$ and $\overleftrightarrow{CD}$ are cut by transversal $\overleftrightarrow{EF}$ at *P* and *Q*, respectively.

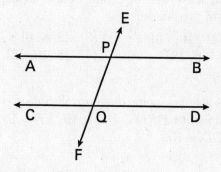

Which statement must always be true?

(1) m∠*APE* = m∠*CQF*
(2) m∠*APE* < m∠*CQF*
(3) m∠*APE* + m∠*CQF* = 90
(4) m∠*APE* + m∠*CQF* = 180

26 What is the distance between points (6,−9) and (−3,4)?

(1) $\sqrt{34}$ (3) $\sqrt{178}$
(2) $\sqrt{106}$ (4) $\sqrt{250}$

27　Which equation represents the axis of symmetry of the graph of the equation $y = x^2 - 6x + 5$?

(1)　$y = 3$ 　　　　　(3)　$x = 3$
(2)　$y = -3$ 　　　　(4)　$x = -3$

28　If the statements $\sim(n \wedge \sim c)$ and n are true, then which statement is a logical conclusion?

(1)　c 　　　　　　(3)　$\sim n \wedge c$
(2)　$\sim c$ 　　　　　(4)　$\sim n \vee \sim c$

29　Which set of numbers may be the measure of the sides of a triangle?

(1)　{10, 10, 20} 　　　(3)　{2, 4, 6}
(2)　{4, 6, 12} 　　　　(4)　{8, 10, 12}

30　In the accompanying diagram, altitude $\overline{EH}$ is drawn in trapezoid $DEFG$, $DE = 10$, $EF = 9$, $FG = 8$, and $GD = 15$.

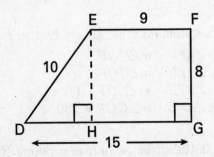

What is $m\angle D$ to the *nearest degree*?

(1) 37 　　　　　　(3) 60
(2) 53 　　　　　　(4) 80

31 Which set is closed under the operation of subtraction?

(1) odd numbers   (3) integers
(2) counting numbers   (4) prime numbers

32 What are the roots of the equation $x^2 - 2x - 1 = 0$?

(1) $x = -1 - \sqrt{2}$ (3) $x = -1 - 2\sqrt{2}$
(2) $x = 1 - \sqrt{2}$ (4) $x = 1 - 2\sqrt{2}$

33 What are the coordinates of the image of point $(-1,2)$ under a dilation of 3 with respect to the origin?

(1) $(-6,3)$ (3) $(3,6)$
(2) $(6,-3)$ (4) $(-3,6)$

34 The number of degrees in the measure of one exterior angle of a regular pentagon is

(1) 72   (3) 360
(2) 108   (4) 540

Directions (35): Leave all construction lines on the answer sheet.

35 *On the answer sheet*, construct the perpendicular bisector of $\overline{AB}$, a chord of circle O.

Part II

Answer three questions from this part. Clearly indicate the necessary steps, including appropriate formula substitutions, diagrams, graphs, charts, etc. Calculations that may be obtained by mental arithmetic or the calculator do not need to be shown. [30]

36 *a* On graph paper, draw the graph of the equation $y = x^2 + 2x - 3$ for all values in the interval $-4 \le x \le 2$.   [6]

    b On the same set of axes, draw the graph of the equation $(x + 1)^2 + (y + 4)^2 = 16$.   [3]

    c Determine the total number of points the graphs drawn in parts *a* and *b* have in common.   [1]

37 Solve the following system of equations algebraically and check:
$$y = x^2 + 2x - 4$$
$$y - 5 = 2x \qquad\qquad [8,2]$$

38 Five students will be selected to represent their school at a conference. The principal has nominated 4 students graduating in 1998, 2 in 1999, 2 in 2000, and 1 in 2001.

a How many five-student groups can be formed from the nine students? [2]

b What is the probability that all of the five students selected will graduate before 2000? [2]

c What is the probability that of the five students selected 2 will graduate in 1998, 1 in 1999, 1 in 2000, and 1 in 2001? [4]

d What is the probability that all of the five students selected will graduate after 1999? [2]

39 In the accompanying diagram, *ABCD* is a trapezoid with altitudes $\overline{DW}$ and $\overline{CZ}$ drawn, *CD* = 17.3, *DA* = 8.6, m∠*A* = 68, and m∠*B* = 53. Find, to the *nearest tenth*, the perimeter of *ABCD*. [10]

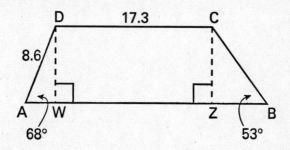

40 *a* In the accompanying diagram of $\triangle CAT$, W is a point on $\overline{AC}$ and G is a point on $\overline{TC}$ such that $\overline{WG}$ is parallel to $\overline{AT}$, $TG = x$, $GC = x - 1$, $CW = x + 5$, and $WA = 2x + 6$. Find the length of $\overline{TG}$. [*Only an algebraic solution will be accepted.*] [6]

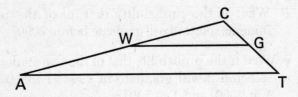

b For all values of y for which these expressions are defined, express the product in simplest form.

$$\frac{y^2 - 49}{y^2 - 3y - 28} \cdot \frac{3y + 12}{y^2 + 5y - 14} \qquad [4]$$

Part III

Answer one question from this part. Clearly indicate the necessary steps, including appropriate formula substitutions, diagrams, graphs, charts, etc. Calculations that may be obtained by mental arithmetic or the calculator do not need to be shown.

[10]

41 Given: If I get a summer job, then I will earn money.
  If I fail mathematics, then I will not earn money.
  I get a summer job or I am not happy.
  I am happy or I am not successful.
  I am successful.

Let J represent: "I get a summer job."
Let E represent: "I will earn money."
Let F represent: "I fail mathematics."
Let H represent: "I am happy."
Let S represent: "I am successful."

Prove: I did not fail mathematics. [10]

42 Quadrilateral $ABCD$ has vertices $A(-3,6)$, $B(6,0)$, $C(9,-9)$, and $D(0,-3)$. Prove that $ABCD$ is

a a parallelogram [8]

b *not* a rhombus [2]

ANSWERS AND EXPLANATIONS
JANUARY 1998
ANSWER KEY

Part I

1. 5
2. 4.8
3. 14
4. $2(x + 3)(x - 3)$
5. 21
6. $\overline{MC}$
7. 110
8. 2
9. $5\sqrt{2}$
10. III
11. (1,3)
12. 2

13. 6
14. −1.5
15. (1)
16. (3)
17. (3)
18. (2)
19. (4)
20. (2)
21. (2)
22. (3)
23. (1)
24. (1)

25. (4)
26. (4)
27. (3)
28. (1)
29. (4)
30. (2)
31. (3)
32. (2)
33. (4)
34. (1)
35. construction

Part II

36. *a* see explanations
    b see explanations
    c 2
37. (3,11), (−3,−1)
    Check
38. *a* 126

    b $\dfrac{6}{126}$

    c $\dfrac{24}{126}$

    d 0
39. 62.4
40. *a* 3

    b $\dfrac{3}{y - 2}$

Part III

41. see explanations
42. see explanations

EXPLANATIONS
Part I

1. 5

They've already defined the function for you, so just plug in $a = 6$ and $b = 3$:

$$6 \star 3 = \frac{2(6) + 3}{3} = \frac{15}{3} = 5$$

2. 4.8

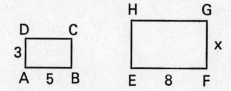

Opposite sides of a rectangle have the same length, so AD and BC both equal 3. Now you can set up a proportion comparing corresponding sides of the two triangles:

$$\frac{AB}{EF} = \frac{BC}{FG} = \frac{5}{8} = \frac{3}{x}$$

Cross multiply, then solve for x:

$$5x = 24$$

$$x = 4.8$$

3. 14

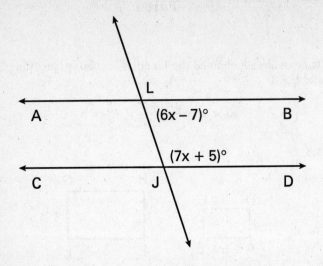

Whenever two parallel lines are cut by a transversal, the sum of the measures of one big angle and one little angle is 180°. Thus, $m\angle JLB + m\angle LJD = 180$. Plug in the algebraic terms and solve for x:

$$(6x - 7) + (7x + 5) = 180$$
$$13x - 2 = 180$$
$$13x = 182$$
$$x = 14$$

4. $2(x + 3)(x - 3)$

Factor 2 out of both terms first:

$$2x^2 - 18 = 2(x^2 - 9)$$

The second term is a difference of squares, so you can factor it like this:

$$2(x^2 - 9) = 2(x + 3)(x - 3)$$

5. 21

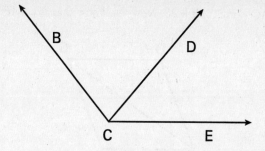

From the Angle Addition Postulate, you know that m∠ECD + m∠DCB = m∠ECB. Plug in the given values and solve for x:

$$(3x - 11) + 74 = 6x$$
$$3x + 63 = 6x$$
$$63 = 3x$$
$$21 = x$$

6. $\overline{MC}$

Whenever the test doesn't give you a diagram, draw one:

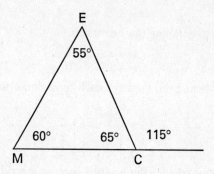

The exterior angle at C is supplementary to ∠ECM, so m∠ECM = 65. The sum of the measures of the three angles in △MEC is 180°, so m∠E = 55. In any triangle, the shortest side is opposite from the smallest angle. Since ∠E is the smallest angle, the side opposite ∠E, or $\overline{MC}$, is the shortest side.

7. 110

The diagonal of a rhombus bisects the interior angles, so
$m\angle DAC = m\angle CAB = 35$. Now you know that $m\angle DAB = 70$.

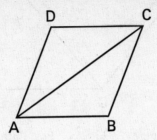

Any two adjacent angles in a rhombus (which is also a parallelogram) are
supplementary, so $m\angle CDA + m\angle DAB = 180$. Also, opposite angles are
equal, and a diagonal divides them equally. Thus, $\angle ABC = \angle CDA =
180 - 2(35) = 110$.

8. 2

Whenever two fractions are equal to each other, you can cross-multiply:

$$\frac{1}{x-1} = \frac{x+2}{4}$$
$$(x - 1)(x + 2) = 4$$

Use FOIL to combine the two terms:

$$x^2 + x - 2 = 4$$
$$x^2 + x - 6 = 0$$

Factor the equation, then set each term equal to zero to find the
two roots:

$$(x + 3)(x - 2) = 0$$
$$x + 3 = 0 \qquad x - 2 = 0$$
$$x = -3 \qquad x = 2$$

The question asks for the positive root, so get rid of –3. Now, plug
in 2 to make sure it works.

9. $5\sqrt{2}$

Draw your square like this:

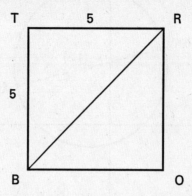

The most basic way to find the length of diagonal $\overline{BR}$ is to use the Pythagorean Theorem on right triangle BRT:

$$(BR)^2 = (BT)^2 + (TR)^2$$
$$(BR)^2 = 5^2 + 5^2$$
$$(BR)^2 = 50$$
$$BR = \sqrt{50} = 5\sqrt{2}$$

Note: You can do this faster if you realize that ΔBRT is a 45:45:90 triangle.

10. III

First, find the image of $(4,-7)$ under the translation $(x - 6, y + 3)$, which shifts the x-coordinate 6 units to the left and the y-coordinate up 3 units:

$$(4 - 6, -7 + 3) = (-2, -4)$$

In Quadrant III, both the x- and y-coordinates are negative. Thus, $(-2, -4)$ is in Quadrant III.

11. **(1,3)**

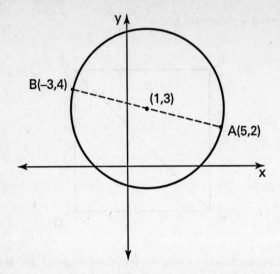

The center of a circle is the midpoint of a diameter. Use the formula for the midpoint of a line segment:

$$(\overline{x}, \overline{y}) = \left(\frac{x_1 + x_2}{2}, \frac{y_1 + y_2}{2} \right)$$

For this problem, let $(x_1, y_1) = (5,2)$ and $(x_2, y_2) = (-3,4)$:

$$\overline{x} = \frac{x_1 + x_2}{2} \qquad \overline{y} = \frac{y_1 + y_2}{2}$$

$$= \frac{5 + (-3)}{2} \qquad = \frac{2 + 4}{2}$$

$$= \frac{2}{2} = 1 \qquad = \frac{6}{2} = 3$$

The coordinates of the center of the circle are (1,3)·

12. 2

The fastest way to solve this one is to find the lowest common denominator of the three fractions (which is $3x$) and multiply it by every term in the equation:

$$\frac{2}{x} \bullet (3x) + \frac{4}{3} \bullet (3x) = \frac{14}{3x} \bullet (3x)$$

$$6 + 4x = 14$$

$$4x = 8$$

$$x = 2$$

Be sure to plug 2 into the equation to make sure that it works

13. 6

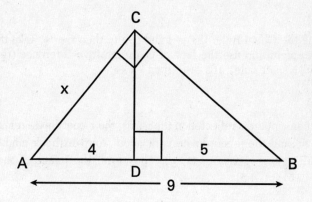

The altitude $\overline{CD}$ of $\triangle ABC$ divides it into two triangles each of which is similar to $\triangle ABC$. (This is a property of right triangles.) Thus:

$$\frac{AD}{AC} = \frac{AC}{AB}$$

$$\frac{4}{x} = \frac{x}{9}$$

$$x^2 = 36$$

$$x = 6$$

14. –1.5

To find the slope of the line between two points, use the slope formula:

$$m = \frac{y_2 - y_1}{x_2 - x_1}$$

For this problem, let $(x_1, y_1) = (-6, 8)$ and $(x_2, y_2) = (2, -4)$:

$$m = \frac{-4 - 8}{2 - (-6)} = \frac{-12}{8} = -\frac{3}{2} = -1.5$$

Make sure that whichever point you start at when you subtract the y's, you start at the same point when you subtract the x's.

Multiple Choice

15. (1)

Use the Chain Rule: If $s \to t$ and $t \to u$, then $s \to u$. Take this new statement and use the Law of Contrapositive Inference (the Flip-and-Negate rule). If $s \to u$, then $\sim u \to \sim s$.

16. (3)

When a point is reflected in the x-axis, the x-coordinate remains the same and the y-coordinate is negated. Your textbook might put it this way: $r_{x\text{-axis}}(x,y) \to (x,-y)$. Therefore, the image of the point $(-4,-5)$ is $(-4,5)$.

17. (3)

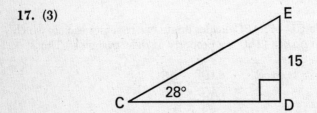

The four choices involve only the sides opposite and adjacent to $\angle C$. This eliminates choices (1) and (2). Choice (3) is the correct ratio $\left(\dfrac{opposite}{adjacent} \right)$ for a tangent.

18. (2)

The expression $n!$ represents the product of every integer between n and 1, inclusive. The expression looks like this:

$$\frac{12!}{8!4!} = \frac{12 \cdot 11 \cdot 10 \cdot 9 \cdot 8 \cdot 7 \cdot 6 \cdot 5 \cdot 4 \cdot 3 \cdot 2 \cdot 1}{8 \cdot 7 \cdot 6 \cdot 5 \cdot 4 \cdot 3 \cdot 2 \cdot 1 \cdot (4 \cdot 3 \cdot 2 \cdot 1)} = \frac{12 \cdot 11 \cdot 10 \cdot 9}{4 \cdot 3 \cdot 2 \cdot 1} = 495$$

Note: If your calculator can calculate factorial expression, this problem becomes a lot easier.

19. (4)

The locus of all points at a given distance d from a line is two lines parallel to the given line, each of which is that certain distance away from the original line:

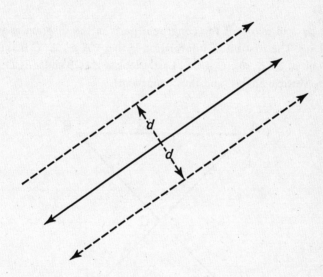

20. (2)

If a line is in the standard form $y = mx + b$, m represents the line's slope and b is its y-intercept. The slope of the line $y = -2x - 5$ is -2, and the y-intercept is -5. (Eliminate (1) and (3)). Parallel lines have the same slope, so any line that is parallel to $y = -2x - 5$ must have a slope of -2. Thus, $y = 2x + 5$ is not parallel to the original line.

21. (2)

To find the number of possible arrangements of the letters in a word with n letters, in which one letter appears p times and a different letter appears q times, the formula looks like this:

$$\frac{n!}{p!\,q!}$$

MUUMUU (which is a loose, floppy dress, in case you were wondering) has six letters, but there are four U's and two M's. Therefore, you can express the number of arrangements as:

$$\frac{6!}{4!\,2!} = \frac{6 \cdot 5 \cdot 4 \cdot 3 \cdot 2 \cdot 1}{4 \cdot 3 \cdot 2 \cdot 1 \cdot (2 \cdot 1)} = 15$$

22. (3)

It pays to mark off the congruent parts in the diagram as you go along. The first bit of information is that $\angle A \cong \angle E$. C is the midpoint of $\overline{ACE}$, so $\overline{AC} \cong \overline{CE}$. Lastly, look at $\angle ACB$ and $\angle ECD$, which are vertical angles (and thus congruent).

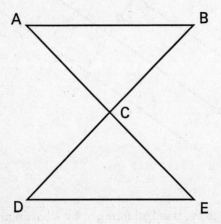

From the diagram, you can see that the congruency theorem to use is Angle-Side-Angle.

23. (1)

Take it one step at a time. This problem follows the rules of PEMDAS: Parentheses first. To find the value of $(P \blacksquare S)$, find P in the far-left column, and run your finger to the right along that row until you get to the column headed by S, like this:

$\blacksquare$	P	L	U	S
P	U	S	P	L
L	S	P	L	U
U	P	L	U	S
S	L	U	S	P

Thus, $P \blacksquare S = L$. Using the same process, you can determine that $L \blacksquare U = L$. Substituting L for both $(P \blacksquare S)$ and $(L \blacksquare U)$ in $(P \blacksquare S) \blacksquare (L \blacksquare U)$ gives $L \blacksquare L$. Applying the same operations to this function gives P.

24. (1)

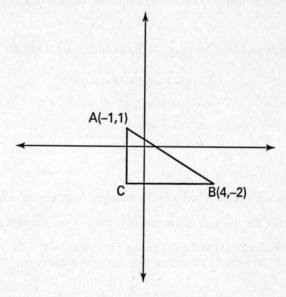

A(−1,1)

C

B(4,−2)

Since C is in Quadrant III, both its x and y coordinates must be negative. Only the coordinates in (1) are both negative.

25. (4)

Whenever you see two parallel lines cut by a transversal, you know that (1) all the little angles are congruent; (2) all the big angles are congruent; and (3) the sum of a little angle and a big angle is 180°. $\angle APE$ is a big angle, and $\angle CQF$ is a little angle, so the sum of their measures is 180°.

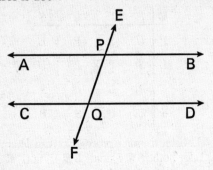

26. (4)

To find the distance between two points, use the distance formula:

$$d = \sqrt{(x_2 - x_1)^2 + (y_2 - y_1)^2}$$

For this problem, let $(x_1, y_1) = (6, -9)$ and $(x_2, y_2) = (-3, 4)$:

$$
\begin{aligned}
d &= \sqrt{(-3 - 6)^2 + [4 - (-9)]^2} \\
&= \sqrt{(-9)^2 + (13)^2} \\
&= \sqrt{81 + 169} \\
&= \sqrt{250}
\end{aligned}
$$

27. (3)

When a parabola is given in the standard form $y = ax^2 + bx + c$, the formula for the axis of symmetry is $x = -\dfrac{b}{2a}$. (At this point, you can eliminate (1) and (2).) In the parabola $y = x^2 - 6x + 5$, $a = 1$, $b = -6$, and $c = 5$. Therefore, the axis of symmetry is:

$$x = -\frac{-6}{2(1)} = 3$$

28. (1)

Using De Morgan's Law:

$$\sim(n \wedge \sim c) \to \sim n \vee c$$

Since the symbol $\vee$ means "or," the translation of this statement is: "Either n is false OR c is true." But we are told that n is true. Thus, c must be true. You can use the Law of Disjunctive Inference like this:

$$[(\sim n \vee c) \wedge n)] \to c$$

29. (4)

The rule for the lengths of the sides of a triangle states that the sum of the lengths of any two sides must be greater than the length of the third side. Consider each of the four choices:

(1) 10 + 10 is not greater than 20

(2) 4 + 6 is not greater than 12

(3) 2 + 4 is not greater than 6

Only the triangle of answer choice (4) obeys the rule.

30. (2)

You can do this one of two ways.

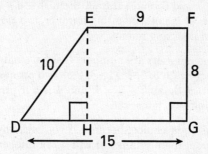

Method One: Since opposite sides of a rectangle are congruent, $FG = EH = 8$. Within $\triangle EDH$, you know the length of the side opposite $\angle D$ ($EH = 8$) and the hypotenuse ($DE = 10$). Use the sine:

$$\sin \angle D = \frac{8}{10} = 0.8$$

With your calculator, determine the corresponding measure in degrees.

$$m\angle D = 53.13°$$

Method Two: Since opposite sides of a rectangle are congruent, $EF = HG = 9$. Since $DG = 15$, $DH = 6$. Within $\triangle EDH$, you know the length of side adjacent to $\angle D$ ($DH = 6$) and the hypotenuse ($DE = 10$). Use the cosine:

$$\cos \angle D = \frac{6}{10} = 0.6$$

With your calculator, determine the corresponding measure in degrees.

$$m\angle D = 53.13°$$

In each case, you can round off your answer to 53°.

31. **(3)**

If a set is "closed" under a certain operation, (if you take any two numbers in the set and perform the operation) the result will also be within the original set. Look at the four answer choices:

(1) Pick two odd numbers (say, 7 and 3) and subtract one from the other: $7 - 3 = 4$, and 4 is not a member of the set of odd numbers.

(2) Counting numbers are the same as whole numbers—integers that start at 0 and get bigger (0, 1, 2, 3, 4...). Pick two of these (say, 7 and 3) and subtract them: $7 - 3 = 4$, but $3 - 7 = -4$. Since -4 is not a counting number, it is not a member of the set of counting numbers.

(3) Prime numbers are numbers that have only themselves and 1 as factors (2, 3, 5, 7, 11...). Pick two primes (say, 7 and 3) and subtract them: $7 - 3 = 4$, and 4 is not prime, and therefore not in the original set.

(4) is the right choice, because if you take any two integers and subtract them, the result will be an integer. (Remember that integers are like counting numbers, but they include negative numbers. Thus, -2 is an integer, but it's not a counting number.)

32. **(2)**

Rearranging $x^2 - 2x - 1 = 0$ makes it look like this:

$$x^2 - 2x = 1$$

Let us plug in choice (2), $x = 1 \pm \sqrt{2}$:

$$\left(1 \pm \sqrt{2}\right)^2 - 2\left(1 \pm \sqrt{2}\right) = 1$$
$$1 + 2 \pm 2\sqrt{2} - 2 \pm 2\sqrt{2} = 1$$
$$1 = 1$$

So choice (2) works in the equation. Plug the other choices in to make sure they don't work.

33. **(4)**

Under a dilation of 3 with respect to the origin, the coordinates of a point are each multiplied by 3. Therefore, the image of the point $(-1,2)$ after that dilation is $(-3,6)$.

34. **(1)**

If you know that a pentagon has five sides, you can estimate the answer just by drawing a regular pentagon like this:

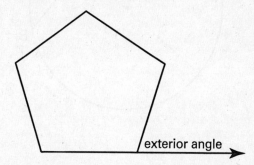

The exterior angle clearly measures less than 90°, so the only possible answer is (1). For the heck of it, though, you can also use the formula. If a regular polygon has n sides, then the measure of each interior angle equals:

$$\frac{180(n-2)}{n}$$

$$\frac{180(5-2)}{5} = \frac{180(3)}{5} = 108$$

The interior angle is 108°. The complementary external angle is 72°.

35.

This is a simple construction of a perpendicular bisector; the segment you're bisecting just happens to be a chord of a circle. Making sure your compass is at least two-thirds as long as AB, place the pointy end on point A and make two arcs. Then, without changing the width of the compass, place the pointy end on point B and make arcs that intersect the first arcs, like this:

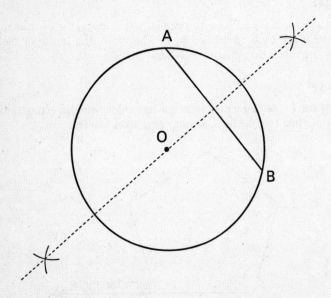

Connect the two points of intersection, and you're done.

Part II

36. *a*

x	$x^2 + 2x - 3$	y
–4	$(-4)^2 + 2(-4) - 3$	5
–3	$(-3)^2 + 2(-3) - 3$	0
–2	$(-2)^2 + 2(-2) - 3$	–3
–1	$(-1)^2 + 2(-1) - 3$	–4
0	$(0)^2 + 2(0) - 3$	–3
1	$(1)^2 + 2(1) - 3$	0
2	$(2)^2 + 2(2) - 3$	5

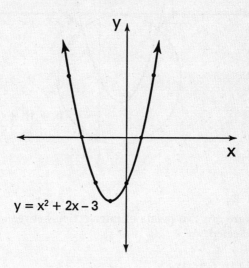

$y = x^2 + 2x - 3$

b

The first curve is a parabola. The second is a circle. In standard form, $(x - h)^2 + (y - k)^2 = r^2$, (h,k) is the center of the circle and r is the radius. Therefore, the circle is centered at $(-1,-4)$ and has a radius of 4:

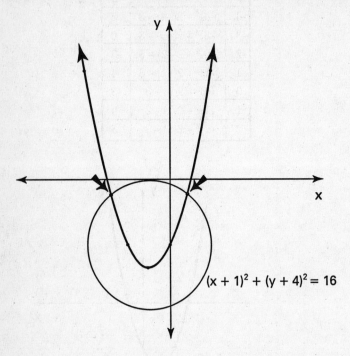

$(x + 1)^2 + (y + 4)^2 = 16$

c 2

There are two points of intersection between the two points, as indicated.

37. **(3,11), (-3,-1)**

Change the second equation by adding 5 to both sides:

$$y = 2x + 5$$

Now you have two equations equal to y, so set them equal to each other:

$$x^2 + 2x - 4 = 2x + 5$$
$$x^2 - 9 = 0$$

This equation contains a difference of squares, so factor it like this:

$$x^2 - 9 = 0$$
$$(x - 3)(x + 3) = 0$$
$$x = \{3, -3\}$$

Plug each value into the second statement to find the corresponding value of y:

$$y = 2(3) + 5 \qquad y = 2(-3) + 5$$
$$y = 11 \qquad\qquad y = -1$$

The two points are $(3,11)$ and $(-3,-1)$. Make sure you get the last two points of credit; check the values of x and y by plugging them into the first equation:

$$11 = (3)^2 + 2(3) - 4 \qquad -1 = (-3)^2 + 2(-3) - 4$$
$$11 = 9 + 6 - 4 \qquad\qquad -1 = 9 - 6 - 4$$
$$11 = 11 \qquad\qquad\qquad -1 = -1$$

38. *a* **126**

This is a basic combinations problem. There are nine students, and you have to choose five. Use the formula $_nC_r = \dfrac{n!}{r!(n-r)!}$ and plug in $n = 9$ and $r = 5$:

$$_9C_5 = \frac{9!}{5!4!} = \frac{9 \cdot 8 \cdot 7 \cdot 6 \cdot 5 \cdot 4 \cdot 3 \cdot 2 \cdot 1}{5 \cdot 4 \cdot 3 \cdot 2 \cdot 1 \cdot (4 \cdot 3 \cdot 2 \cdot 1)} = \frac{9 \cdot 8 \cdot 7 \cdot 6}{4 \cdot 3 \cdot 2 \cdot 1} = 126$$

b $\dfrac{6}{126}$

From Part A, you know that there are 126 possible combinations. There are six students who will graduate before 2000 (four in 1998 and two in 1999), and you have to determine the number of ways you can choose five of them:

$$_6C_5 = \frac{6!}{5!1!} = \frac{6 \cdot 5 \cdot 4 \cdot 3 \cdot 2 \cdot 1}{5 \cdot 4 \cdot 3 \cdot 2 \cdot 1 \cdot (1)} = 6$$

Since there are 126 total combinations (from Part A) and six of them involve the five students who will graduate before 2000, the probability is $\dfrac{6}{126}$ (or $\dfrac{1}{21}$ if you reduce).

c $\dfrac{24}{126}$

Find out the number of combinations involving each class. There are four students graduating in 1998, and you need to choose two of them:

$$_4C_2 = \frac{4!}{2!\,2!} = \frac{4 \cdot 3 \cdot 2 \cdot 1}{2 \cdot 1 \cdot (2 \cdot 1)} = 6$$

There are two students who will graduate in 1999, and you need to choose one of them:

$$_2C_1 = \frac{2!}{1!\,1!} = \frac{2 \cdot 1}{1 \cdot 1} = 2$$

This makes sense; if you're choosing one of two people, you take one or the other. The same holds true for the students who will graduate in 2000:

$$_2C_1 = \frac{2!}{1!\,1!} = \frac{2 \cdot 1}{1 \cdot 1} = 2$$

And there's just one student graduating in 2001, so the number of combinations is 1. Multiply all these numbers together to find the final number of combinations: $6 \cdot 2 \cdot 2 \cdot 1 = 24$. Since there are 126 total combinations (from Part A) and 24 of them follow the directions specified in the question, the probability is $\dfrac{24}{126}$ (or $\dfrac{4}{21}$ if you reduce).

d **0**

Only three students will graduate after 1999: two in 2000 and one in 2001. There is zero chance that all five students will graduate after 1999.

39. 62.4

This one's going to take a lot of trigonometry. You'll need to make four trigonometric calculations, then add up all the sides.

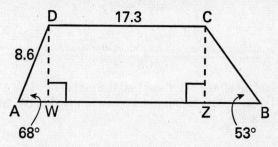

1. In △ADW, you know the angle measures and the length of the hypotenuse. You want to find the opposite side, so use sine (the SOH in SOHCAHTOA):

$$\sin 68° = \frac{DW}{AD}$$

$$0.9272 = \frac{DW}{8.6}$$

$$DW = 7.97$$

2. Still in △ADW: You know the opposite side, and you want the adjacent side. Use tangent:

$$\tan 68° = \frac{DW}{AW}$$

$$2.4751 = \frac{7.97}{AW}$$

$$AW = 3.22$$

DCWZ is a rectangle, so DW = CZ = 7.97, and DC = WZ = 17.3. Now shift to △CZB.

3. You have an angle measure in △CBZ and the opposite leg. To find the adjacent side, ZB, use tangent:

$$\tan 53° = \frac{CZ}{ZB}$$

$$1.327 = \frac{7.97}{ZB}$$

$$CB = 6$$

4. Still in $\triangle CBZ$: You know the adjacent side ZB, and you need the hypotenuse CB. Use cosine (the CAH in SOHCAHTOA):

$$\cos 53° = \frac{ZB}{CB}$$

$$0.6018 = \frac{6}{CB}$$

$$CB = 9.97$$

Now add up all the sides and find the perimeter: 17.3 + 9.97 + 6 + 17.3 + 3.22 + 8.6 = 62.39, which when rounded to the nearest tenth equals 62.4.

40. *a* **3**

Triangles CWG and CAT are similar, so you can set up a proportion relating corresponding parts of each triangle:

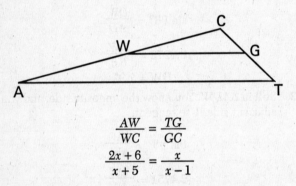

$$\frac{AW}{WC} = \frac{TG}{GC}$$

$$\frac{2x+6}{x+5} = \frac{x}{x-1}$$

When two fractions are equal, you can cross-multiply:

$$(2x+6)(x-1) = x(x+5)$$

$$2x^2 + 4x - 6 = x^2 + 5x$$

$$x^2 - x - 6 = 0$$

Factor the equation and solve for x:

$$(x-3)(x+2) = 0$$

$$x = \{3, -2\}$$

Since distances are positive values, get rid of –2. Your answer is 3, and it pays to plug 3 back into your original equation to make sure it works.

b $\dfrac{3}{y-2}$

Factor each of the terms like this:

$$y^2 - 49 = (y-7)(y+7)$$
$$y^2 - 3y - 28 = (y-7)(y+4)$$
$$3y + 12 = 3(y+4)$$
$$y^2 + 5y - 14 = (y+7)(y-2)$$

Rewrite the product and cancel out the like terms:

$$\frac{(y-7)(y+7)}{(y-7)(y+4)} \cdot \frac{3(y+4)}{(y+7)(y-2)} = \frac{3}{y-2}$$

Part III

41. Symbolize the terms first:

"If I get a summer job, then I will earn money." $J \rightarrow E$

"If I fail mathematics, then I will not earn money." $F \rightarrow \sim E$

"I get a summer job or I am not happy." $J \vee \sim H$

"I am happy or I am not successful." $H \vee \sim S$

"I am successful." S

Prove: "I did not fail mathematics." $\sim F$

Now write the proof:

Statements	Reasons
1. $H \vee \sim S$ S	1. Given
2. H	2. Law of Disjunctive Inference
3. $J \vee \sim H$	3. Given
4. J	4. Law of Disjunctive Inference (2, 3)
5. $J \rightarrow E$	5. Given
6. E	6. Law of Detachment (4, 5)
7. $F \rightarrow \sim E$	7. Given
8. $\sim F$	8. Law of *Modus Tollens* (6, 7)

Note: If you never learned the Law of *Modus Tollens*, you can use the Law of Contrapositive Inference on Statement 7 (so it goes from $F \rightarrow \sim E$ to $E \rightarrow \sim F$) then use the Law of Detachment.

42. *a*

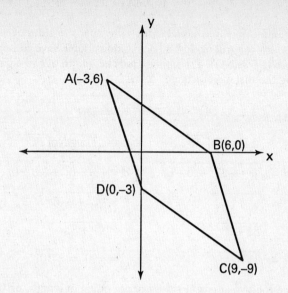

A parallelogram has two pairs of opposite parallel sides. To prove that *ABCD* is a parallelogram, you have to show that each pair of opposite sides are parallel. To do this, find the slope of each of the sides using the slope formula:

$$m = \frac{y_2 - y_1}{x_2 - x_1}$$

Slope of $\overline{AB}$:

$$m = \frac{0 - 6}{6 - (-3)}$$

$$= \frac{-6}{9}$$

$$= -\frac{2}{3}$$

Slope of $\overline{BC}$:

$$m = \frac{-9 - 0}{9 - 6}$$

$$= \frac{-9}{3}$$

$$= -3$$

Slope of $\overline{CD}$:

$$m = \frac{-3 - (-9)}{0 - 9}$$

$$= \frac{-6}{9}$$

$$= -\frac{2}{3}$$

Slope of $\overline{AD}$:

$$m = \frac{-6 - (-3)}{-3 - 0}$$

$$= \frac{9}{-3}$$

$$= -3$$

Since $\overline{AB}$ and $\overline{CD}$ have the same slope, $-\frac{2}{3}$, those two sides are parallel. The other two sides also have the same slope, −3, so they're parallel as well. Thus, quadrilateral *ABCD* is a parallelogram

b

A rhombus has four equal sides. The opposite sides of a parallelogram are congruent, but adjacent sides don't have to be. To prove that $ABCD$ is NOT a rhombus, find the length of two adjacent sides using the distance formula:

$$d = \sqrt{\left(x_2 - x_1\right)^2 + \left(y_2 - y_1\right)^2}$$

Length of $\overline{AB}$:

$$d = \sqrt{[6 - (-3)]^2 + (0 - 6)^2}$$

$$= \sqrt{9^2 + (-6)^2}$$

$$= \sqrt{81 + 36}$$

$$= \sqrt{117}$$

Length of $\overline{BC}$:

$$d = \sqrt{[9 - 6]^2 + (-9 - 0)^2}$$

$$= \sqrt{3^2 + (-9)^2}$$

$$= \sqrt{9 + 81}$$

$$= \sqrt{90} = 3\sqrt{10}$$

Since the two adjacent sides are not equal in length, $ABCD$ is NOT a rhombus.

Or here's another way to think about it: The diagonals of a rhombus are perpendicular to each other, while those in a parallelogram are not.

Continue to use slope to show that the slope of the diagonals are not negative reciprocals, therefore not those of a rhombus.

EXAMINATION
JUNE 1998

Part I

Answer 30 questions from this part. Each correct answer will receive 2 credits. No partial credit will be allowed. Write your answers in the spaces provided on the separate answer sheet. Where applicable, answers may be left in terms of π or in radical form. [60]

1 What is the image of (6,–1) after a reflection in the x-axis?

2 In the accompanying diagram, $\overline{AB}$ intersects $\overline{CD}$ at E, $\overline{AC}$ and $\overline{BD}$ are drawn, m∠A = 85, m∠C = 45, and m∠D = 110. Find m∠B.

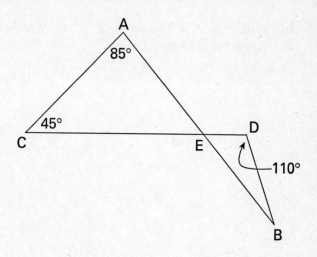

3 In the accompanying diagram, line k is parallel to line n, and line l is a transversal that intersects lines k and n. If m$\angle 1 = x + 25$ and m$\angle 2 = 5x - 25$, find x.

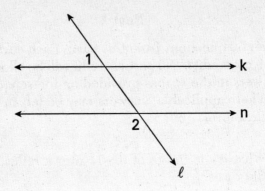

4 A translation maps (x,y) to $(x - 4,y + 5)$. What are the coordinates of A', the image of point $A(5,-3)$ under this translation.

5 In $\triangle ABC$, m$\angle A = 62$ and m$\angle B = 54$. Which is the longest side of the triangle?

6 In the accompanying diagram, m∠ABD = 72 and
$\overrightarrow{FBE}$ bisects ∠ABD. Find m∠ABF.

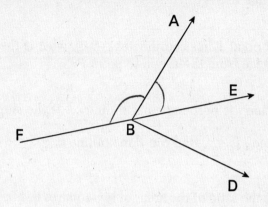

7 The operation ✳ for the set {M,A,T,H} is defined
in the table below. What is the identity element
for ✳?

✳	M	A	T	H
M	H	M	A	T
A	M	A	T	H
T	A	T	H	M
H	T	H	M	A

8 For the binary operation $a \otimes b = \dfrac{\sqrt{a}}{\sqrt{b}}$, find the
value of $8 \otimes 2$ in simplest form.

9 In rectangle *DATE*, diagonals $\overline{DT}$ and $\overline{AE}$ intersect at *S*. If *AE* = 40 and *ST* = *x* + 5, find the value of *x*.

10 If point *P* has coordinates (–8,6), what is the distance from the origin to point *P*?

11 Line *j* is perpendicular to line *k*. If the slope of line *j* is $\frac{5}{2}$, find the slope of line *k*.

12 If the ratio of the areas of two squares is 4:9, what is the ratio of the perimeter of the smaller square to the perimeter of the larger square?

13 If $_nC_2 = 28$, what is the value of *n*?

14 Solve for *x*: $\frac{1}{3x} + 1 = \frac{7}{6}$

Directions (15–34): For *each* question chosen, write on the separate answer sheet the *numeral* preceding the word or expression that best completes the statement or answers the question.

15 In the accompanying diagram, $\overline{AC} \parallel \overline{DE}$, $AB = 4$, $BC = 6$, and $BD = 3$.

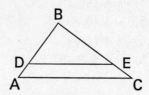

What is the length of $\overline{BE}$?

(1) 1   (3) 4.5
(2) 1.5   (4) 5

16 Which statement is the negation of $a \wedge {\sim} b$?

(1) ${\sim}a \vee b$ (3) ${\sim}a \wedge b$
(2) ${\sim}a \vee {\sim}b$ (4) ${\sim}a \wedge {\sim}b$

17 The greatest number of different 5-letter arrangements can be made from the letters in the word

(1) ANGLE   (3) DADDY
(2) ORDER   (4) ADAPT

18 If M is the midpoint of $\overline{AB}$, then which statement is *false*?

(1) $\dfrac{AB}{2} = MB$ (3) $AB - MB = AM$

(2) $AM = MB$ (4) $AM + AB = MB$

19 Which transformation represents a dilation?

(1) $A(-3,5) \rightarrow A'(-6,10)$
(2) $A(-3,5) \rightarrow A'(5,-3)$
(3) $A(-3,5) \rightarrow A'(1,9)$
(4) $A(-3,5) \rightarrow A'(-3,-5)$

20 In the accompanying diagram, $\triangle RST$ is a right triangle, $\overline{SU}$ is the altitude to hypotenuse $\overline{RT}$, $RU = 4$, and $UT = 12$.

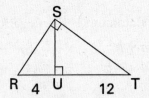

What is the length of $\overline{RS}$?

(1) 8   (3) $\sqrt{160}$

(2) $\sqrt{48}$ (4) 24

21 If $(2x - 3)$ and $(x + 5)$ are multiplied to form the trinomial $ax^2 + bx + c$, what is the value of b?

(1) –15   (3) 7

(2) 2   (4) 4

22 If $A \rightarrow \sim B$ and B are both true statements, then which conclusion must be true?

(1) $\sim B$ (3) A

(2) $\sim A$ (4) $\sim A \rightarrow \sim B$

23 The coordinates of the midpoint of $\overline{AB}$ are $(-7,6)$. If the coordinates of A are $(2,-4)$ and the coordinates of B are $(-16,y)$, what is the value of y?

(1) 8   (3) –14

(2) –2   (4) 16

24 The equation of the locus of points 5 units from the origin is

(1) $x^2 + y^2 = 5$ (3) $x = 5$

(2) $x^2 + y^2 = 25$ (4) $y = 5$

25 If side $\overline{AB}$ of $\triangle ABC$ is extended from point B to point D, then $m\angle DBC$ is always

(1) smaller than $(m\angle A + m\angle BCA)$

(2) greater than $(m\angle A + m\angle BCA)$

(3) equal to $2m\angle A$

(4) greater than $m\angle BCA$

26 What is the slope of a line that passes through points $(-4,2)$ and $(6,8)$?

(1) $-\dfrac{3}{5}$

(3) $\dfrac{5}{3}$

(2) $\dfrac{3}{5}$

(4) $-\dfrac{5}{3}$

27 What are the coordinates of the turning point for the graph of the parabola whose equation is $y = x^2 - 4$?

(1) $(0,-2)$

(3) $(0,-4)$

(2) $(0,2)$

(4) $(0,4)$

28 The vertices of $\triangle ABC$ are $A(0,0)$, $B(0,k)$, and $C(k,0)$. The area of this triangle can be expressed as

(1) $\dfrac{k^2}{2}$

(3) k^2

(2) $\dfrac{k^2}{4}$

(4) $2k$

29 The roots of the equation $x^2 + 8x + 3 = 0$ are

(1) $4 \pm \sqrt{13}$

(3) $4 \pm \sqrt{19}$

(2) $-4 \pm \sqrt{13}$

(4) $-4 \pm \sqrt{19}$

30 Which statement is the inverse of "If a quadrilateral is a square, then it has four right angles"?

(1) If a quadrilateral has four right angles, then it is a square.
(2) If a quadrilateral is not a square, then it has four right angles.
(3) If a quadrilateral does not have four right angles, then it is not a square.
(4) If a quadrilateral is not a square, then it does not have four right angles.

31 An intersection of the graphs of the equations $y = -x$ and $y = x^2 - 2$ is

(1) $(-1,-1)$ (3) $(2,2)$
(2) $(-2,2)$ (4) $(1,1)$

32 A parallelogram must be a rectangle if its diagonals

(1) bisect each other
(2) bisect the angles to which they are drawn
(3) are perpendicular to each other
(4) are congruent

33 The sum of the measures of the interior angles of a regular pentagon is

(1) 180°   (3) 540°
(2) 360°   (4) 720°

34 In right triangle ABC, $m\angle C = 90$, $m\angle A = 55$, and $CA = 10$. What is the length of $\overline{AB}$ to the *nearest integer*?

(1) 6   (3) 17
(2) 14   (4) 24

Directions (35): Leave all construction lines on the answer sheet.

35 *On the answer sheet*, construct an equilateral triangle with sides of length $\overline{CD}$.

C   D

Part II

Answer three questions from this part. Clearly indicate the necessary steps, including appropriate formula substitutions, diagrams, graphs, charts, etc. Calculations that may be obtained by mental arithmetic or the calculator do not need to be shown. [30]

36 Answer both *a* and *b*.

   a Simplify for all values of x for which this expression is defined:

   $$\frac{x^2 - x - 20}{x^2 + 7x + 12} \bullet \frac{2x^2 + 6x}{x^2 - 25} \quad [5]$$

   b Solve for the positive value of y:

   $$\frac{3 + y}{2y} = \frac{y - 1}{y} \quad [5]$$

37 Solve the following system of equations algebraically and check:

   $$x^2 + y^2 = 52$$
   $$x - y = -2 \quad [8,2]$$

38 From a vase containing 4 yellow roses, 3 pink roses, and 5 red roses, a combination of 3 roses is randomly selected.

  a How many combinations of 3 roses are possible? [2]

  b What is the probability of choosing 3 roses that are all the same color? [4]

  c What is the probability of choosing *exactly* one rose of each color in the 3-rose selection? [4]

39 a On graph paper, draw the graph of the equation $y = -x^2 + 4x + 3$ for all values of x in the interval $-1 \leq x \leq 5$. [6]

  b On the same set of axes, draw the image of the graph drawn in part *a* after a reflection in the y-axis and label it b. [2]

  c Write the equation for the axis of symmetry for the parabola drawn in part b. [2]

40 In the accompanying diagram of square MARY, $\overline{ME}$ is drawn to side $\overline{YR}$, m∠EMY = 40, and YE = 12.

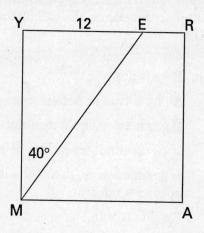

a Find the area of polygon MARE to the *nearest integer*. [7]

b If diagonal $\overline{AY}$ is drawn, will $\overline{AY}$ be perpendicular to $\overline{ME}$? Explain your answer. [3]

Part III

Answer one question from this part. Clearly indicate the necessary steps, including appropriate formula substitutions, diagrams, graphs, charts, etc. Calculations that may be obtained by mental arithmetic or the calculator do not need to be shown. [10]

41 Given: Beta is not true.

Alpha is true or beta is true.

If gamma is not true, then alpha is not true.

If sigma is not true, then delta is true.

If gamma is true, then delta is not true or epsilon is not true.

Epsilon is true.

Let A represent: "Alpha is true."

Let B represent: "Beta is true."

Let G represent: "Gamma is true."

Let D represent: "Delta is true."

Let E represent: "Epsilon is true."

Let S represent: "Sigma is true."

Prove: Sigma is true. [10]

42 Quadrilateral $DRAW$ has vertices $D(-3,6)$, $R(6,3)$, $A(6,-2)$, and $W(-6,2)$. Using coordinate geometry, prove that quadrilateral $DRAW$ is an isosceles trapezoid. [10]

ANSWERS AND EXPLANATIONS
JUNE 1998
ANSWER KEY

Part I

1. (6,1)
2. 20
3. 30
4. (1,2)
5. $\overline{AB}$
6. 144
7. A
8. 2
9. 15
10. 10
11. $-\dfrac{2}{5}$

12. 2:3
13. 8
14. 2
15. (3)
16. (1)
17. (1)
18. (4)
19. (1)
20. (1)
21. (3)
22. (2)
23. (4)

24. (2)
25. (4)
26. (2)
27. (3)
28. (1)
29. (2)
30. (4)
31. (2)
32. (4)
33. (3)
34. (3)
35. construction

Part II

36. a $\dfrac{2x}{x+5}$

    b 5

37. (−6,−4), (4,6)

    Check

38. a 220

    b $\dfrac{15}{220}$

    c $\dfrac{60}{220}$

39. a see explanations

    b see explanations

    c $x = -2$

40. a 119

    b No. Explanations will vary.

Part III

41. see explanations
42. see explanations

EXPLANATIONS
Part I

1. (6,1)

Whenever a point is reflected in the x-axis, the x-coordinate remains the same and the y-coordinate is negated. In other words:

$$r_{x\text{-axis}}(x,y) \to (x,-y).$$

Thus, the image of $(6,-1)$ after a reflection in the x-axis is $(6,1)$.

2. 20

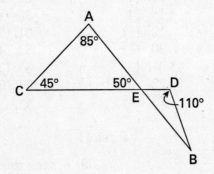

Consider $\triangle ACE$ first. The sum of the three angles in a triangle is 180, so find the measure of $\angle AEC$:

$$\text{m}\angle A + \text{m}\angle C + \text{m}\angle AEC = 180$$
$$85 + 45 + \text{m}\angle AEC = 180$$
$$\text{m}\angle AEC = 50$$

Since $\angle AEC$ and $\angle DEB$ are vertical angles, they have the same measure. Thus, $\text{m}\angle DEB = 50$. Now you can use the rule of 180 to find $\angle B$:

$$\text{m}\angle D + \text{m}\angle B + \text{m}\angle DEB = 180$$
$$110 + \text{m}\angle B + 50 = 180$$
$$\text{m}\angle B = 20$$

3. 30

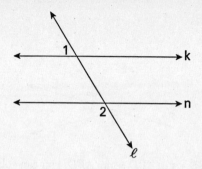

Whenever two parallel lines are cut by a transversal, the sum of the measures of one big angle and one small angle is 180°. In the above diagram, $\angle 1$ is a small angle and $\angle 2$ is a big angle. Plug in the algebraic terms and solve for x:

$$m\angle 1 + m\angle 2 = 180$$
$$(x + 25) + (5x - 25) = 180$$
$$6x = 180$$
$$x = 30$$

4. (1,2)

The translation $(x - 4, y + 5)$ shifts the x-coordinate 4 units to the left and the y-coordinate up 5 units. Therefore, the image of $A(5,-3)$ is:

$$(5 - 4, -3 + 5) = (1,2).$$

5. $\overline{AB}$

The sum of the measures of the three angles in $\triangle ABC$ is 180°, so $m\angle C = 64$. In any triangle, the longest side is opposite the longest angle. Since $\angle C$ is the largest angle, the side opposite $\angle C$, or $\overline{AB}$, is the longest side.

6. 144

Since FBE bisects $\angle ABF$, $m\angle ABE = m\angle EBD$. Set the measure of each angle equal to x:

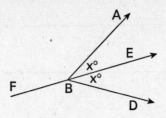

Since $m\angle ABE + m\angle EBD = m\angle ABD$, you can solve for x:

$$x + x = 72$$
$$2x = 72$$
$$x = 36$$

Now look at $\angle ABF$ and $\angle ABE$. Since they're supplementary, the sum of their measures is 180:

$$m\angle ABF + m\angle ABE = 180$$
$$m\angle ABF + 36 = 180$$
$$m\angle ABF = 144$$

7. A

Look at each of the rows: The elements in the A row are the same as the elements at the top of the operation table:

$*$	M	A	T	H
M	H	M	A	T
A	M	A	T	H
T	A	T	H	M
H	T	H	M	A

Thus, A is the identity element of the operation.

8. 2

Just plug in $a = 8$ and $b = 2$; the result is: $\dfrac{\sqrt{8}}{\sqrt{2}}$

This isn't in its simplest form yet. Simplify the term like this

$$\frac{\sqrt{8}}{\sqrt{2}} = \sqrt{\frac{8}{2}} = \sqrt{4} = 2.$$

9. 15

Whenever the test doesn't provide you with a diagram, draw one

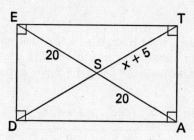

The diagonals of a rectangle bisect each other, so ST is half as long as AE, or 20. Set ST equal to 20 and solve for x:

$$x + 5 = 20$$
$$x = 15$$

10. 10

If you graph the point on the coordinate axes, you might be able to answer this without doing too much math:

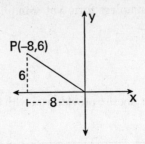

You've graphed a right triangle with legs that measure 6 and 8. At this point, you might recognize that this is a 3:4:5 triangle. Thus, since the legs measure 3 • 2 and 4 • 2, the hypotenuse must measure 5 • 2, or 10.

If this is a little too high-tech, just use the distance formula:

$$d = \sqrt{(x_2 - x_1)^2 + (y_2 - y_1)^2}$$

Let $(x_1, y_1) = (-8, 6)$ and $(x_2, y_2) = (0,0)$:

$$d = \sqrt{[0 - (-8)]^2 + (0 - 6)^2}$$
$$= \sqrt{8^2 + (-6)^2}$$
$$= \sqrt{64 + 36}$$
$$= \sqrt{100} = 10$$

11. $-\dfrac{2}{5}$

The slopes of any two perpendicular lines are negative reciprocals (that is, their product is –1). Therefore, any line that is perpendicular to a line with a slope of $\dfrac{5}{2}$ has a slope of $-\dfrac{2}{5}$.

12. 2:3

Draw two squares, one with an area of 4 and the other with an area of 9:

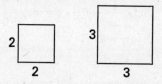

Each side of the small square is 2 units long, so its perimeter is 8. Each side of the large square is 3 units long, so its perimeter is 12. The ratio of the two perimeters is 8:12, which reduces to 2:3.

13. 8

This requires a little experimentation. You'll have to estimate what n equals and plug that into the formula:

$$_nC_r = \frac{n!}{r!(n-r)!}$$

Let's say that $n = 10$:

$$_{10}C_2 = \frac{10!}{2!\,8!} = \frac{10 \cdot 9 \cdot 8 \cdot 7 \cdot 6 \cdot 5 \cdot 4 \cdot 3 \cdot 2 \cdot 1}{2 \cdot 1 \cdot (8 \cdot 7 \cdot 6 \cdot 5 \cdot 4 \cdot 3 \cdot 2 \cdot 1)} = \frac{10 \cdot 9}{2 \cdot 1} = 45$$

That's too big, so x must be smaller. Try $x = 8$:

$$_8C_2 = \frac{8!}{2!\,6!} = \frac{8 \cdot 7 \cdot 6 \cdot 5 \cdot 4 \cdot 3 \cdot 2 \cdot 1}{2 \cdot 1 \cdot (6 \cdot 5 \cdot 4 \cdot 3 \cdot 2 \cdot 1)} = \frac{8 \cdot 7}{2 \cdot 1} = 28$$

Bingo, $n=8$!

14. 2

The lowest common denominator of the three fractions is $6x$, so multiply each of the terms by $6x$:

$$(6x) \cdot \frac{1}{3x} + (6x) \cdot 1 = (6x) \cdot \frac{7}{6}$$
$$2 + 6x = 7x$$
$$2 = x.$$

As always, plug your answer back into the equation to make sure it's right:

$$\frac{1}{3 \cdot 2} + 1 = \frac{7}{6}$$
$$\frac{1}{6} + 1 = \frac{7}{6}$$
$$\frac{7}{6} = \frac{7}{6}$$

Multiple Choice

Don't forget that one of the best techniques on these Multiple Choice questions is to use Process of Elimination to get rid of answer choices that aren't possible.

15. (3)

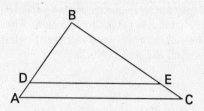

Since $\overline{AC}$ is parallel to $\overline{DE}$, $\triangle BDE$ and $\triangle BAC$ are similar (and corresponding parts are proportional). Set up the proportion:

$$\frac{BD}{AB} = \frac{BE}{BC}$$

Now, substitute all the values you know:

$$\frac{3}{4} = \frac{BE}{6}$$

Cross-multiply and solve for BE:

$$4(BE) = 18$$
$$BE = 4.5$$

16. (1)

Whenever you negate a statement with a " $\wedge$ " or a " $\vee$ " in it, use De Morgan's Law:

$$\sim(a \wedge \sim b) \rightarrow \sim a \vee b$$

17. (1)

To find the number of possible arrangements of the letters in a word with n letters, in which one letter appears p times (and p is greater than 1), the formula looks like this:

$$\frac{n!}{p!}$$

Each of the four answer choices contains five letters, but ANGLE is the only one that doesn't repeat any letters. Therefore, ANGLE has the greatest number of ways to rearrange the letters. You don't have to bother with all the math.

18. (4)

The fastest way to grasp this question is to draw a diagram like this:

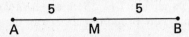

If $AB = 10$, then both AM and MB equal 5. Now, plug those values into each statement; answer choice (4) has the only equation that doesn't work ($5 + 10 \neq 5$).

19. (1)

Whenever a point undergoes a dilation, each of the coordinates of the point is multiplied by a constant, which is called the scale factor of the dilation. To find the correct answer here, look for the answer choice in which the coordinates of the image are multiples of the coordinates of the original point.

In answer choice (1), if the point $(-3,5)$ undergoes a dilation of scale factor 2, the coordinates of the image are $(-3 \bullet 2, 5 \bullet 2)$, or $(-6,10)$

20. (1)

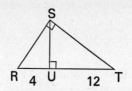

Whenever you draw the altitude of a right triangle, you create three similar right triangles—$\triangle RSU$(small), $\triangle SUT$(medium), and the original $\triangle RST$(large). Corresponding parts of the triangles are proportional. To find RS, look at the similar triangles: In the small triangle, RU is the small leg and RS is the hypotenuse. In the large triangle, RS is the small leg and RT is the hypotenuse. Set up the proportion (and remember that $RT = RU + UT$, or 16):

$$\frac{RU}{RS} = \frac{RS}{RT}$$
$$\frac{4}{RS} = \frac{RS}{16}$$
$$(RS)^2 = 64$$
$$RS = 8$$

21. (3)

Multiply the two terms using FOIL:

$$(2x - 3)(x + 5) =$$
$$2x^2 + 10x - 3x - 15 =$$
$$2x^2 + 7x - 15$$

In this standard format, b is the coefficient of the x term. Thus, $b = 7$.

22. (2)

Use the Law of Contrapositive Inference on the first statement: If $A \rightarrow \sim B$, then $B \rightarrow \sim A$. If B is a true statement, then $\sim A$ must be true due to the Law of Detachment.

23. (4)

Use the formula for the midpoint of a line segment:

$$(\bar{x}, \bar{y}) = \left(\frac{x_1 + x_2}{2}, \frac{y_1 + y_2}{2} \right)$$

For this problem, the midpoint $(\bar{x}, \bar{y})$ is $(-7, 6)$, and you can let (x_1, y_1) = $A(2, -4)$ and (x_2, y_2) = $B(-16, y)$. However, you only need to deal with the y-coordinate:

$$\bar{y} = \frac{y_1 + y_2}{2}$$

$$6 = \frac{-4 + y}{2}$$

$$12 = -4 + y$$

$$16 = y$$

24. (2)

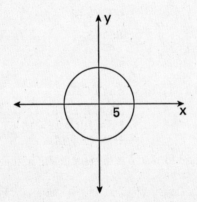

The locus of points that are a specific distance from a certain fixed point is a circle, so you can get rid of (3) and (4), which are both lines. The formula of a circle centered at the origin is $x^2 + y^2 = r^2$, in which r is the radius of the circle. Since the radius of the circle you're looking for is 5, the equation of the circle is $x^2 + y^2 = 25$.

25. (4)

You have to draw this before you can answer it. Draw it like this:

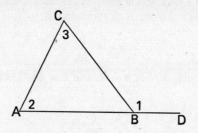

$$m<1 = m<2 + m<3$$

Since the measure of exterior angle $\angle DBC$ is equal to the sum of non-adjacent interior angles $\angle CAB$ and $\angle BCA$, it must be true that $m\angle DBC$ is greater than $m\angle BCA$.

26. (2)

To find the slope of the line between two points, use the slope formula:

$$m = \frac{y_2 - y_1}{x_2 - x_1}$$

For this problem, let $(x_1, y_1) = (-4, 2)$ and $(x_2, y_2) = (6, 8)$:

$$m = \frac{8 - 2}{6 - (-4)} = \frac{6}{10} = \frac{3}{5}$$

27. (3)

Find the x-coordinate of the turning point by finding the axis of symmetry. When a parabola is given in the standard form $y = ax^2 + bx + c$, the formula for the axis of symmetry is:

$$x = -\frac{b}{2a}$$

In this parabola, $a = 1$, $b = 0$, and $c = -4$. Therefore, the axis of symmetry is:

$$x = -\frac{0}{2(1)} = 0$$

(**Note**: This should be no surprise, because the x-coordinate of each answer choice is 0.)

Now, plug $x = 0$ into the equation to find the corresponding y-coordinate:

$$y = (0)^2 - 4$$
$$y = -4$$

The coordinates of the turning point are $(0,-4)$.

28. (1)

Plug in for k first. If you let $k = 3$, the graph of the triangle looks like this:

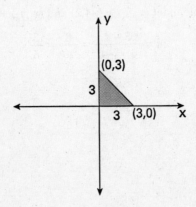

As you can see, $\triangle ABC$ is a right triangle. The area of the triangle is $\frac{1}{2}bh$; the height of the triangle is 3, and so is the length of the base. Therefore, the area of the triangle is:

$$\frac{1}{2}(3)(3) = \frac{9}{2}$$

If you plug $k = 3$ into each answer choice, answer choice (1) equals $\frac{9}{2}$.

29. (2)

Since the answer choices all contain square root signs, you should take the hint that you can't factor the equation—you need to use the Quadratic Formula:

$$x = \frac{-b \pm \sqrt{b^2 - 4ac}}{2a}$$

This equation is in standard $ax^2 + bx + c = 0$, and $a = 1$, $b = 8$, and $c = 3$:

$$x = \frac{-8 \pm \sqrt{8^2 - 4(1)(3)}}{2(1)}$$

$$= \frac{-8 \pm \sqrt{64 - 12}}{2} = \frac{-8 \pm \sqrt{52}}{2}$$

This answer doesn't match any of the choices, so you have to reduce the square root.

$$\sqrt{52} = \sqrt{4 \cdot 13} = \sqrt{4} \cdot \sqrt{13} = 2\sqrt{13}$$

Now, plug $2\sqrt{13}$ into the fraction and reduce:

$$x = \frac{-8 \pm 2\sqrt{13}}{2} = \frac{2(-4 \pm \sqrt{13})}{2} = -4 \pm \sqrt{13}$$

30. (4)

The inverse of the statement $A \rightarrow B$ is $\sim A \rightarrow \sim B$. Let $A =$ "A quadrilateral is a square," and $B =$ "The quadrilateral has four right angles." Thus, the inverse of the original statement is "If a quadrilateral is *not* a square, then it does *not* have four right angles."

31. (2)

The quick way to answer this is to plug each of the answer choices into the first statement $y = -x$. The only coordinates that satisfy this equation are in answer choice (2).

The long way goes like this:

Since $-x$ and $x^2 - 2$ are both equal to y, you can set them equal to each other:

$$-x = x^2 - 2$$
$$x^2 + x - 2 = 0$$

Now factor it and set each factor equal to zero so you can solve for x:

$$(x + 2)(x - 1) = 0$$
$$x = \{-2, 1\}$$

These are the two possible values of x. Plug each into the first equation to find the corresponding y-coordinates:

$$y = -(-2) \qquad\qquad y = -(1)$$
$$y = 2 \qquad\qquad\qquad y = -1$$

The two points of intersection are $(-2, 2)$ and $(1, -1)$.

32. (4)

Each of the first three answer choices is a characteristic of a rhombus:

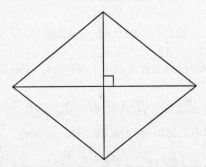

The diagonals bisect each other, they bisect the angles to which they are drawn, and they are perpendicular to each other. However, diagonals of a rectangle are congruent, so any parallelogram with congruent diagonals must be a rectangle.

33. (3)

The formula for finding the sum of the measures of all interior angles of a regular polygon the following (*n* equals the number of sides of the polygon):

$$180(n - 2)$$

A pentagon has five sides, so *n* = 5:

$$180(5 - 2) = 180 \times 3 = 540$$

34. (3)

Draw the diagram like this:

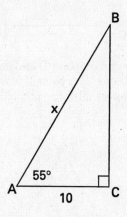

You want to find the hypotenuse of the triangle, and you know the length of the adjacent side (*AC* = 10). Use cosine (the CAH in SOHCAHTOA):

$$\cos 55° = \frac{10}{AB}$$

$$0.5736 = \frac{10}{AB}$$

$$AB = \frac{10}{0.5736}$$

$$AB = 17.43$$

When you round this off to the nearest integer, as instructed, you get 17.

35.

This one's pretty easy. Take the pointy end of your compass and place it on point C, and adjust the compass so the pencil point is on point D Then make an arc above $\overline{CD}$ like this·

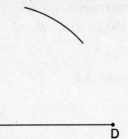

Now put the pointy end on point D and make a second arc that intersects with the first one. This point of intersection is the third point of the triangle. Connect all three points like this, and you're finished:

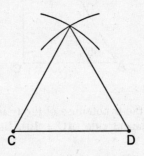

Part II

36. *a* $\dfrac{2x}{x+5}$

Simplify all the elements in the expression like this:

$$x^2 - x - 20 = (x - 5)(x + 4)$$
$$x^2 + 7x + 12 = (x + 3)(x + 4)$$
$$2x^2 + 6x = 2x(x + 3)$$
$$x^2 - 25 = (x + 5)(x - 5)$$

The expression now looks like this:

$$\frac{(x - 5)(x + 4)}{(x + 3)(x + 4)} \bullet \frac{2x(x + 3)}{(x + 5)(x - 5)}$$

Once you cancel out all the elements that appear both on the top and bottom, you're left with this:

$$\frac{2x}{x + 5}$$

_b_ 5

Whenever two fractions are equal to each other, you can cross-multiply:

$$\frac{3 + y}{2y} = \frac{y - 1}{y}$$
$$2y(y - 1) = y(3 + y)$$
$$2y^2 - 2y = 3y + y^2$$
$$y^2 - 5y = 0$$

Now factor the equation and set each factor equal to zero:

$$y(y - 5) = 0$$
$$y = \{0, 5\}$$

Zero is not positive, so get rid of it. Also, $y = 0$ is an extraneous solution since each side of the original equation would be undefined with this value of y. The only positive value that satisfies the equation is 5, and you should plug it back into the equation to make sure it works:

$$\frac{3+5}{2(5)} = \frac{5-1}{5}$$

$$\frac{8}{10} = \frac{4}{5}$$

$$\frac{4}{5} = \frac{4}{5}$$

37. $(-6,-4), (4,6)$

If you add y to both sides of the second equation, the equation becomes $x = y - 2$. Now substitute this equation into the first equation:

$$(y - 2)^2 + y^2 = 52$$
$$y^2 - 4y + 4 + y^2 = 52$$
$$2y^2 - 4y + 4 = 52$$
$$2y^2 - 4y - 48 = 0$$

Divide each term in the equation by 2, then factor it and solve for y:

$$y^2 - 2y - 24 = 0$$
$$(y + 4)(y - 6) = 0$$
$$y = \{-4, 6\}$$

These are the two possible values of y. Plug these values into the second equation to find the corresponding x-coordinates:

$$y = -4 \qquad\qquad\qquad y = 6$$
$$x - (-4) = -2 \qquad\qquad x - 6 = -2$$
$$x = -6 \qquad\qquad\qquad x = 4$$

The two solutions are $(-6,-4)$ and $(4,6)$. Be sure to check these numbers and *show your work*, or you'll lose two points off your score.

38. *a* **220**

This is a basic combinations problem. There are twelve roses, and you have to choose three. Use the formula $_nC_r = \dfrac{n!}{r!(n-r)!}$ and plug in $n = 12$ and $r = 3$

$$_{12}C_3 = \frac{12!}{3!\,9!} = \frac{12 \bullet 11 \bullet 10 \bullet 9 \bullet 8 \bullet 7 \bullet 6 \bullet 5 \bullet 4 \bullet 3 \bullet 2 \bullet 1}{3 \bullet 2 \bullet 1 \bullet (9 \bullet 8 \bullet 7 \bullet 6 \bullet 5 \bullet 4 \bullet 3 \bullet 2 \bullet 1)} = \frac{12 \bullet 11 \bullet 10}{3 \bullet 2 \bullet 1} = 220$$

b $\dfrac{15}{220}$

This is a bit more complicated, but not much. You have to find out how many of the combinations you just figured out in part *a* consist of all the same flower. There are four yellow roses, and you want to know how many combinations of three yellow roses are possible:

$$_4C_3 = \frac{4!}{3!\,1!} = \frac{4 \cdot 3 \cdot 2 \cdot 1}{3 \cdot 2 \cdot 1 \cdot (1)} = 4$$

There are only three pink roses, so there's only one way to select all three of them:

$$_3C_3 = \frac{3!}{3!\,0!} = \frac{3 \cdot 2 \cdot 1}{3 \cdot 2 \cdot 1 \cdot (1)} = 1$$

(Remember that 0! = 1.) Finally, there are five red roses:

$$_5C_3 = \frac{5!}{3!\,2!} = \frac{5 \cdot 4 \cdot 3 \cdot 2 \cdot 1}{3 \cdot 2 \cdot 1 \cdot (2 \cdot 1)} = 10$$

There are four ways to select three yellow roses, one way to select three pink roses, and ten ways to select three red roses. Thus, there are a total of fifteen ways to select three roses of the same color. There are 220 possible three-rose combinations, so the probability that the roses are the same color is $\dfrac{15}{220}$.

c $\dfrac{60}{220}$

Each combination that contains a rose of each color could contain one of four yellows, three pinks, and five reds. Therefore, there are $3 \cdot 4 \cdot 5$, or 60, combinations that contain one yellow, one pink, and one red. There are 220 possible three-rose combinations, so the probability that the roses are all different colors is $\dfrac{60}{220}$. (You could reduce this to $\dfrac{3}{11}$, but you don't have to, so don't bother. Why open up the possibility for a silly mistake that could cost you after all this work?)

39. *a*

Create a chart by plugging in every number within the given range and finding the coordinates of the parabola.

x	$-x^2 + 4x + 3y$	y
–1	$-(-1)^2 + 4(-1) + 3$	–2
0	$-(0)^2 + 4(0) + 3$	3
1	$-(1)^2 + 4(1) + 3$	6
2	$-(2)^2 + 4(2) + 3$	7
3	$-(3)^2 + 4(3) + 3$	6
4	$-(4)^2 + 4(4) + 3$	3
5	$-(5)^2 + 4(5) + 3$	–2

Now graph it like this:

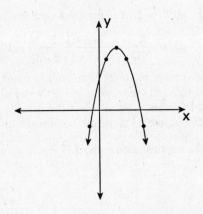

b

Whenever a point is reflected in the y-axis, the x-coordinate is negated and the y-coordinate remains the same. In other words, $r_{y\text{-axis}}$ $(x,y) \rightarrow (-x,y)$. The new points look like this:

(–1,–2) becomes (1,–2)
(0,3) becomes (0,3)
(1,6) becomes (–1,6)
(2,7) becomes (–2,7)
(3,6) becomes (–3,6)
(4,3) becomes (–4,3)
(5,–2) becomes (–5,–2)

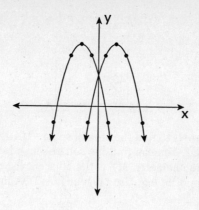

c $x = -2$

When a parabola is given in the standard form $y = ax^2 + bx + c$, the formula for the axis of symmetry is $x = -\dfrac{b}{2a}$. In the original parabola, $a = -1$, $b = 4$, and $c = 3$. Therefore, the axis of symmetry is:

$$x = -\frac{4}{2(-1)} = 2$$

Since the parabola in part b is a reflection of the original parabola in the y-axis, the axis of symmetry of part b's parabola is $x = -2$.

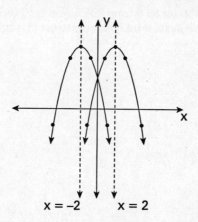

$x = -2$ $x = 2$

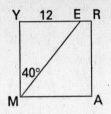

The plan here is to find the area of square *MARY*, then subtract the area of $\triangle MEY$. You can find the square's area by finding the length *MY* using trigonometry. *MY* is the adjacent leg of the triangle, and *EY* is the opposite leg. Use tangent (the TOA in SOHCAHTOA):

$$\tan 40° = \frac{EY}{MY}$$

$$0.8391 = \frac{12}{MY}$$

$$MY = 14.3$$

The area of the square equals $(MY)^2$, or 204.5

The area of the right triangle is $\frac{1}{2}bh$:

$$A = \frac{1}{2}(12)(14.3)$$

$$A = 85.8$$

Once you subtract 85.8 from 204.5, you get 118.7. When you round this off to the nearest integer, as instructed, you get 119.

b **No**

MARY is a square; therefore, it is also a rhombus. The diagonals of a rhombus are perpendicular, so diagonal $\overline{AY}$ is perpendicular to diagonal $\overline{MR}$. Since $\overline{MR}$ is not parallel to $\overline{ME}$, $\overline{ME}$ can't possibly be perpendicular to $\overline{AY}$:

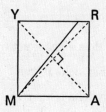

Part III

41.

Use the letters provided to symbolize all the clues first:

Beta is not true:	$\sim B$
Alpha is true or beta is true.	$A \vee B$
If gamma is not true, then alpha is not true.	$\sim G \rightarrow \sim A$
If sigma is not true, then delta is true.	$\sim S \rightarrow D$
If gamma is true, then delta is not true	
or epsilon is not true.	$G \rightarrow (\sim D \vee \sim E)$
Epsilon is true.	E

Now write the proof:

Statements	Reasons
1. $\sim B$; $A \vee B$	1. Given
2. A	2. Law of Disjunctive Inference (1)
3. $\sim G \rightarrow \sim A$	3. Given
4. $A \rightarrow G$	4. Law of Contrapositive Inference (3)
5. G	5. Law of Detachment (2, 4)
6. $G \rightarrow (\sim D \vee \sim E)$	6. Given
7. $\sim D \vee \sim E$	7. Law of Detachment (5, 6)
8. E	8. Given
9. $\sim D$	9. Law of Disjunctive Inference (7, 8)
10. $\sim S \rightarrow D$	10. Given
11. S	11. Law of *Modus Tollens* (9, 10)

42.

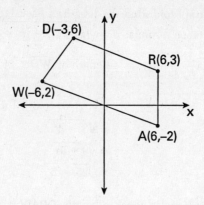

A trapezoid has exactly one pair of opposite parallel sides. To prove that *DRAW* is a trapezoid, you have to show that one pair of opposite sides are parallel and the other pair are not. To do this, find the slope of each of the sides using the slope formula:

$$m = \frac{y_2 - y_1}{x_2 - x_1}.$$

Slope of $\overline{DR}$: Slope of $\overline{RA}$: Slope of $\overline{AW}$: Slope of $\overline{WD}$:

$$m = \frac{3 - 6}{6 - (-3)} \qquad m = \frac{-2 - 3}{6 - 6} \qquad m = \frac{2 - (-2)}{-6 - 6} \qquad m = \frac{6 - 2}{-3 - (-6)}$$

$$= \frac{-3}{9} \qquad\qquad = \frac{-5}{0} \qquad\qquad = \frac{4}{-12} \qquad\qquad = \frac{4}{-3 + 6}$$

$$= -\frac{1}{3} \qquad\qquad = \infty \qquad\qquad = -\frac{1}{3} \qquad\qquad = \frac{4}{3}$$

Since $\overline{AW}$ and $\overline{DR}$ have the same slope, those two sides are parallel. The other two sides don't have the same slope (the slope of $\overline{RA}$ is undefined, so it's parallel to the *y*-axis), so they are not parallel. Thus, quadrilateral *DRAW* is a trapezoid.

The sides of a trapezoid that are not parallel are called legs, and the legs of an isosceles trapezoid are congruent. To prove that $DRAW$ is an isosceles trapezoid, find the length of each leg ($\overline{RA}$ and $\overline{WD}$) using the distance formula: $d = \sqrt{(x_2 - x_1)^2 + (y_2 - y_1)^2}$

Length of $\overline{RA}$:

$$d = \sqrt{(6-6)^2 + (-2-3)^2}$$
$$= \sqrt{0^2 + (-5)^2}$$
$$= \sqrt{0 + 25}$$
$$= \sqrt{25} = 5$$

Length of $\overline{WD}$:

$$d = \sqrt{[-3-(-6)]^2 + (6-2)^2}$$
$$= \sqrt{3^2 + 4^2}$$
$$= \sqrt{9 + 16}$$
$$= \sqrt{25} = 5$$

Since the two legs are equal in length, $DRAW$ is an isosceles trapezoid.

EXAMINATION
AUGUST 1998

Part I

Answer 30 questions from this part. Each correct answer will receive 2 credits. No partial credit will be allowed. Write your answers in the spaces provided on the separate answer sheet. Where applicable, answers may be left in terms of π or in radical form.   [60]

1 One angle is four times as large as a second angle. If the angles are supplementary, find the number of degrees in the smaller angle.

2 In the accompanying diagram, $\overline{DCB}$, $\overleftrightarrow{AB} \parallel \overleftrightarrow{CE}$, and m$\angle ECD$ = 47. Find m$\angle CBA$.

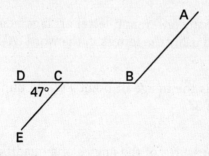

3 If $c \, \heartsuit \, b$ is defined as $\sqrt{c^2 - b^2}$, evaluate 13 $\heartsuit$ 5.

4 Solve for the positive value of x: $\dfrac{x-3}{4} = \dfrac{4}{x+3}$

5 The base $\overline{BC}$ of isosceles triangle ABC is extended through C to D. If m$\angle ACD = 108$, what is the number of degrees in the measure of vertex angle A?

6 The number of degrees in a pair of vertical angles is represented by x and $3x - 48$. What is the value of x?

7 The lengths of the sides of scalene triangle PQR are 10, 11, and 17. What is the perimeter of the triangle formed by joining the midpoints of the sides of triangle PQR?

8 If the slope of $\overleftrightarrow{JK}$ is $\dfrac{3}{4}$ and $\overleftrightarrow{JK} \perp \overleftrightarrow{PQ}$, what is the slope of $\overleftrightarrow{PQ}$?

9 How many different 6-letter arrangements can be formed using the letters in the word "AUGUST"?

10 What is the image of point $P(2,-1)$ under a dilation of 3?

11 The measures of the angles of a quadrilateral are in the ratio 2:3:6:7. Find the number of degrees in the largest angle of the quadrilateral.

12 In right triangle RST, $\overline{TP}$ is the altitude to hypotenuse $\overline{RS}$. If $RP = 11$ and $SP = 21$, find the length of $\overline{TP}$ to the *nearest tenth*.

Directions (13–34): For *each* question chosen, write on the separate answer sheet the *numeral* preceding the word or expression that best completes the statement or answers the question.

13 If $x = 1$ is a solution of $x^2 + cx + 2 = 0$, what is the value of c?

(1) –3   (3) 3
(2) –2   (4) –4

14 Which statement is the negation of $\sim p \vee q$?

(1) $p \wedge \sim q$ (3) $p \vee q$
(2) $p \vee \sim q$ (4) $\sim p \wedge q$

15 A quadrilateral whose diagonals are always congruent is a

(1) parallelogram   (3) rhombus
(2) rectangle   (4) trapezoid

16 Which set of numbers may represent the lengths of the sides of a triangle?

(1) {1, 3, 4}   (3) {5, 7, 9}
(2) {4, 4, 9}   (4) {8, 5, 3}

17 Which statement is the contrapositive of "If a regular polygon is a regular hexagon, each angle measures 120°"?

(1) If each angle of a regular polygon measures
120°, the polygon is a regular hexagon.
(2) If each angle of a regular polygon does not
measure 120°, the polygon is not a regular
hexagon.
(3) If a polygon is not a regular hexagon, each
angle does not measure 120°.
(4) If a polygon is a regular hexagon, the polygon has six equal sides.

18 Which is an equation of the locus of points equidistant from points (–2,0) and (4,0)?

(1) $x = 1$ (3) $y = 1$
(2) $x = -1$ (4) $y = -1$

19 The corresponding altitudes of two similar triangles
are 6 and 14. If the perimeter of the *smaller* triangle is 21, what is the perimeter of the larger
triangle?

(1) 9   (3) 49
(2) 27   (4) 64

20 The coordinates of the center of a circle are (−2,−3), and a diameter of the circle has one endpoint at (−5,−2). What are the coordinates of the other endpoint of the diameter?

(1) (9,8) (3) (−8,−1)

(2) (1,−4) (4) $\left(-3\frac{1}{2}, -2\frac{1}{2}\right)$

21 Which transformation represents a reflection in the origin?

(1) $(x,y) \rightarrow (x + h, y + k)$
(2) $(x,y) \rightarrow (kx, -ky)$
(3) $(x,y) \rightarrow (y,x)$
(4) $(x,y) \rightarrow (-x,-y)$

22 What is the length of the line segment that joins points (4,−1) and (7,5)?

(1) 5 (3) $\sqrt{29}$

(2) $\sqrt{13}$ (4) $\sqrt{45}$

23 In rectangle $ABCD$, $AD = 10$ and diagonal $AC = 26$. What is the perimeter of $ABCD$?

(1) 34 (3) 240
(2) 68 (4) 260

24 Two angles of a triangle measure 72° and 46°. What is the measure of an exterior angle of this triangle?

(1) 46° (3) 108°
(2) 62° (4) 144°

25 In the accompanying diagram of right triangle ABC, legs AC and BC are 12 and 5, respectively, and hypotenuse AB is 13.

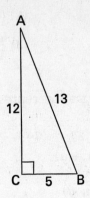

What is tan B?

(1) $\dfrac{12}{5}$

(3) $\dfrac{5}{13}$

(2) $\dfrac{12}{13}$

(4) $\dfrac{5}{12}$

26 Expressed in simplest form, $\dfrac{x^2 - x - 6}{x^2 - 9}, x \neq \pm 3$, is equivalent to

(1) $\dfrac{x + 2}{x - 3}$

(3) $\dfrac{x - 2}{x - 3}$

(2) $\dfrac{x + 2}{x + 3}$

(4) $\dfrac{x - 2}{x + 3}$

27 Which equation represents a line parallel to the line whose equation is $y = \frac{2}{3}x + 3$?

(1) $y = 2x - 3$

(3) $y + 4 = \frac{2}{3}x$

(2) $y = \frac{1}{3}x + 3$

(4) $2y - 4 = 3x$

28 The roots of the equation $3x^2 + 8x - 2 = 0$ are

(1) $\dfrac{8 \pm \sqrt{88}}{6}$

(3) $\dfrac{8 \pm \sqrt{40}}{6}$

(2) $\dfrac{-8 \pm \sqrt{88}}{6}$

(4) $\dfrac{-8 \pm \sqrt{40}}{6}$

29 What are the coordinates of the turning point of the parabola whose equation is $y = x^2 - 6x + 5$?

(1) $(-3,-4)$

(3) $(3,14)$

(2) $(-3,32)$

(4) $(3,-4)$

30 If two isosceles triangles have congruent vertex angles, the triangles must be

(1) congruent

(3) right

(2) equilateral

(4) similar

31 In the accompanying diagram of rhombus $ABCD$, $\overline{AC}$ and $\overline{BD}$ are diagonals intersecting at point M.

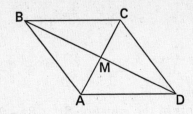

What is the perimeter of the rhombus if m∠DAB = 120 and AC = 12?

(1) 48

(3) $24\sqrt{3}$

(2) $48\sqrt{3}$

(4) 24

32 When drawn on the same set of axes, which pair of equations will result in two points of intersection?

(1) $y = x$ and $y = -x$
(2) $y = 3$ and $x = -3$
(3) $y = x^2$ and $y = -x^2$
(4) $y = x$ and $x^2 + y^2 = 1$

33 Which of these arguments is *not* valid?

(1) $x \rightarrow y$
    $z \rightarrow \sim y$
    $\therefore x \rightarrow \sim z$

(3) $x \vee y$
    x
    $\therefore y$

(2) $x \rightarrow y$
    $\sim y$
    $\therefore \sim x$

(4) $x \rightarrow y$
    x
    $\therefore y$

34 In the accompanying diagram of isosceles triangle
    ABC, $\angle ACB$ is the vertex angle, $\overline{CM} \perp \overline{AB}$, and
    M is the midpoint of $\overline{AB}$.

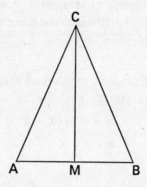

Which statement can *not* be used to justify
$\triangle ACM \cong \triangle BCM$?

(1) HL $\cong$ HL   (3) SSS $\cong$ SSS
(2) AAS $\cong$ AAS   (4) AAA $\cong$ AAA

Directions (35): Leave all construction lines on the answer
sheet.

35 *On the answer sheet*, using a straightedge and com-
    pass, locate the center of the circle on diameter
    $\overline{AB}$.

Part II

Answer three questions from this part. Clearly indicate the necessary steps, including appropriate formula substitutions, diagrams, graphs, charts, etc. Calculations that may be obtained by mental arithmetic or the calculator do not need to be shown.   [30]

36 Solve the following system of equations algebraically or graphically and check:

$$y = x^2 - 6x + 2$$
$$y + x = 2 \qquad [8,2]$$

37 *a* Find, to the *nearest tenth*, all values of x for which the expression is defined.

$$\frac{2x}{x-4} = \frac{x-6}{x-2} \qquad [5]$$

b A committee of 5 is to be selected from 12 students: 5 sophomores, 4 juniors, and 3 seniors.

(1) How many committees of 5 students can be formed?   [2]

(2) What is the probability that the committee will consist of 2 sophomores, 2 juniors, and 1 senior?   [3]

38 In the accompanying diagram of $\triangle ABD$, m$\angle B$ = 90, $\overline{BCD}$, m$\angle ACB$ = 58, m$\angle D$ = 23, and BC = 60 meters.

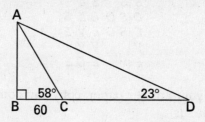

a   Find, to the *nearest meter*, the length of $\overline{AB}$. [3]

b   Using the result from part *a*, find the perimeter of $\triangle ABD$ to the *nearest meter*. [7]

39 In the table below, operation ♦ is commutative.

♦	S	O	L	V	E
S	S		S	L	
O	S	O	O	L	S
L	S	O	L	V	E
V			V	V	
E	V		E	O	E

a On your answer paper, copy and complete the table. [2]

b What is the identity element for the operation ♦? [2]

c What is the inverse for element O under the operation ♦? [2]

d Solve for x: $(L ♦ O) ♦ x = V ♦ S$ [2]

e Explain why element E does *not* have an inverse. [2]

40 *a* On graph paper, draw the graph of circle O, which is represented by the equation $(x - 1)^2 + (y + 3)^2 = 16$. [3]

b On the same set of axes, draw the image of circle O after the translation $(x,y) \rightarrow (x - 2, y + 4)$ and label it O'. [2]

c Write an equation of circle O'. [2]

d Write an equation of the line that passes through the centers of circle O and circle O'. [3]

Part III

Answer one question from this part. Clearly indicate the necessary steps, including appropriate formula substitutions, diagrams, graphs, charts, etc. Calculations that may be obtained by mental arithmetic or the calculator do not need to be shown.   [10]

41   Given: $\angle CDE \cong \angle CED$, $\overline{AD} \cong \overline{EB}$

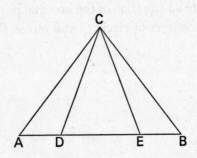

Prove: $\angle ACD \cong \angle BCE$ [10]

42   The coordinates of the vertices of quadrilateral ABCD are A(0,–4), B(8,–3), C(4,4) and D(–4,3). Prove that quadrilateral ABCD is

a a rhombus   [7]

b *not* a rectangle   [3]

ANSWERS AND EXPLANATIONS
AUGUST 1998
ANSWER KEY

Part I

1. 36
2. 133
3. 12
4. 5
5. 36
6. 24
7. 19
8. $-\dfrac{4}{3}$
9. 360
10. (6,–3)
11. 140
12. 15.2

13. (1)
14. (1)
15. (2)
16. (3)
17. (2)
18. (1)
19. (3)
20. (2)
21. (4)
22. (4)
23. (2)
24. (3)

25. (1)
26. (2)
27. (3)
28. (2)
29. (4)
30. (4)
31. (1)
32. (4)
33. (3)
34. (4)
35. construction

Part II

36. (0,2)(5,–3)
    Check
37. *a* 2.7, –8.7
    b (1) 792
       (2) $\dfrac{180}{792}$
38. *a* 96
    b 568

39. *a* see explanations
    b L
    c V
    d V
    e Answers will vary.

40. *a* see explanations
    b see explanations
    c $(x + 1)^2 + (y - 1)^2 = 16$
    d $y = -2x - 1$

Part III

41. see explanations
42. see explanations

EXPLANATIONS
Part I

1. 36

Let the measures of the two angles be x and y. The question gives you two equations. Since one angle is four times the other, you can write the first equation: $y = 4x$. The two angles are supplementary, so the sum of their measures is 180°; equation number 2 becomes $x + y = 180$. Substitute the first equation into the second and solve like this:

$$x + (4x) = 180$$
$$5x = 180$$
$$x = 36.$$

2. 133

The diagram is a little incomplete; add to it like this:

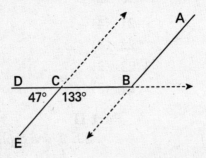

DCB is a line, so $\angle DCE$ and $\angle ECB$ are supplementary. Therefore, $m\angle ECB = 180 - 47$, or 133. If you tilt the page a bit, you'll see that DB is a transversal and $\angle ECB$ and $\angle CBA$ are alternate interior angles (which have the same measure).

3. 12

They've already defined the function for you, so just plug in $c = 13$ and $b = 5$:

$$c \, \heartsuit \, b = \sqrt{13^2 - 5^2} = \sqrt{169 - 25} = \sqrt{144} = 12$$

4. 5

Whenever two fractions are equal to each other, you can cross-multiply:

$$\frac{x-3}{4} = \frac{4}{x+3}$$
$$(x+3)(x-3) = 16$$
$$x^2 - 9 = 16$$
$$x^2 = 25$$
$$x = \pm 5$$

Since you want the positive value, throw out –5. You're left with 5, and you should plug in $x = 5$ to make sure:

$$\frac{5-3}{4} = \frac{4}{5+3}$$
$$\frac{1}{2} = \frac{1}{2}$$

5. 36

Draw a diagram like this:

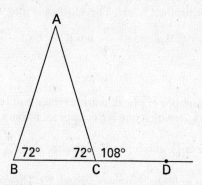

The exterior angle at ACD is supplementary to $\angle ACB$, so m$\angle ACB = 72$. Since $\angle A$ is the vertex angle, the other two angles, $\angle ABC$ and $\angle ACB$ are the base angles (which are congruent). Thus, the measure of $\angle ABC$ is also 72. Now you have to find the measure of the vertex angle, $\angle A$. The sum of the three angles in a triangle is 180:

$$m\angle A + m\angle ABC + m\angle ACB = 180$$
$$m\angle A + 72 + 72 = 180$$
$$m\angle A = 36$$

6. 24

Since vertical angles have the same measure, you can set the measures equal to each other and solve:

$$x = 3x - 48$$
$$-2x = -48$$
$$x = 24$$

7. 19

If you connect the midpoints of the three sides of a triangle, the perimeter of the smaller triangle is exactly half the perimeter of the original triangle. Since the perimeter of the original triangle is $10 + 11 + 17$, or 38, then the perimeter of the smaller triangle is half of 38, or 19.

8. $-\dfrac{4}{3}$

The slopes of any two perpendicular lines are negative reciprocals (that is, their product is -1). Therefore, any line that is perpendicular to a line with a slope of $\dfrac{3}{4}$ has a slope of $-\dfrac{4}{3}$.

9. 360

To find the number of possible arrangements of the letters in a word with n letters, in which one letter appears p times (remember that p is greater than 1), the formula looks like this: $\dfrac{n!}{p!}$

AUGUST has six letters, but there are two U's. Therefore, you can express the number of arrangements as:

$$\frac{6!}{2!} = \frac{6 \cdot 5 \cdot 4 \cdot 3 \cdot 2 \cdot 1}{2 \cdot 1} = \frac{720}{2} = 360$$

10. (6,–3)

Under a dilation of 3 with respect to the origin, the coordinates of a point are each multiplied by 3. Therefore, the image of the point (2,–1) after that dilation is (6,–3).

11. 140

This one's pretty weird-looking, but it's not bad. The sum of the measures of any quadrilateral (a four-sided figure) is 360°. If the ratio of the four angles is 2:3:6:7, you can set up an equation like this:

$$2x + 3x + 6x + 7x = 360$$
$$18x = 360$$
$$x = 20$$

You're not done yet. The biggest angle is $7x$, so substitute $x = 20$ and find the measure:

$$7 \times 20 = 140$$

12. 15.2

Drawing your own diagram like this will help illustrate the problem:

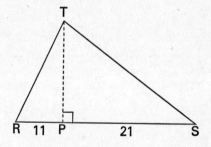

Whenever you draw the altitude of a right triangle, you create three similar right triangles—$\triangle RPT$(small), $\triangle PST$(medium), and the original $\triangle RST$ (large). Corresponding parts of the triangles are proportional. To find TP, look at the similar triangles: In the small triangle, RP is the small leg and TP is the long leg. In the medium triangle, RS is the small leg and PS is the long leg. Set up the proportion:

$$\frac{RP}{TP} = \frac{TP}{PS}$$

$$\frac{11}{TP} = \frac{TP}{21}$$

$$(TP)^2 = 231$$

$$TP = 15.198$$

When you round this off to the nearest tenth, as instructed, you get 15.2.

Multiple Choice

Don't forget that one of the best techniques on these Multiple Choice questions is to use Process of Elimination to get rid of answer choices that aren't possible.

13. (1)

If $x = 1$ is a solution of the equation $x^2 + cx + 2 = 0$, you can plug $x = 1$ into the equation and solve for c:

$$(1)^2 + c(1) + 2 = 0$$
$$1 + c + 2 = 0$$
$$c = -3$$

14. (1)

Whenever you negate a statement with a " $\wedge$ " or a " $\vee$ " in it, use De Morgan's Law:

$$\sim(\sim p \vee q) \rightarrow p \wedge \sim q$$

15. (2)

If you're not sure about the lengths of the diagonals of each of the quadrilaterals in the answer choices, draw each one of them and look for yourself. A parallelogram has parallel and congruent sides, a rhombus has four congruent sides, a rectangle is a parallelogram with four right angles, and a trapezoid has one pair of parallel sides and one pair of non-parallel sides:

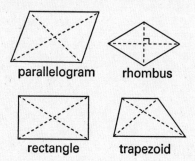

parallelogram   rhombus

rectangle   trapezoid

Only the diagonals of a rectangle are congruent.

16. (3)

The rule for the lengths of the sides of a triangle states that the sum of the lengths of any two sides must be greater than the length of the third side. First consider choices (1), (2), and (4):

(1) 1 + 3 is not greater than 4

(2) 4 + 4 is not greater than 9

(4) 3 + 5 is not greater than 8

Therefore, each of these is not a viable triangle. If look at the lengths in answer choice (3), you'll see that the sum of any two sides is greater than the third:

$$5 + 7 > 9$$
$$5 + 9 > 7$$
$$7 + 9 > 5$$

17. (2)

Let A = "A regular polygon is a hexagon," and B = "Each angle of a regular polygon measures 120°." The contrapositive (which is also sometimes referred to as the Law of Contrapositive Inference) of the statement $A \rightarrow B$ is $\sim B \rightarrow \sim A$. Thus, the contrapositive of the original statement is "If each angle of a regular polygon does *not* measure 120°, then the regular polygon is *not* a regular hexagon."

18. (1)

The locus of points equidistant from any two points is the perpendicular bisector of the segment that connects the two points.

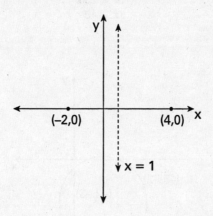

In this problem, the perpendicular bisector is vertical, so the equation must have the form $x = k$, where k is a constant. Eliminate (3) and (4). The constant k must also be halfway between 1 and 7. The average of –2 and 4 is 1 (because $\frac{-2 + 4}{2} = 1$), so the equation of the line is $x = 1$.

19. (3)

Draw some sample triangles like these:

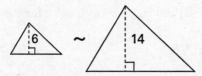

Whenever you have two similar triangles, all linear measures of corresponding parts of the triangles are proportional. Since the ratio of the altitudes is 6:14, then the ratio of every set of corresponding sides is 6:14. Therefore, the ratio of the perimeters is 6:14. Set up the proportion:

$$\frac{6}{14} = \frac{21}{x}$$

Cross-multiply and solve:

$$6x = 294$$
$$x = 49$$

20. (2)

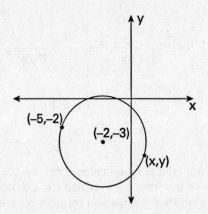

The midpoint of the diameter of a circle is the center of that circle. Use the formula for the midpoint of a line segment:

$$(\overline{x}, \overline{y}) = \left(\frac{x_1 + x_2}{2}, \frac{y_1 + y_2}{2} \right)$$

For this problem, the midpoint $(\overline{x}, \overline{y})$ is $(-2, -3)$, and you can let $(x_1, y_1) = (-5, -2)$ and $(x_2, y_2) = (x, y)$. Solve for x and y like this:

$$\overline{x} = \frac{x_1 + x_2}{2} \qquad\qquad \overline{y} = \frac{y_1 + y_2}{2}$$
$$-2 = \frac{-5 + x}{2} \qquad\qquad -3 = \frac{-2 + y}{2}$$
$$-4 = -5 + x \qquad\qquad -6 = -2 + y$$
$$1 = x \qquad\qquad -4 = y$$

The coordinates of the point are $(1, -4)$.

21. (4)

Whenever a point is reflected in the origin, both coordinates of that point are negated. In other words, $r_{(0,0)}(x,y) \rightarrow (-x,-y)$.

22. (4)

To find the distance between two points, use the distance formula:

$$d = \sqrt{(x_2 - x_1)^2 + (y_2 - y_1)^2}$$

Let $(x_1, y_1) = (4, -1)$ and $(x_2, y_2) = (7, 5)$:

$$d = \sqrt{(7 - 4)^2 + [5 - (-1)]^2}$$
$$= \sqrt{3^2 + 6^2}$$
$$= \sqrt{9 + 36}$$
$$= \sqrt{45}$$

23. (2)

Draw the diagram like this:

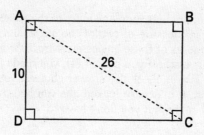

Look at right triangle ADC: You can use the Pythagorean Theorem to find the length of DC:

$$(AC)^2 = (AD)^2 + (DC)^2$$
$$26^2 = 10^2 + (DC)^2$$
$$676 = 100 + (DC)^2$$
$$576 = (DC)^2$$
$$24 = DC$$

Note: You can do this faster if you realize that $\triangle ADC$ is a 5:12:13 triangle.

You're not done yet. Opposite sides of a rectangle are congruent, so $AB = 24$ and $BC = 10$. Add up the four sides, and you'll get the perimeter: $10 + 24 + 10 + 24 = 68$.

24. (3)

An exterior angle extends out from the vertex like this:

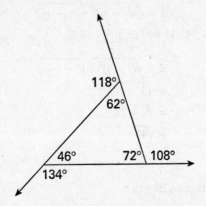

Each exterior angle is supplementary to the adjacent interior angle. You know the measure of two of the angles already: 72° and 46°. The supplements of these angles measure 108° and 134° (Be careful with your math; if you picked (4), you made a careless subtraction error.) If you check the answer choices, you'll find that (3) is 108°. At first, it may have looked like you had to find the measure of the third angle, but you don't have to.

25. (1)

The tangent of an angle is the ratio of the opposite side over the adjacent side (the TOA in SOHCAHTOA). Since the side opposite $\angle B$ is 12 and the adjacent leg is 5, the tangent of $\angle B$ is $\dfrac{12}{5}$.

26. (2)

Reduce the top and bottom of the fraction like this:

$$x^2 - x - 6 = (x - 3)(x + 2)$$
$$x^2 - 9 = (x - 3)(x + 3)$$

Rewrite the fraction like this and cancel out the like term

$(x - 3)$: $\dfrac{(x - 3)(x + 2)}{(x - 3)(x + 3)} = \dfrac{x + 2}{x + 3}$

27. (3)

If a line is in the standard form $y = mx + b$, m represents the line's slope and b is its y-intercept. The slope of the line $y = \dfrac{2}{3}x + 3$ is $\dfrac{2}{3}$. Parallel lines have the same slope, so the slope of the right answer will also be $\dfrac{2}{3}$. Answer choices (1) and (2) are already in standard form and neither slope is 3, so you can eliminate them. If you subtract 4 from both sides of answer choice (3), the equation becomes $y = \dfrac{2}{3}x - 4$. The slope of this line is $\dfrac{2}{3}$, so it's parallel to the original equation.

28. (2)

Since the answer choices all contain square root signs, you should take the hint that you can't factor the equation—you need to use the Quadratic Formula:

$$x = \dfrac{-b \pm \sqrt{b^2 - 4ac}}{2a}$$

This equation is in standard $y = ax^2 + bx + c$ format, and $a = 3$, $b = 8$, and $c = -2$:

$$x = \dfrac{-8 \pm \sqrt{(8)^2 - 4(3)(-2)}}{2(3)}$$

$$= \dfrac{-8 \pm \sqrt{64 + 24}}{6} = \dfrac{-8 \pm \sqrt{88}}{6}$$

29. (4)

Find the x-coordinate of the turning point by finding the axis of symmetry. When a parabola is given in the standard form $y = ax^2 + bx + c$, the formula for the axis of symmetry is:

$$x = -\frac{b}{2a}$$

In this parabola, $a = 1$, $b = -6$, and $c = 5$. Therefore, the axis of symmetry is:

$$x = -\frac{-6}{2(1)} = \frac{6}{2} = 3$$

You know that the x-coordinate is 3, so you can eliminate answer choices (1) and (2). Now, plug $x = 3$ into the equation to find the corresponding y-coordinate:

$$y = (3)^2 - 6(3) + 5$$
$$y = 9 - 18 + 5$$
$$y = -4$$

The coordinates of the turning point are $(3,-4)$.

30. (4)

An isosceles triangle has two congruent base angles and a vertex angle (see question 34). Draw a diagram like this and give each vertex angle a value. Let's say that each vertex angle measures 40°:

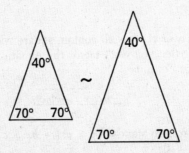

In each case, the base angles measure 70° (remember that the two base angles are congruent and the sum of the three angles must be 180). Thus, you've got two triangles that are the same shape, but not necessarily the same size.

31. (1)

There are four characteristics of a rhombus that you have to know to answer this one:

(1) The diagonals of a rhombus are perpendicular, so every rhombus is made up of four congruent right triangles. (2) The diagonals bisect each other, so if $AC = 12$ then $AM = MC = 6$. (3) The diagonals bisect their angles of origin. Therefore, if m∠$DAB = 120°$, then angles BAM and MAD each measure 60°:

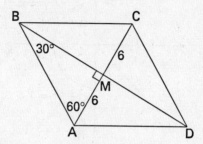

Look at △BAM: $AM = 6$, and AM is the short leg of the 30:60:90 triangle. Since the hypotenuse of a 30:60:90 triangle is twice the length of the short leg, $BA = 12$. This is where the fourth characteristic of a rhombus kicks in: (4) All four sides of a rhombus are congruent, so the perimeter of $ABCD$ is 4 • 12, or 48.

32. (4)

You might be able to answer this one quickly if you recognize that $y = x$ is a line that goes through the origin and $x^2 + y^2 = 1$ is a circle centered at the origin:

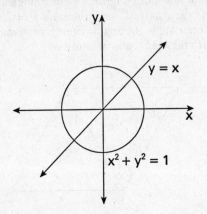

There are two points of intersection.

Here are the graphs of the three other answer choices:

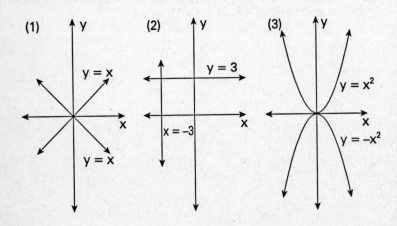

33. (3)

The first statement of answer choice (3) is $x \lor y$, which reads, "either x or y is true." The second statements asserts that x is true. Since the first statement is satisfied, you don't know anything about y; it could be true or false. Let's review the other three choices:

(1) Using the Law of Contrapositive Inference, you can rewrite the second statement as $y \rightarrow {\sim}z$. Thus, $x \rightarrow {\sim}z$ becomes valid because of the Chain Rule.

(2) Using the Law of Contrapositive Inference, you can rewrite the first statement as ${\sim}y \rightarrow {\sim}x$. Since ${\sim}y$ is the second statement, ${\sim}x$ becomes valid because of the Law of Detachment (or *Modus Ponens*). (You can also use the Law of *Modus Tollens* here.)

(4) You can infer that y is true because of the Law of Detachment (or *Modus Ponens*).

34. (4)

Angle-Angle-Angle is *never* a valid statement to prove that two triangles are congruent. You can use Angle-Angle to prove that two triangles are similar, but not congruent. As you know, every triangle congruence theorem must contain reference to at least one side.

35.

The center of the circle is the midpoint of the diameter, so all you
have to do is construct the perpendicular bisector of diameter AB
and indicate the point of intersection. Make sure the width of your
compass is at least two-thirds as long as AB, place the pointy end of
your compass on point A, and make two arcs. Then, without changing the width of the compass, place the pointy end on point B and
make arcs that intersect the first arcs, like this·

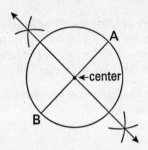

Connect the two points of intersection. The point where the perpendicular bisector intersects diameter AB is the center of the circle.

Part II

36. (0,2) and (5,–3)

Let's look at the algebraic solution first. First, subtract x from both sides of the second equation. It now looks like this:

$$y = -x + 2$$

Since you have two equations that are equal to y, you can set the two of them equal to each other:

$$x^2 - 6x + 2 = -x + 2$$
$$x^2 - 5x = 0$$

Factor x out of the left side of the equation and find the roots of the equation:

$$x(x - 5) = 0$$
$$x = \{0, 5\}$$

The two x-coordinates are 0 and 5; plug each of them into the first equation to find their corresponding y-coordinates:

$x = 0$:
$y = (0)^2 - 6(0) + 2$
$y = 2$

$x = 5$:
$y = (5)^2 - 6(5) + 2$
$y = 25 - 30 + 2$
$y = -3$

The two sets of coordinates are (0,2) and (5,–3).

The graphic solution looks like this:

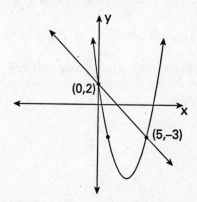

Be sure to check your work, or you'll lose two points.

37. *a*   2.7, –8.7

When two fractions equal each other, you can cross-multiply:

$$\frac{2x}{x-4} = \frac{x-6}{x-2}$$
$$2x(x-2) = (x-4)(x-6)$$
$$2x^2 - 4x = x^2 - 10x + 24$$
$$x^2 + 6x - 24 = 0$$

You can't factor this, so you have to use the Quadratic Formula:

$$x = \frac{-b \pm \sqrt{b^2 - 4ac}}{2a}$$

This equation is in standard $y = ax^2 + bx + c$ format, and $a = 1, b = 6$, and $c = -24$:

$$x = \frac{-6 \pm \sqrt{(6)^2 - 4(1)(-24)}}{2(1)}$$
$$= \frac{-6 \pm \sqrt{36 + 96}}{2} = \frac{-6 \pm \sqrt{132}}{2}$$

Substitute $\sqrt{132} \approx 11.49$ into the fraction and find the numerical values:

$$x = \frac{-6 + 11.49}{2} = \frac{5.49}{2} = 2.74$$
$$x = \frac{-6 - 11.49}{2} = \frac{-17.49}{2} = -8.74$$

When you round these off to the nearest tenth, as instructed, you get 2.7 and –8.7. Plug these values back into the original fraction to check your work.

b **(1) 792**

This is a basic combinations problem. There are twelve students, and you have to choose five. Use the formula $_nC_r = \dfrac{n!}{r!(n-r)!}$ and plug in $n = 12$ and $r = 5$:

$$_{12}C_5 = \frac{12!}{5!\,7!} = \frac{12 \cdot 11 \cdot 10 \cdot 9 \cdot 8 \cdot 7 \cdot 6 \cdot 5 \cdot 4 \cdot 3 \cdot 2 \cdot 1}{5 \cdot 4 \cdot 3 \cdot 2 \cdot 1 \cdot (7 \cdot 6 \cdot 5 \cdot 4 \cdot 3 \cdot 2 \cdot 1)}$$
$$= \frac{12 \cdot 11 \cdot 10 \cdot 9 \cdot 8}{5 \cdot 4 \cdot 3 \cdot 2 \cdot 1} = 792$$

(2) $\dfrac{180}{792}$

This is a bit more complicated, but not much. You have to find out how many of the combinations you just figured out in part *a* consist of two sophomores, two juniors, and one senior. There are five sophomores, and you want to know how many combinations of two sophomores are possible:

$$_5C_2 = \frac{5!}{2!\,3!} = \frac{5 \cdot 4 \cdot 3 \cdot 2 \cdot 1}{2 \cdot 1 \cdot (3 \cdot 2 \cdot 1)} = 10$$

There are four juniors, and you want to choose two of them:

$$_4C_2 = \frac{4!}{2!\,2!} = \frac{4 \cdot 3 \cdot 2 \cdot 1}{2 \cdot 1 \cdot (2 \cdot 1)} = 6$$

Finally, you have to choose one out of three seniors:

$$_3C_1 = \frac{3!}{1!\,2!} = \frac{3 \cdot 2 \cdot 1}{1 \cdot (2 \cdot 1)} = 3$$

There are ten ways to select two sophomores, six ways to select two juniors, and three ways to select one senior. Thus, there are a total of $10 \cdot 6 \cdot 3$, or 180, ways to select two sophomores, two juniors, and one senior. From part (1), you know that there are 792 possible combinations, so the probability is $\dfrac{180}{792}$.

38. ***a*** **96**

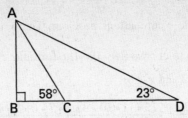

It's trigonometry time. The first place to look is $\triangle ABC$. You want to find AB, which is the side opposite $\angle ACB$, which measures $58°$. You know the length of adjacent side BC, so use tangent (the TOA in SOHCAHTOA):

$$\tan 58 = \frac{AB}{BC}$$

$$1.6 = \frac{AB}{60}$$

$$96 = AB$$

b **568**

Find BD using trigonometry one more time. Forget about AC for a second, and concentrate on right triangle ABD. You know the side opposite $\angle ADB$, and you want to find the adjacent side BD. Use tangent again:

$$\tan 23 = \frac{AB}{BD}$$

$$0.4245 = \frac{96}{BD}$$

$$BD = 226.15$$

You have a choice now. You can use trig again to find AD, or you can use the Pythagorean Theorem like this:

$$(AD)^2 = (AB)^2 + (BD)^2$$
$$(AD)^2 = (96)^2 + (226.15)^2$$
$$(AD)^2 = 9216 + 51143.82$$
$$(AD)^2 = 60359.82$$
$$AD = 245.68$$

Now you know the lengths of all three sides. Just add 'em up, and you're done:

$$96 + 226.15 + 245.68 = 567.83$$

When you round this off to the nearest meter, as instructed, you get 568.

39. *a*

Since the operation is commutative, the array is symmetrical along the diagonal line from the upper left to the lower right. The diagram looks like this:

®	S	O	L	V	E
S	S	S	S	L	V
O	S	O	O	L	S
L	S	O	L	V	E
V	L	L	V	V	O
E	V	S	E	O	E

b **L**

If you look at the middle row (with the *L* character at the far left), you'll see that the letters along that row match the headings above them. Therefore, *L* is the identity element.

c **V**

The identity element is *L*, so you want to find the value that turns *O* into *L*. Look at the completed system: Since $(O \blacklozenge V) = L$, the inverse of *O* is *V*.

d **V**

Start from the parentheses:

$$(L \blacklozenge O) \blacklozenge x = V \blacklozenge S$$
$$O \blacklozenge x = L$$

Since $O \blacklozenge V = L$, it must be true that $x = V$.

e

The identity element of the operation is *L*, and *L* does not appear in the bottom row (the row that corresponds to the element *E*). Thus, *E* has no identity element.

40. *a*

The graph is a circle in the standard formula $(x - h)^2 + (y - k)^2 = r^2$, in which (h,k) is the center of the circle and r is the radius. Therefore, the circle is centered at $(1,-3)$ and has a radius of 4:

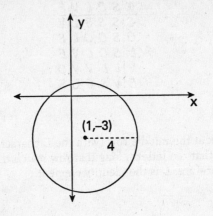

b

Under the translation $(x - 2, y + 4)$, each point shifts 2 units to the left and 4 units up. Since the center of the first circle is $(1,-3)$, the image under the translation is $(1 - 2, -3 + 4)$, or $(-1,1)$. The radius is still 4, so the graph looks like this:

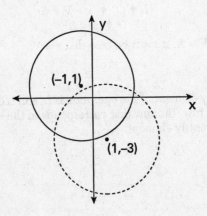

c $(x + 1)^2 + (y - 1)^2 = 16$

Use the standard formula $(x - h)^2 + (y - k)^2 = r^2$; the center of the new circle is (−1,1) and the radius is 4:

$$[x - (-1)]^2 + (y - 1)^2 = 4^2$$
$$(x + 1)^2 + (y - 1)^2 = 16$$

d $y = -2x - 1$

The two points to work with are the center of each circle: (1,−3) and (−1,1). Find the slope between the two points using the slope formula:

$$m = \frac{y_2 - y_1}{x_2 - x_1}$$

In this case, let $(x_1, x_2) = (1, -3)$ and $(x_2, y_2) = (-1, 1)$:

$$m = \frac{1 - (-3)}{-1 - 1} = \frac{4}{-2} = -2$$

You can plug the slope into the standard $y = mx + b$ format. The equation thus far is:

$$y = -2x + b$$

Now, plug one of the points into the equation and solve for *b*. We'll choose (−1,1):

$$1 = -2(-1) + b$$
$$1 = 2 + b$$
$$-1 = b$$

The equation is $y = -2x - 1$.

Part III

41.

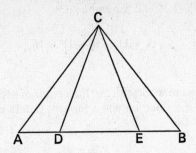

The plan: ∠ACD and ∠BCE are corresponding parts of ΔACD and ΔBCE. Prove that the two triangles are congruent using Side-Angle-Side, then use CPCTC.

Statements	Reasons
1. $\overline{AD} \cong \overline{EB}$ (side)	1. Given
2. ∠CDE ≅ ∠CED	2. Given
3. ∠ADC is supplementary to ∠CDE; ∠CED is supplementary to ∠CEB	3. Definition of supplementary angles
4. ∠ADC ≅ ∠CEB (angle)	4. Angles that are supplementary to congruent angles are congruent.
5. $\overline{CD} \cong \overline{CE}$ (side)	5. In a triangle sides opposite congruent angles are congruent.
6. ΔADC ≅ ΔBCE	6. SAS ≅ SAS
7. ∠ACD ≅ ∠BCE	7. Corresponding parts of congruent triangles are congruent.

42. *a*

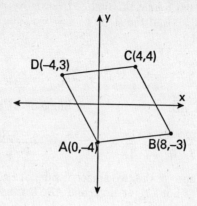

To prove that *ABCD* is a rhombus, find the length of each side using the distance formula

$$d = \sqrt{(x_2 - x_1)^2 + (y_2 - y_1)^2} :$$

$AB = \sqrt{(8 - 0)^2 + [-3 - (-4)]^2}$

$\quad = \sqrt{8^2 + 1^2}$

$\quad = \sqrt{64 + 1}$

$\quad = \sqrt{65}$

$BC = \sqrt{(4 - 8)^2 + [4 - (-3)]^2}$

$\quad = \sqrt{(-4)^2 + 7^2}$

$\quad = \sqrt{16 + 49}$

$\quad = \sqrt{65}$

$CD = \sqrt{(-4 - 4)^2 + (3 - 4)^2}$

$\quad = \sqrt{(-8)^2 + (-1)^2}$

$\quad = \sqrt{64 + 1}$

$\quad = \sqrt{65}$

$AD = \sqrt{(-4 - 0)^2 + [3 - (-4)]^2}$

$\quad = \sqrt{(-4)^2 + 7^2}$

$\quad = \sqrt{16 + 49}$

$\quad = \sqrt{65}$

All four sides of the quadrilateral have the same length, so *ABCD* is a rhombus.

b

A rectangle has four right angles. In order to prove that *ABCD* is not a rectangle, find the slope of any two adjacent sides using the slope formula:

$$m = \frac{y_2 - y_1}{x_2 - x_1}$$

Slope of $\overline{AB}$:

$$m = \frac{-3 - (-4)}{8 - 0} = \frac{1}{8}$$

Slope of $\overline{BC}$:

$$m = \frac{4 - (-3)}{4 - 8} = \frac{7}{-4} = -\frac{7}{4}$$

Since the slopes of the two adjacent sides are *not* negative reciprocals, $\angle ABC$ is not a right angle and *ABCD* is *not* a rectangle.

EXAMINATION
JANUARY 1999

Part I

Answer 30 questions from this part. Each correct answer will receive 2 credits. No partial credit will be allowed. Write your answers in the spaces provided on the separate answer sheet. Where applicable, answers may be left in terms of π or in radical form. [60]

1 In the accompanying diagram, $\overline{AB}$ is extended to C, m$\angle DBC$ = 142, and $\overleftrightarrow{AE} \parallel \overleftrightarrow{DB}$. Find m$\angle EAB$.

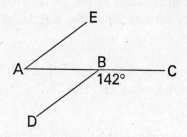

2 The corresponding altitudes of two similar triangles are 6 and 4. If the perimeter of the larger triangle is 18, what is the perimeter of the smaller triangle?

3 What is the identity element for the operation @ in the following system?

@	A	B	C	D
A	D	A	B	C
B	A	B	C	D
C	B	C	D	A
D	C	D	A	B

4 What are the coordinates of P', the image of $P(2,-5)$ after a reflection in the y-axis?

5 Parallelogram $STAR$ has coordinates $S(0,0)$, $T(6,-1)$, $A(4,2)$, and $R(-2,3)$. What are the coordinates of the point of intersection of the diagonals?

6 If the operation $\odot$ is defined as $a \odot b = \sqrt{a} + b^2$, what is the value of $16 \odot 3$?

7 In the accompanying diagram of isosceles triangle BAC, vertex angle A measures $70°$ and $\overline{AC}$ is extended to D. Find $m\angle BCD$.

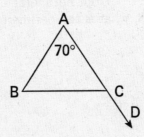

8 In the accompanying diagram of right triangle OAP, the coordinates of P are $(6,k)$. Find the value of k if the area of $\triangle OAP$ is 12.

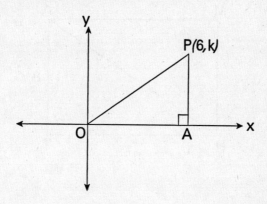

9 In the accompanying diagram, the lengths of the bases of isosceles trapezoid $ABCD$ are 7 and 15. Each leg makes an angle of 45° with the longer base. Find the length of the altitude of the trapezoid

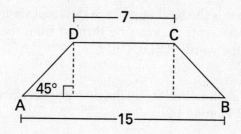

10 If $x + 15$ and $2x + 27$ represent the number of degrees in the measures of two consecutive angles of a parallelogram, find the value of x.

11 In rectangle *MATH*, *AT* = 8 and *TH* = 12. Find the length of diagonal $\overline{HA}$ to the *nearest tenth*.

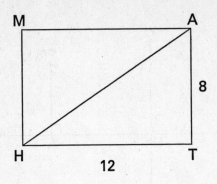

12 Solve for the positive value of x: $\dfrac{4}{x+2} = \dfrac{x-2}{15}$

13 Write an equation of the line that passes through point (8,3) and is parallel to the x-axis.

14 What is the total number of different six-letter arrangements that can be formed from the letters of the word "REDUCE"?

15 Find, in radical form, the distance between points (−3,7) and (4,2).

Directions (16–34): For *each* question chosen, write on the separate answer sheet the *numeral* preceding the word or expression that best completes the statement or answers the question.

16 The measure of an exterior angle of a triangle can *not* be

(1) less than 90°
(2) between 90° and 180°
(3) exactly 90°
(4) greater than 180°

17 If two angles of a triangle measure 56° and 68°, the triangle is

(1) scalene   (3) obtuse
(2) isosceles   (4) right

18 Which statement is logically equivalent to $\sim(p \wedge \sim q)$?

(1) $\sim p \wedge q$ (3) $\sim p \wedge \sim q$
(2) $\sim p \vee q$ (4) $\sim p \vee \sim q$

19 If two sides of a scalene triangle measure 10 and 12, the length of the third side could be

(1) 10   (3) 15
(2) 2   (4) 22

20 In the accompanying diagram, $\overline{ABC}$, $\overline{DBE}$, and $\overline{EC}$ are drawn and m∠ABD = 3x.

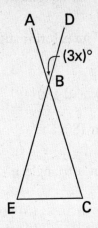

What is the sum of m∠C and m∠E?

(1) 2x

(3) 180 − x

(2) 3x

(4) 180 − 3x

21 In the accompanying diagram of right triangle ABC, m$\angle C$ = 90, m$\angle BAC$ = 48, $AC = x$, and CB = 16.3.

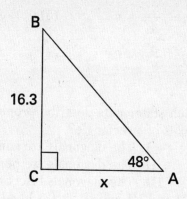

Which equation could be used to find the length of $\overline{AC}$?

(1) $\sin 48 = \dfrac{16.3}{x}$ (3) $\tan 48 = \dfrac{16.3}{x}$

(2) $\cos 48 = \dfrac{x}{16.3}$ (4) $\tan 48 = \dfrac{x}{16.3}$

22 What is the image of (4,–1) after a dilation of 2?
   (1) (6,1)   (3) (6,–1)
   (2) (2,–3)   (4) (8,–2)

23 Which expression is a factored form of $2x^2 - 2x - 12$?
   (1) $2(x + 2)(x - 3)$ (3) $2(x + 3)(x - 2)$
   (2) $2(x + 6)(x - 1)$ (4) $2(x + 1)(x - 6)$

24 What is the slope of the line $y + 6x = 3$?
   (1) –6   (3) 3
   (2) –3   (4) 6

25 The graph of which equation passes through points (0,6) and (4,−1)?

(1) $y = \dfrac{7}{4}x + 6$ 　　　 (3) $y = -\dfrac{7}{4}x + 6$

(2) $y = \dfrac{4}{7}x + 6$ 　　　 (4) $y = -\dfrac{4}{7}x + 6$

26 Which statements describe properties of the diagonals of a rectangle?
　　　　I. The diagonals are congruent.
　　　　II. The diagonals are perpendicular.
　　　　III. The diagonals bisect each other.
(1) II and III, only 　　　 (3) I and III, only
(2) I and II, only 　　　 (4) I, II, and III

27 Given: $d \rightarrow \sim e$
　　　　　e
　　　　$\sim d \rightarrow c$

Which statement is true?
(1) $d \vee \sim c$ 　　　 (3) d
(2) c 　　　 (4) $c \wedge \sim e$

28 What are the roots of the equation $x^2 - 6x - 3 = 0$?

(1) $3 \pm 2\sqrt{3}$ 　　　 (3) 3,1

(2) 3,2 　　　 (4) $-3 \pm 2\sqrt{3}$

29 What is an equation of the axis of symmetry of the graph of the parabola $y = -3x^2 + 12x - 17$?
(1) $x = -2$ 　　　 (3) $x = -4$
(2) $x = 2$ 　　　 (4) $x = 4$

30 In $\triangle PQR$, $m\angle P = 51$ and $m\angle Q = 57$. Which expression is true?

(1) $QR > PQ$ (3) $PQ = QR$

(2) $PR > PQ$ (4) $PQ > QR$

31 The expression $_6C_2$ is equivalent to

(1) 360   (3) $_6C_4$

(2) $_2C_6$ (4) $_6P_2$

32 Which statement is the converse of "If quadrilateral $ABCD$ is a trapezoid, then it has only two opposite sides that are parallel"?

(1) If quadrilateral $ABCD$ is not a trapezoid, then it does not have two and only two opposite sides that are parallel.

(2) If quadrilateral $ABCD$ has only two opposite sides that are parallel, then it is a trapezoid.

(3) If quadrilateral $ABCD$ is a trapezoid, then it does not have two and only two opposite sides that are parallel.

(4) If quadrilateral $ABCD$ does not have two and only two opposite sides that are parallel, then it is not a trapezoid.

33 Which equation is represented by the graph drawn
    in the accompanying diagram?

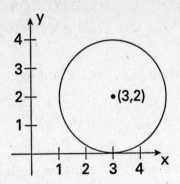

(1) $(x + 3)^2 + (y + 2)^2 = 4$
(2) $(x - 3)^2 + (y - 2)^2 = 2$
(3) $(x + 3)^2 + (y + 2)^2 = 2$
(4) $(x - 3)^2 + (y - 2)^2 = 4$

34 Which statement is an illustration of the commu
    tative property of real numbers?
    (1) $5 + 3 = 3 + 5$
    (2) $5(6 + 7) = 5(6) + 5(7)$
    (3) $\left(\dfrac{1}{2} + \dfrac{1}{3}\right) + \dfrac{1}{4} = \dfrac{1}{2} + \left(\dfrac{1}{3} + \dfrac{1}{4}\right)$
    (4) $-5 + 0 = -5$

Directions (35): Leave all construction lines on the answer sheet.

35 *On the answer sheet,* construct the bisector of obtuse angle *MAE*.

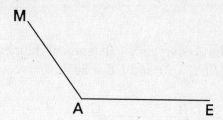

Part II

Answer three questions from this part. Clearly indicate the necessary steps, including appropriate formula substitutions, diagrams, graphs, charts, etc. Calculations that may be obtained by mental arithmetic or the calculator do not need to be shown.

[30]

36 In the accompanying diagram of rhombus *RUDE*, m∠*RUE* = 21 and *UE* = 20.

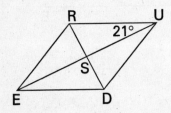

Find, to the *nearest tenth*, the

a length of $\overline{RD}$ [5]

b perimeter of *RUDE*   [5]

37 In the accompanying diagram, M is the midpoint of $\overline{AB}$.

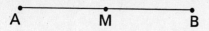

A   M   B

  a Describe fully the locus of points in a plane that are

    (1) equidistant from A and B [2]

    (2) 4 units from $\overleftrightarrow{AB}$ [3]

    (3) d units from M [3]

  b For which value of d will there be exactly two points that satisfy all the conditions in part *a*? [2]

38 Solve the following system of equations either graphically or algebraically and check.

$$y = x^2 - 4x + 9$$
$$2x - y + 1 = 0 \quad\quad [8,2]$$

39 Find the area of quadrilateral $MATH$, whose vertices are $M(4,5)$, $A(9,7)$, $T(11,2)$, and $H(2,1)$. [10]

40 In the accompanying diagram of right triangle ABC, altitude $\overline{CD}$ is drawn to hypotenuse $\overline{AB}$, $CA = 6$, and AB is 7 more than AD.

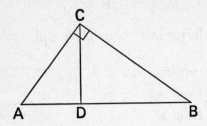

a Find AD to the *nearest hundredth*. [7]

b Using the results from part *a*, find the length of altitude $\overline{CD}$ to the *nearest tenth*. [3]

Part III
Answer one question from this part. Clearly indicate the necessary steps, including appropriate formula substitutions, diagrams, graphs, charts, etc. Calculations that may be obtained by mental arithmetic or the calculator do not need to be shown. [10]

41 Given: isosceles triangle CAT, $\overline{CT} \cong \overline{AT}$, $\overline{ST}$ bisects $\angle CTA$, and $\overline{SC}$ and $\overline{SA}$ are drawn.

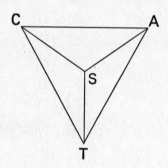

   Prove $\angle SCA \cong \angle SAC$ [10]

42 Given: $A \rightarrow \sim B$
   $\qquad D \rightarrow \sim C$
   $\qquad (\sim D \wedge \sim E) \rightarrow F$
   $\qquad C \vee B$
   $\qquad A$
   $\qquad \sim F$

   Prove: E [10]

ANSWERS AND EXPLANATIONS
JANUARY 1999
ANSWER KEY

Part I

1. 38
2. 12
3. *B*
4. (−2,−5)
5. (2,1)
6. 13
7. 125
8. 4
9. 4
10. 46
11. 14.4
12. 8

13. $y = 3$
14. 360
15. $\sqrt{74}$
16. (4)
17. (2)
18. (2)
19. (3)
20. (4)
21. (3)
22. (4)
23. (1)
24. (1)

25. (3)
26. (3)
27. (2)
28. (1)
29. (2)
30. (4)
31. (3)
32. (2)
33. (4)
34. (1)
35. construction

Part II

36. *a* 7.7
    b 42.8
37. *a* (1) the perpendicular bisector of $\overline{AB}$
    (2) two lines parallel to $\overline{AB}$ and 4 units from it
    (3) a circle with center at *M* having a radius of *d*
    b 4

38. (2,5) and (4,9)
    Check
39. 31.5
40. *a* 3.45
    b 4.9

Part III

41. see explanations
42. see explanations

EXPLANATIONS
Part I

1. 38

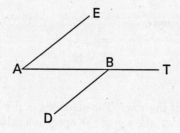

The sum of two supplementary angles is 180°, so find the measure of ∠ABD first:

m∠ABD + m∠DBC = 180

m∠ABD + 142 = 180

m∠ABD = 38

Now look at ∠EAB and ∠ABD. Since *AE* and *DB* are parallel, these two angles are alternate interior angles, which also have the same measure. Thus, m∠EAB = 38.

2. 12

Draw some sample triangles like these:

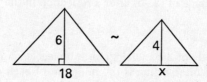

Whenever you have two similar triangles, all linear measures of corresponding parts of the triangles are proportional. Since the ratio of
the altitudes is 6:4, then the ratio of every set of corresponding sides
is also 6:4. Therefore, the ratio of the perimeters is 6:4. Set up the

proportion: $\dfrac{6}{4} = \dfrac{18}{x}$

Cross-multiply and solve:

$$6x = 72$$
$$x = 12$$

3. **B**

Look at each of the rows: The elements in the *B* row are the same
as the elements at the top of the operation table:

@	A	B	C	D
A	D	A	B	C
B	A	B	C	D
C	B	C	D	A
D	C	D	A	B

Thus, *B* is the identity element of the operation.

4. **(−2,−5)**

Whenever a point is reflected in the *y*-axis, the *x*-coordinate is negated and the *y*-coordinate remains the same. In other words:

$$r_{y\text{-axis}}\,(x,y) \rightarrow (-x,y)$$

Thus, the image of (2,−5) after a reflection in the *y*-axis is (−2,−5).

5. **(2,1)**

The diagonals of a parallelogram intersect each other. Therefore,
the point of intersection is the midpoint of each diagonal. To find
the point of intersection, pick a pair of opposite points and use the
midpoint formula:

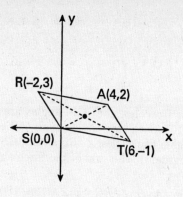

$$\left(\overline{x}, \overline{y}\right) = \left(\frac{x_1 + x_2}{2}, \frac{y_1 + y_2}{2}\right)$$

For this problem, the midpoint $\left(\overline{x}, \overline{y}\right)$ is (x,y), and you can let $(x_1, y_1) = S(0,0)$ and $(x_2, y_2) = A(4,2)$. Solve for x and y like this:

$\overline{x} = \dfrac{x_1 + x_2}{2}$

$x = \dfrac{0 + 4}{2}$

$x = 2$

$\overline{y} = \dfrac{y_1 + y_2}{2}$

$y = \dfrac{0 + 2}{2}$

$y = 1$

The coordinates of the point are $(2,1)$.

Note: You can use $T(6,-1)$ and $R(-2,3)$ as well:

$\overline{x} = \dfrac{x_1 + x_2}{2}$

$x = \dfrac{6 + (-2)}{2}$

$x = \dfrac{4}{2}$

$x = 2$

$\overline{y} = \dfrac{y_1 + y_2}{2}$

$y = \dfrac{-1 + 3}{2}$

$y = \dfrac{2}{2}$

$y = 1$

6. 13

They've already defined the function for you, so just plug in $a = 16$ and $b = 3$:

$$16 \; ❂ \; 3 = \sqrt{16} + 3^2 = 4 + 9 = 13$$

7. 125

Since $\triangle ABC$ is isosceles, the base angles are equal. Therefore, $180° - 70° = 110°$. Each base angle equals $55°$. Since $\angle A$ is the vertex angle, the other two angles, $\angle ABC$ and $\angle ACB$ are the base angles (which are congruent). The sum of the three angles in a triangle is 180:

$$m\angle A + m\angle ABC + m\angle ACB = 180$$
$$70 + x + x = 180$$
$$2x = 110$$
$$x = 55$$

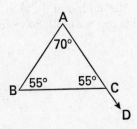

Each of the base angles measures $55°$; now use that information to find the measure of the exterior angle BCD, which is supplementary to $\angle ACB$:

$$m\angle ACB + m\angle BCD = 180$$
$$55 + m\angle BCD = 180$$
$$m\angle BCD = 125$$

8. 4

Since $\triangle OAP$ is a right angle, you can use the measures of the two legs to find the area. Also, the coordinates of point P are $(6,k)$, so $OA = 6$ and $AP = k$:

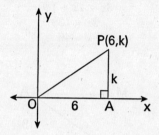

The formula for the area of a triangle is $A = \frac{1}{2}bh$. Plug in $A = 12$, $b = 6$, and $h = k$:

$$12 = \frac{1}{2}(6)h$$
$$12 = 3h$$
$$4 = h$$

9. 4

Label the points at which the altitudes meet the base of the trapezoid X and Y, like this:

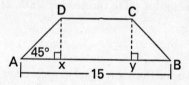

The altitudes are perpendicular to the two parallel sides DC and AB, so $XDCY$ is a rectangle. Therefore, $XY = 7$. Since $ABCD$ is an isosceles trapezoid, $AX = YB$. Figure out the length of each like this:

$$AX + XY + YB = 15$$
$$x + 7 + x = 15$$
$$2x = 8$$
$$x = 4$$

Now look at $\triangle AXD$. Since it's a 45:45:90 triangle, its two legs have the same length. Thus, AX and XD both are 4 units long.

10. 46

The sum of any two consecutive angles is 180°, so plug in the two algebraic terms you've been given and solve for x:

$$(x + 15) + (2x + 27) = 180$$
$$3x + 42 = 180$$
$$3x = 138$$
$$x = 46$$

11. 14.4

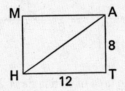

Look at right triangle ATH: Since triangle ATH is a right triangle, you can use the Pythagorean Theorem to find the length of HA:

$$(HA)^2 = (HT)^2 + (AT)^2$$
$$(HA)^2 = 12^2 + 8^2$$
$$(HA)^2 = 144 + 64$$
$$(HA)^2 = 208$$

Now use your calculator to find the right answer:

$$HA = 14.422$$

When you round this off to the *nearest tenth*, as instructed, you get 14.4.

12. 8

Whenever two fractions are equal to each other, you can cross-multiply:

$$\frac{4}{x + 2} = \frac{x - 2}{15}$$
$$(x + 2)(x - 2) = 4 \cdot 15$$

Combine the terms on the left using FOIL, then solve for x:

$$x^2 - 4 = 60$$
$$x^2 = 64$$
$$x = \pm 8$$

Since you only want the positive value, get rid of -8.

13. $y = 3$

Any line that is parallel to the x-axis has a slope of 0. Since you're given a point, you can plug the slope into the standard $y = mx + b$ format:

$$y = (0)x + b$$

Now, plug the coordinates of the point into the equation and solve for b:

$$3 = (0)8 + b$$
$$3 = 0 + b$$
$$3 = b$$

The equation is $y = (0)x + 3$, or more simply, $y = 3$.

14. 360

To find the number of possible arrangements of the letters in a word with n letters, in which one letter appears p times (remember that p is greater than 1), the formula looks like this: $\dfrac{n!}{p!}$

REDUCE has six letters, but there are two E's. Therefore, you can express the number of arrangements as:

$$\frac{6!}{2!} = \frac{6 \cdot 5 \cdot 4 \cdot 3 \cdot 2 \cdot 1}{2 \cdot 1} = \frac{720}{2} = 360$$

15. $\sqrt{74}$

To find the distance between any two points, use the distance formula: $d = \sqrt{(x_2 - x_1)^2 + (y_2 - y_1)^2}$

In this case, $(x_1, y_1) = (-3,7)$ and $(x_2, y_2) = (4,2)$:

$$d = \sqrt{[4 - (-3)]^2 + (2 - 7)^2}$$
$$= \sqrt{7^2 + (-5)^2}$$
$$= \sqrt{49 + 25}$$
$$= \sqrt{74}$$

The question asks for the answer in radical form, so you don't have to do any more work.

Multiple Choice

Don't forget that one of the best techniques on these Multiple Choice questions is to use Process of Elimination to get rid of answer choices that aren't possible.

16. (4)

All exterior angles of a triangle are supplementary to one of the triangle's interior angles.

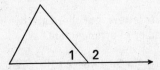

In any case, the sum of the measures of $\angle 1$ and $\angle 2$ equal 180. Since there's no such thing as an angle with a negative measure on this exam, it's impossible for either angle to be bigger than 180°.

17. (2)

The sum of the three angles in a triangle is 180. Use this formula to determine the measure of the third angle:

$$m\angle 1 + m\angle 2 + m\angle 3 = 180$$
$$56 + 68 + x = 180$$
$$x = 56$$

Since the triangle has two angles that have the same measure (56°), it is an isosceles triangle.

18. (2)

Whenever you negate a statement with a "∧" or a "∨" in it, use De Morgan's Law:

$$\sim(p \wedge \sim q) \rightarrow \sim p \vee q$$

19. (3)

The length of a third side of a triangle must be larger than the difference between the two known sides and less than their sum. In other words:

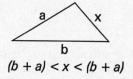

(b + a) < x < (b + a)

Since the two known sides are 10 and 12, the length of the third side must be between 12 – 10, or 2, and 12 + 10, or 22. You can eliminate (2), because the third side has to be greater than 2, not equal to 2. For the same reason, you can get rid of (4).

The other two numbers are within range, but a scalene triangle has three sides of different lengths. There already is a side with length 10, so the third side can't be 10 as well. That eliminates (1).

20. (4)

Since $\overline{ABC}$ and $\overline{EBD}$ are straight lines, $\angle ABD$ and $\angle EBC$ are vertical angles, which have the same measure. Thus, m$\angle EBC = 3x$.

Now look at $\triangle BEC$. The sum of the three angles in a triangle is 180:

$$\text{m}\angle E + \text{m}\angle C + \text{m}\angle EBC = 180$$
$$\text{m}\angle E + \text{m}\angle C + 3x = 180$$

Once you subtract $3x$ from both sides of the equation, you'll get your answer:

$$\text{m}\angle E + \text{m}\angle C = 180 - 3x$$

Note: You can also work with this problem by plugging in.

21. (3)

You know the length of the opposite side of $\angle A$ ($BC = 10$), and you want to find the length of the adjacent side, x. You want to use tangent (the TOA in SOHCAHTOA), so you can eliminate (1) and (2). Now plug in the variables for TOA, and remember that m$\angle A = 48$:

$$\tan 48 = \frac{16.3}{x}$$

22. (4)

Under a dilation of 2 with respect to the origin, the coordinates of a point are each multiplied by 2. Therefore, the image of the point $(4,-1)$ after that dilation is $(8,-2)$.

23. (1)

When working with this trinomial (which is just a high-falutin' name for a thing with three terms in it), factor the 2 out of each term first:

$$2x^2 - 2x - 12 = 2(x^2 - x - 6)$$

Now, factor the term in the parentheses (you might have to resort to trial-and-error, but you'll get it eventually):

$$x^2 - x - 6 = (x + 2)(x - 3)$$

Therefore, the final factorization is $2(x + 2)(x - 3)$.

24. (1)

Before you can determine the slope of a line, you have to put the equation into the standard $y = mx + b$ format. In this case, all you have to do is subtract $6x$ from both sides:

$$y + 6x = 3$$
$$y = -6x + 3$$

The slope of the line is –6.

Note: Whatever you do, don't fall asleep and pick (4)! It's a trap for kids who aren't paying attention.

25. (3)

Each answer choice is in the standard $y = mx + b$ format, and the only difference among them is the slope (m). So, all you have to do is find the slope of the line that contains the two points using the slope formula:

$$m = \frac{y_2 - y_1}{x_2 - x_1}$$

In this case, let $(x_1, x_2) = (0,6)$ and $(x_2, y_2) = (4,-1)$:

$$m = \frac{-1 - 6}{4 - 0} = \frac{-7}{4} = -\frac{7}{4}$$

The only line with a slope of $-\dfrac{7}{4}$, so the answer is (3).

26. (3)

Draw a rectangle and its diagonals, like this:

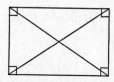

Now consider each of the statements one at a time:

  I. The diagonals of a rectangle are congruent; eliminate (1).

  II. The diagonals are perpendicular; eliminate (2) and (4).

  III. The diagonals bisect each other

The only answer left is (3).

27. (2)

Here's what a logical proof might look like:

Statements	Reasons
1. $d \rightarrow \sim e$	1. Given
2. $e \rightarrow \sim d$	2. Law of Contrapositive Inference
3. e	3. Given
4. $\sim d$	4. Law of Detachment (2, 3)
5. $\sim d \rightarrow c$	5. Given
6. c	6. Law of Detachment (4, 5)

Since c is your result, the answer is (2). **Note:** You can also combine statements 1 and 3 using the Law of *Modus Tollens* like this:

$$[(d \rightarrow \sim e) \wedge e] \rightarrow \sim d$$

28. (1)

Try the integers first by plugging them back into the equation. Since 3 is in both answer choices (2) and (3), try it first:

$$(3)^2 - 6(3) - 3 = 0$$
$$9 - 18 - 3 = 0$$
$$-12 = 0$$

Since 3 doesn't work, you can eliminate (2) and (3) and begin work with the Quadratic Formula:

$$x = \frac{-b \pm \sqrt{b^2 - 4ac}}{2a}$$

This equation is in standard $ax^2 + bx + c$ format, and $a = 1$, $b = -6$, and $c = -3$:

$$x = \frac{-(-6) \pm \sqrt{(-6)^2 - 4(1)(-3)}}{2(1)}$$

$$= \frac{6 \pm \sqrt{36 + 12}}{2}$$

$$= \frac{6 \pm \sqrt{48}}{2}$$

$$= \frac{6 \pm 4\sqrt{3}}{2} = 3 \pm 2\sqrt{3}$$

29. (2)

When a parabola is given in the standard form $y = ax^2 + bx + c$, the formula for the axis of symmetry is:

$$x = -\frac{b}{2a}$$

In this parabola, $a = -3$, $b = 12$, and $c = -17$. Therefore, the axis of symmetry is:

$$x = -\frac{12}{2(-3)} = -\frac{12}{-6} = 2$$

30. (4)

First, find the measure of $\angle R$. The sum of the three angles in a triangle is 180:

$$m\angle P + m\angle Q + m\angle R = 180$$
$$51 + 57 + x = 180$$
$$108 + x = 180$$
$$m\angle R = 72$$

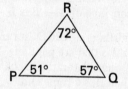

In any triangle, the shortest side is opposite from the smallest angle, and the largest side is opposite from the largest angle. Since $\angle R$ is the largest angle, the side opposite $\angle R$, or PQ, is largest. Also, $\angle P$ is the smallest angle, so QR is the smallest side. Given this info, you can tell that $PQ > QR$.

31. (3)

The fastest way to do this one is to remember the formula about combinations: $_nC_r = {}_nC_{n-r}$. From this, you can determine that $_6C_2 = {}_6C_4$.

Otherwise, use the formula $_nC_r = \dfrac{n!}{r!\,(n-r)!}$ and plug in $n = 6$ and $r = 2$:

$$_6C_2 = \frac{6!}{2!\,4!} = \frac{6 \cdot 5 \cdot 4 \cdot 3 \cdot 2 \cdot 1}{2 \cdot 1 \cdot (4 \cdot 3 \cdot 2 \cdot 1)} = \frac{6 \cdot 5}{2 \cdot 1} = 15$$

Eliminate (1). Answer choice is not possible, because n must be greater than r. And the permutation in answer choice (4) is also impossible, because of this:

$$_6P_2 = \frac{6!}{2!} = 6 \cdot 5 \cdot 4 \cdot 3 = 720$$

32. (2)

To form the converse of a logic statement, just flip the elements. In other words, the converse of $A \rightarrow B$ is $B \rightarrow A$.

Now let A = "Quadrilateral $ABCD$ is a trapezoid" and B = "It has only two opposite sides that are parallel." The converse of the statement will read, "If quadrilateral $ABCD$ has only two opposite sides that are parallel, then it is a trapezoid."

33. (4)

Before you use the formula, you have to determine the radius of the circle. Since the circle is tangent to the x-axis, the radius of the circle is 2:

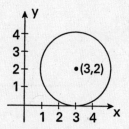

Now, use the standard formula $(x - h)^2 + (y - k)^2 = r^2$; the center of the circle is $(3,2)$ and the radius is 2:

$$(x - 3)^2 + (y - 2)^2 = 2^2$$
$$(x - 3)^2 + (y - 2)^2 = 4$$

34. (1)

The commutative property of real numbers says that the sum or product any two numbers is the same, regardless of the order in which they appear. In other words:

$$a + b = b + a \qquad\qquad a \bullet b = b \bullet a$$

Therefore, the best illustration of the commutative property is answer choice (1).

35. construction

This is about as simple a construction as there is. Take your compass, put the metal end on point A, and make an arc that intersects AM and AE. Label those points X and Y like this:

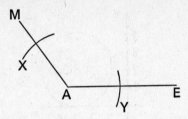

Widen your compass a little bit, put the metal end on point X, and make a second arc within the angle. Then put the metal end on point Y and make a third arc that intersects the second arc. Label that point of intersection Z:

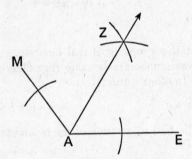

Now draw in ray AZ. This is the angle bisector.

Part II

36. ***a*** **7.7**

Since the diagonals of a rhombus are perpendicular to each other, every rhombus is made up of four right triangles. The diagonals also bisect each other; since $UE = 20$, then $SU = 10$.

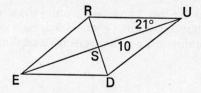

Now it's time for a little trig on right triangle RSU. You want to find the length of the side opposite $\angle RUS$, and you know the length of the adjacent leg, so use tangent (the TOA in SOHCAHTOA):

$$\tan 21° = \frac{RS}{SU}$$

$$0.3839 = \frac{RS}{10}$$

$$3.839 = RS$$

Since RS is half as long as RD (remember that the diagonals bisect each other), then $RD = 2 \cdot 3.839$, or 7.677. When you round this off to the nearest tenth, as instructed, the answer is 7.7.

b **42.8**

You can use trig now, but you don't have to. If you keep your attention on right triangle RSU, you know $RS = 3.8$ and $SU = 10$. Find RU using the Pythagorean Theorem:

$$(RU)^2 = (RS)^2 + (SU)^2$$
$$(RU)^2 = (3.8)^2 + 10^2$$
$$(RU)^2 = 14.44 + 100$$
$$(RU)^2 = 114.44$$
$$RU = 10.697$$

A rhombus has four equal sides, so multiply *RU* by four to get the perimeter:

$$4 \cdot 10.697 = 42.788$$

When you round this off to the nearest tenth, as instructed, the answer is 42.8.

37. *a* (1) the perpendicular bisector of $\overline{AB}$

In situations like this, a picture is worth a thousand words. The perpendicular bisector of a line segment is defined as the locus of points that are equidistant from the segment's endpoints, like this:

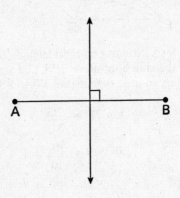

(2) two lines parallel to $\overline{AB}$ and 4 units from it

The two lines look like this:

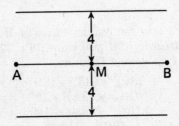

(3) a circle with center _M_ having a radius of _d_

A circle is defined as a locus of points a specific distance from a certain point, like this:

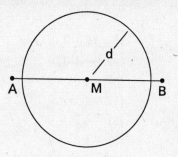

b **4**

The composite diagram of all three loci looks like this, and the two points are labeled _X_ and _Y_:

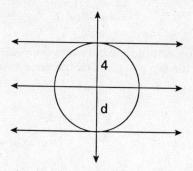

Since _X_ and _Y_ are on the two parallel lines in part (2) of the last question, they are 4 units away from point _M_. Therefore, the radius of the circle centered at _M_ must be 4.

38. (2,5) and (4,9)

<u>The Graphic Solution:</u>

Make a chart for the graph of the first equation, which is a parabola, like this:

x	$x^2 - 4x + 9$	y
-1	$(-1)^2 - 4(-1) + 9$	13
0	$(0)^2 - 4(0) + 9$	9
1	$(1)^2 - 4(1) + 9$	6
2	$(2)^2 - 4(2) + 9$	5
3	$(3)^2 - 4(3) + 9$	6
4	$(4)^2 - 4(4) + 9$	9
5	$(5)^2 - 4(5) + 9$	13

Before you graph the line, play with it a bit until it's in standard $y = mx + b$ format:

$$2x - y + 1 = 0$$
$$-y = -2x - 1$$
$$y = 2x + 1$$

Now you know that the line intersects the y-axis at 1 and has a slope of 2. Graph the two equations on the same axes, like this:

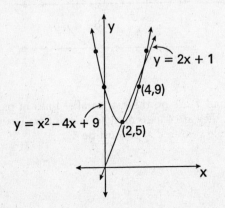

The graphs intersect at (2,5) and (4,9).

The Algebraic Solution:

Convert the second equation into $y = 2x + 1$ as you did above, then set the two equations equal to each other:

$$x^2 - 4x + 9 = 2x + 1$$
$$x^2 - 6x + 8 = 0$$

Factor this and solve for the values of x:

$$(x - 2)(x - 4) = 0$$
$$x = \{2, 4\}$$

Substitute these two values into the first equation and solve for y:

$$y = (2)^2 - 4(2) + 9 \qquad y = (4)^2 - 4(4) + 9$$

$$y = 4 - 8 + 9 \qquad y = 16 - 16 + 9$$

$$y = 5 \qquad y = 9$$

The two points of intersection are (2,5) and (4,9).

39. **31.5**

Graph the four points, then pencil in the rectangle that contains the quadrilateral like this:

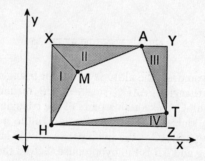

The fastest to find the area of *MATH* is to find the area of the big rectangle (which appears as *HXYZ*) and then subtract the areas of the four triangles like this:

Area of rectangle $HXYZ$: $6 \cdot 9 = 54$

Area of Triangle I ($\triangle MXH$): $\dfrac{1}{2}(6)(2) = 6$

Area of Triangle II ($\triangle MAX$): $\dfrac{1}{2}(7)(2) = 7$

Area of Triangle III ($\triangle AYT$): $\dfrac{1}{2}(5)(2) = 5$

Area of Triangle IV ($\triangle HZT$): $\dfrac{1}{2}(9)(1) = 4.5$

The area of quadrilateral $MATH$ equals $54 - (6 + 7 + 5 + 4.5)$, or 31.5.

40. ***a*** **3.45**

Labeling this diagram properly will make your life much easier. Since $AB = AD + DB$, and AB is 7 more than AD, then $AD = x$ and $DB = 7$:

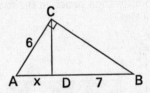

Whenever you draw the altitude of a right triangle, you create three similar right triangles—$\triangle ADC$ (small), $\triangle CDB$ (medium), and the original $\triangle ABC$ (large). Corresponding parts of the triangles are proportional. To find AD, look at the similar triangles: In the small triangle, AD is the small leg and AC is the hypotenuse. In the large triangle, AC is the small leg and AB is the hypotenuse. Set up the proportion:

$$\frac{AD}{AC} = \frac{AC}{AB}$$

$$\frac{x}{6} = \frac{6}{x+7}$$

$$x^2 + 7x = 36$$

$$x^2 + 7x - 36 = 0$$

You can't factor this, so you have to use the Quadratic Formula:

$$x = \frac{-b \pm \sqrt{b^2 - 4ac}}{2a}$$

This equation is in standard $ax^2 + bx + c$ format, and $a = 1$, $b = 7$, and $c = -36$:

$$x = \frac{-7 \pm \sqrt{(7)^2 - 4(1)(-36)}}{2(1)}$$

$$= \frac{-7 \pm \sqrt{49 + 144}}{2}$$

$$= \frac{-7 \pm \sqrt{193}}{2}$$

$$= \frac{-7 + \sqrt{193}}{2}, \frac{-7 - \sqrt{193}}{2}$$

Since $\sqrt{193} = 13.89$, you'll get two values:

$$\frac{-7 + 13.892}{2} = \frac{6.892}{2} = 3.446 \qquad \frac{-7 - 13.892}{2} = \frac{-20.892}{2} = -10.446$$

Throw out the second value, because you're looking for a distance (and distances can't be negative. The only value remaining is 3.446. When you round this off to the nearest *hundredth*, as instructed, you get 3.45.

b **4.9**

From here, it's easier. You know AD and DB, and you're looking for CD. The altitude $\overline{CD}$ of $\triangle ABC$ is the mean proportional to segments $\overline{AD}$ and $\overline{DB}$. Set up the proportion like this:

$$\frac{AD}{CD} = \frac{CD}{DB}$$
$$\frac{3.45}{CD} = \frac{CD}{7}$$
$$(CD)^2 = 24.15$$
$$CD = \sqrt{24.15}$$
$$CD = 4.91$$

When you round this off to the nearest *tenth*, as instructed, you get 4.9.

Part III

41.

The plan: Prove that $\triangle CST$ is congruent to $\triangle AST$ using Side-Angle-Side, show that $\angle SCT$ is congruent to $\angle SAT$, and subtract those congruent angles from congruent angles ACT and CAT.

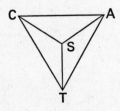

Statements	Reasons
1. $\overline{CT} \cong \overline{AT}$	1. Given
2. $\overline{ST}$ bisects $\angle CTA$	2. Given
3. $\angle CTS \cong \angle ATS$	3. Definition of angle bisector
4. $\overline{ST} \cong \overline{ST}$	4. Reflexive quality of congruence
5. $\triangle CTS \cong \triangle ATS$	5. SAS $\cong$ SAS
6. $\angle SCT \cong \angle SAT$	6. CPCTC
7. $m\angle SCT = m\angle SAT$	7. Definition of congruence
8. $m\angle ACT = m\angle CAT$	8. Angles opposite congruent sides of a triangle are equal in measure
9. $m\angle SCT + m\angle SCA = m\angle ACT$; $m\angle CAS + m\angle SAT = m\angle CAT$	9. Angle Addition Postulate
10. $m\angle SCA = m\angle SAC$	10. Subtraction Property of Equality
11. $\angle SCA \cong \angle SAC$	11. Definition of Congruence

42.

Here's the proof:

Statements	Reasons
1. $A \rightarrow \sim B$; A	1. Given
2. $\sim B$	2. Law of Detachment (1)
3. $(C \vee B)$	3. Given
4. C	4. Law of Disjunctive Inference (2, 3)
5. $D \rightarrow \sim C$	5. Given
6. $\sim D$	6. Law of Modus Tollens (4, 5)
7. $(\sim D \wedge \sim E) \rightarrow F$	7. Given
8. $\sim F \rightarrow \sim(\sim D \wedge \sim E)$	8. Law of Contrapositive Inference (7)
9. $\sim F \rightarrow (D \vee E)$	9. De Morgan's Law
10. $\sim F$	10. Given
11. $(D \vee E)$	11. Law of Detachment (9, 10)
12. E	12. Law of Disjunctive Inference (6, 11)

a

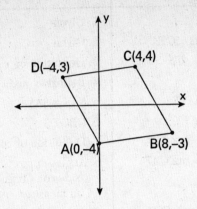

To prove that $ABCD$ is a rhombus, find the length of each side using the distance formula $d = \sqrt{(x_2 - x_1)^2 + (y_2 - y_1)^2}$:

$AB = \sqrt{(8 - 0)^2 + [-3 - (-4)]^2}$

$\quad = \sqrt{8^2 + 1^2}$

$\quad = \sqrt{64 + 1}$

$\quad = \sqrt{65}$

$BC = \sqrt{(4 - 8)^2 + [4 - (-3)]^2}$

$\quad = \sqrt{(-4)^2 + 7^2}$

$\quad = \sqrt{16 + 49}$

$\quad = \sqrt{65}$

$CD = \sqrt{(-4 - 4)^2 + (3 - 4)^2}$

$\quad = \sqrt{(-8)^2 + (-1)^2}$

$\quad = \sqrt{64 + 1}$

$\quad = \sqrt{65}$

$AD = \sqrt{(-4 - 0)^2 + [3 - (-4)]^2}$

$\quad = \sqrt{(-4)^2 + 7^2}$

$\quad = \sqrt{16 + 49}$

$\quad = \sqrt{65}$

All four sides of the quadrilateral have the same length, so $ABCD$ is a rhombus.

b

A rectangle has four right angles. In order to prove that *ABCD* is not a rectangle, find the slope of any two adjacent sides using the slope formula:

$$m = \frac{y_2 - y_1}{x_2 - x_1}$$

Slope of $\overline{AB}$:

$$m = \frac{-3 - (-4)}{8 - 0} = \frac{1}{8}$$

Slope of $\overline{BC}$:

$$m = \frac{4 - (-3)}{4 - 8} = \frac{7}{-4} = -\frac{7}{4}$$

Since the slopes of the two adjacent sides are *not* negative reciprocals, $\angle ABC$ is not a right angle and *ABCD* is *not* a rectangle.

EXAMINATION
JUNE 1999

Part I

Answer 30 questions from this part. Each correct answer will receive 2 credits. No partial credit will be allowed. Write your answers in the spaces provided on the separate answer sheet. Where applicable, answers may be left in terms of π or in radical form. [60]

1 If the operation $\blacklozenge$ is defined as a $\blacklozenge$ b $= 2a - b^2$, evaluate 3 $\blacklozenge$ 2.

2 In the diagram below, $\overleftrightarrow{AB}$ and $\overleftrightarrow{CD}$ intersect at E, m$\angle AEC = 6x - 20$, and m$\angle BED = 4x + 10$. Find the value of x.

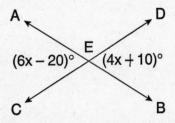

3 In isosceles triangle $ABC, \overline{CA} \cong \overline{CB}$. If side $\overline{CA}$ is extended through A to F and $\overline{FB}$ is drawn, what is the longest side of $\triangle FAB$?

4 The ratio of two complementary angles is 7:2. What is the measure, in degrees, of the larger angle?

5 In the accompanying diagram of $\triangle ABC$, $\overline{DE} \parallel \overline{AB}$, $DE = 8$, $CD = 12$, and $DA = 3$. Find the length of $\overline{AB}$.

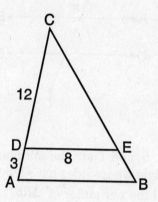

6 Solve for x: $\dfrac{x}{6} + \dfrac{2x}{3} = 5$

7 After a dilation with respect to the origin, the image of point $A(3,4)$ is $A'(9,12)$. What are the coordinates of the image of point $B(2,7)$ after the same dilation?

8 In the accompanying diagram, $\overleftrightarrow{AB}$ is parallel to $\overleftrightarrow{CD}$; transversal $\overleftrightarrow{KL}$ intersects $\overleftrightarrow{AB}$ and $\overleftrightarrow{CD}$ at E and F, respectively; $m\angle BEF = 3x + 40$; and $m\angle DFL = 8x - 10$. Find $m\angle CFL$.

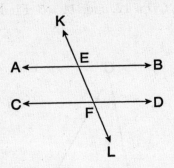

9 Points R, S, and T are the midpoints of the sides of a triangle whose sides have lengths 14, 18, and 20. Find the perimeter of $\triangle RST$.

10 Solve the following system of equations for the positive value of x:

$$y = 5x + 14$$
$$y = x^2$$

11 In the accompanying diagram of right triangle
ABC, $\overline{CD}$ is the altitude to hypotenuse $\overline{AB}$, CD = 6,
and DB = 4. Find the length of $\overline{AD}$.

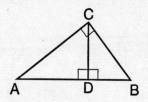

12 In which quadrant does the image of $A(3,-1)$ lie
after the translation $(x,y) \rightarrow (x + 4, y - 2)$?

Directions (13–34): For each question chosen, write on the
separate answer sheet the numeral preceding the word or expression that best completes the statement or answers the question.

13 Given the true statements:

"If Peter is a rabbit, then Felix is a cat."

"Felix is not a cat."

Which statement *must* also be true?

(1) Felix is a cat.
(2) Felix is not a rabbit.
(3) Peter is a cat.
(4) Peter is not a rabbit.

14 Which statement is logically equivalent to $\sim(p \lor \sim r)$?

(1) $p \land \sim r$ (3) $\sim p \land r$

(2) $\sim p \lor r$ (4) $\sim p \lor \sim r$

15 The sum of $\dfrac{4}{5x}$ and $\dfrac{5}{4x}$ is equivalent to

(1) x (3) $\dfrac{41}{9x}$

(2) $41x^2$ (4) $\dfrac{41}{20x}$

16 What are the coordinates of the image of point $(-2,6)$ after a reflection in the y-axis?

(1) $(2,6)$ (3) $(2,-6)$

(2) $(6,-2)$ (4) $(-2,-6)$

17 In isosceles trapezoid $ABCD$, $AD = BC$. What is $m\angle A + m\angle C$?

(1) 45   (3) 180

(2) 90   (4) 360

18 If the turning point of a parabola is $(4,-3)$ and the axis of symmetry is parallel to the y-axis, then the equation of the axis of symmetry is

(1) $x = -3$ (3) $x = 4$

(2) $y = -3$ (4) $y = 4$

19 In the accompanying diagram of $\triangle ABC$, which expression can be used to determine m$\angle A$?

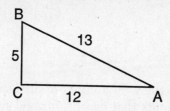

(1) $\sin A = \dfrac{12}{13}$ (3) $\cos A = \dfrac{5}{13}$

(2) $\cos A = \dfrac{12}{5}$ (4) $\tan A = \dfrac{5}{12}$

20 What is the length of the line segment joining points $B(-7, 2)$ and $E(1, 8)$?

(1) $\sqrt{72}$ (3) 12

(2) 10 (4) $\sqrt{164}$

21 Which equation represents the locus of points equidistant from the lines whose equations are $y = 3x + 8$ and $y = 3x - 6$?

(1) $y = 3x - 1$ (3) $y = 3x - 4$

(2) $y = 3x + 1$ (4) $y = 3x + 4$

22 If the diagonals of a rhombus are 12 and 16, then a side of the rhombus will measure

(1) 10 (3) 16

(2) 12 (4) 20

23 How many committees of three students can be formed from a class of nine students?

(1) $_9C_3$

(3) $\dfrac{9!}{3}$

(2) $_9P_3$

(4) $(9 - 3)!$

24 What is the total number of different six-letter arrangements that can be formed from the letters in the word "POWWOW"?

(1) 720
(3) 20
(2) 60
(4) 6

25 If the lengths of two sides of a triangle are 2 and 5, the length of the third side could be

(1) 1
(3) 6
(2) 2
(4) 7

26 Points $A(-1,3)$ and $B(4,1)$ are endpoints of a diameter of a circle. The coordinates of the center of this circle are

(1) (3,4)
(3) (1.5,2)
(2) (2,2)
(4) (0,3.5)

27 A parallelogram must be a rectangle if its diagonals
(1) are congruent
(2) bisect each other
(3) bisect the angles through which they pass
(4) are perpendicular to each other

28 In the diagram below of right triangle
BAC, m∠A = 90, m∠B = 45, and AC = 8.

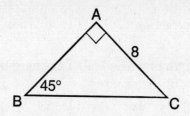

What is the length of $\overline{BC}$?

(1) $8\sqrt{3}$ (3) $4\sqrt{2}$

(2) $8\sqrt{2}$ (4) $16\sqrt{2}$

29 What is the equation of the line that is perpendicular to the line $y - 2x = 4$ and passes through
point (2,4)?

(1) $y = \dfrac{1}{2}x + 4$ (3) $y = \dfrac{1}{2}x + 5$

(2) $y = -\dfrac{1}{2}x + 5$ (4) $y = -2x + 5$

30 What is the slope of the line that passes through
the points (−2,4) and (8,−1)?

(1) $-\dfrac{1}{2}$ (3) $\dfrac{2}{1}$

(2) $\dfrac{1}{2}$ (4) $-\dfrac{2}{1}$

31 Under which operation is the set of odd integers closed?

(1) addition   (3) multiplication
(2) subtraction   (4) division

32 The length of a diagonal of a square is 8. What is the area of the square?

(1) 8   (3) 24
(2) 16   (4) 32

33 Which fraction is expressed in simplest form?

(1) $\dfrac{x-1}{x^2-1}$ (3) $\dfrac{x+1}{x^2-1}$

(2) $\dfrac{x-1}{x^2-2x+1}$ (4) $\dfrac{x+1}{x^2+1}$

34 In regular pentagon $ABCDE$, the measure of an exterior angle at A is

(1) 36°   (3) 72°
(2) 60°   (4) 108°

Directions (35): Leave all construction lines on the answer sheet.

35 *On the answer sheet*, construct the bisector of angle C.

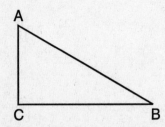

Part II

Answer three questions from this part. Clearly indicate the necessary steps, including appropriate formula substitutions, diagrams, graphs, charts, etc. Calculations that may be obtained by mental arithmetic or the calculator do not need to be shown. [80]

36 Solve the following system of equations graphically and check:

$$(x + 2)^2 + (y - 1)^2 = 16$$
$$x - y = 1 \qquad [8,2]$$

37 *a* Find, to the *nearest tenth*, all values of x for which the expression is defined:

$$\frac{x - 3}{5} = \frac{2}{x + 2} \qquad [5]$$

b A committee of five is to be chosen from 6 freshmen and 8 sophomores. What is the probability that the committee will include 2 freshmen and 3 sophomores? [5]

38. The coordinates of the endpoints of line segment $\overline{ME}$ are $M(-4, -1)$ and $E(5, 4)$.

 a On graph paper, draw and label the graph of $\overline{ME}$. [1]

 b Segment $\overline{ST}$ is the image of $\overline{ME}$ after the transformation $(x, y) \rightarrow (x + 2, y - 6)$, where S is the image of M, and T is the image of E. On the same set of axes, draw and state the coordinates of the endpoints of the graph of $\overline{ST}$. [3]

 c Is quadrilateral *METS* a parallelogram? Justify your answer using coordinate geometry. [1,5]

39. In the tables below, the elements S, A, L, E and the operations $*$ and $\#$ are defined.

$*$	S	A	L	E
S	A	S	E	L
A	S	A	L	E
L	E	L	A	S
E	L	E	S	A

$\#$	S	A	L	E
S	A	L	E	S
A	L	E	S	A
L	E	S	A	L
E	S	A	L	E

 a What is the inverse of L under $\#$? [2]

 b Evaluate: $(A * L) \# (E * S)$ [2]

 c Solve for x: $(x \# L) * L = A$ [2]

 d Find *all* values of x such that $x * x = x \# x$. [4]

40 Trapezoid *ABCD* has coordinates *A*(0,9), *B*(12,9), *C*(8,4), and *D*(0,4).

   a Using coordinate geometry, show that $\overline{AD}$ is *not* parallel to $\overline{BC}$.   [3]

   b Find the area trapezoid *ABCD*.   [2]

   c Find the perimeter of *ABCD* to the *nearest integer*.   [3]

   d Find m∠*ABC* to the *nearest degree*.   [2]

Part III

Answer one question from this part. Clearly indicate the necessary steps, including appropriate formula substitutions, diagrams, graphs, charts, etc. Calculations that may be obtained by mental arithmetic or the calculator do not need to be shown. [10]

41 Given: If Patty plays soccer, then Carl plays football.

If Carl plays football and Dana plays field hockey, then Scott does not play golf.

If Frank does not play volleyball, then Scott plays golf.

Dana plays field hockey.

Frank does not play volleyball.

Let *P* represent: "Patty plays soccer."

Let *C* represent: "Carl plays football."

Let *S* represent: "Scott plays golf."

Let *F* represent: "Frank plays volleyball."

Let *D* represent: "Dana plays field hockey."

Prove: Patty does not play soccer. [10]

42 Given: rhombus RSTV, $\overline{VTX}, \overline{STW}, \overline{SX}, \overline{VW}$, and $\angle RSX \cong \angle RVW$.

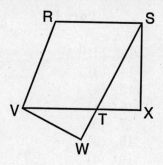

Prove: $\overline{TX} \cong \overline{TW}$ [10]

ANSWERS AND EXPLANATIONS
JUNE 1999
ANSWER KEY
Part I

1. 2	13. (4)	25. (3)
2. 15	14. (3)	26. (3)
3. $\overline{FB}$	15. (4)	27. (1)
4. 70	16. (1)	28. (2)
5. 10	17. (3)	29. (2)
6. 6	18. (3)	30. (1)
7. (6,21)	19. (4)	31. (3)
8. 110	20. (2)	32. (4)
9. 26	21. (2)	33. (4)
10. 7	22. (1)	34. (3)
11. 9	23. (1)	35. construction
12. IV	24. (2)	

Part II

36. (−2,−3), (2,1)
    Check

37. *a* −3.5, 4.5

    b $\dfrac{840}{2002}$

38. *a* see explanations
    b S(−2,−7), T(7,−2)
    c Yes

39. *a* S
    b A
    c E
    d S, L

40. *a* see explanations
    b 50
    c 31
    d 51

Part III

41. see explanations
42. see explanations

EXPLANATIONS
Part I

1. 2

They've already defined the operation for you, so just plug in $a = 3$ and $b = 2$:

$$3 \blacklozenge 2 = 2(3) - 2^2$$
$$= 6 - 4$$
$$= 2$$

2. 15

Since $\angle AEC$ and $\angle DEB$ are vertical angles, their measures are equal. Set the two terms equal to each other an solve for x:

$$6x - 20 = 4x + 10$$
$$2x - 20 = 10$$
$$2x = 30$$
$$x = 15$$

3. $\overline{FB}$

Draw a diagram of the problem making sure you make an *isosceles* triangle, since $\overline{CA} \cong \overline{CB}$. Now extend $\overline{CA}$ through A to point F (the new point) and connect points B and F to create $\triangle FAB$. It can easily be seen that $\overline{FB}$ is the longest side of $\triangle FAB$.

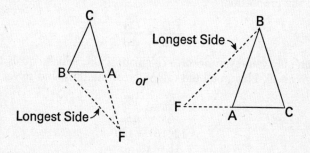

4. 70

When two angles are complementary, the sum of their angles is 90°. Since the ratio of the angles is 7:2, the measures of the angles themselves must be $7x$ and $2x$. Set up this equation and solve:

$$7x + 2x = 90$$
$$9x = 90$$
$$x = 10$$

Since $x = 10$, the measures of the two angles must be $7 \cdot 10$, or 70, and $2 \cdot 10$, or 20. They want the larger of the two angles, so your answer is 70.

5. 10

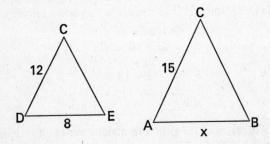

Whenever you have two similar triangles, all linear measures of corresponding parts of the triangles are proportional. In this case, you're comparing the small triangle CDE with the large triangle CAB. Set up the proportion:

$$\frac{CD}{DE} = \frac{CA}{AB}$$

The only value you need to calculate is CA, which equals CD plus DA, or 15. Plug in all the values, cross-multiply, and solve:

$$\frac{12}{8} = \frac{15}{AB}$$
$$12(AB) = 120$$
$$AB = 10 = x$$

6. 6

Solve this problem by first multiplying every term in the equation by 6:

$$(6)\frac{x}{6} + (6)\frac{2x}{3} = (6)5$$
$$x + 4x = 30$$
$$5x = 30$$
$$x = 6$$

7. (6,21)

Whenever a point undergoes a dilation, each of the coordinates of the point is multiplied by a constant. If the image of $A(3,4)$ after a dilation is $A'(9,\underline{12})$, then the point underwent a dilation of 3 (because $3 \cdot 3 = 9$, and $4 \cdot 3 = 12$). If the point $B(2,7)$ undergoes a dilation of 3, the coordinates of the image are $(2 \cdot 3, 7 \cdot 3)$, or $(6,21)$.

8. 110

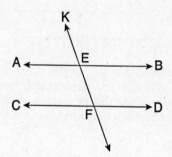

Since $\angle BEF$ and $\angle DFL$ are corresponding angles, they have the same measure. Therefore, you can set the angles measures equal to each other and find the value of x:

$$8x - 10 = 3x + 40$$
$$5x - 10 = 40$$
$$5x = 50$$
$$x = 10$$

You're not done yet. Since $x = 10$, you can find the actual measure of each angle by plugging it into both terms to make sure you're right:

$$8(10) - 10 = 70 \qquad\qquad 3(10) + 40 = 70$$

Whenever two parallel lines are cut by a transversal, the sum of the measures of one big angle and one small angle is 180°. In the above diagram, $\angle BEF$ and $\angle DFL$ are small angles and $\angle CFL$ is a big angle. Since the small angles all measure 70°, then all the big angles, including $\angle CFL$, measure $180 - 70$, or 110°.

9. 26

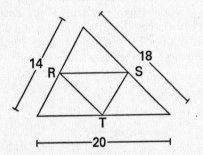

If you connect the midpoints of the three sides of a triangle, the perimeter of the smaller triangle is exactly half the perimeter of the original triangle. Since the perimeter of the original triangle is $14 + 18 + 20$, or 52, then the perimeter of $\triangle RST$ is half of 52, or 26.

10. 7

The two equations you're given both begin with y. Since y equals two different things, you can set those two things equal to each other:

$$x^2 = 5x + 14$$

Subtract $5x$ and 14 from both sides of the equation to put the equation in proper format:

$$x^2 - 5x - 14 = 0$$

Now, you're ready to start the trial and error factoring, until you come up with the following factors:

$$(x - 7)(x + 2) = 0$$

Set each factor equal to zero and solve for x in each case:

$$x - 7 = 0 \qquad\qquad x + 2 = 0$$
$$x = 7 \qquad\qquad\quad x = -2$$

The two factors of the equation are 7 and –2. Since you're only asked for the positive value of x, then $x = 7$.

11. 9

You know CD and DB, and you're looking for AD. The altitude $\overline{CD}$ of $\triangle ABC$ is the mean proportional to segments $\overline{AD}$ and $\overline{DB}$. Set up the proportion, then plug in all the values you know like this:

$$\frac{AD}{CD} = \frac{CD}{DB}$$

$$\frac{AD}{6} = \frac{6}{4}$$

$$4(AD) = 36$$

$$AD = 9$$

12. Quadrant IV

The translation $(x + 4, y - 2)$ shifts the x-coordinate 4 units to the right and the y-coordinate down 2 units. Therefore, the image of $A(3,-1)$ is:

$$(3 + 4, -1 - 2) = (7, -3)$$

The point $(7,-3)$ lies in Quadrant IV.

Part I Multiple Choice

Don't forget that one of the best techniques on these Multiple Choice questions is to use Process of Elimination to get rid of answer choices that aren't possible.

13. (4)

Let P equal "Peter is a rabbit" and F equal "Felix is a cat." You can now map the statement "If Peter is a rabbit, then Felix is a cat" like this:

$$P \to F$$

If you use the Law of Contrapositive Inference on the first statement, you get:

$$\sim F \to \sim P$$

Since the second statement says that Felix is not a cat, you can symbolize it like this:

$$\sim F$$

Now, you can use the Law of Detachment to confirm that $\sim P$ must be true. In other words, Peter is not a rabbit.

14. (3)

Whenever you negate a statement with a "∧" or a "∨" in it, use De Morgan's Law. Negate both terms, and then turn the arrow the other way:

$$\sim(p \lor \sim r) \to \sim p \land r$$

15. (4)

The fastest way to solve this one is to multiply the top and bottom of the first fraction by the second denominator, and multiply the top and bottom the second fraction by the first denominator. In this situation, multiply the first fraction by $\dfrac{4x}{4x}$ and the second by $\dfrac{5x}{5x}$, like this:

$$\frac{4}{5x} + \frac{5}{4x}$$

$$\frac{4}{5x} \cdot \frac{(4x)}{(4x)} + \frac{5}{4x} \cdot \frac{(5x)}{(5x)}$$

Then just multiply, add, and reduce:

$$\frac{16x}{20x^2} + \frac{25x}{20x^2} = \frac{41x}{20x^2} = \frac{41}{20x}$$

16. (1)

Whenever a point is reflected in the y-axis, the x-coordinate is negated and the y-coordinate remains the same. In other words, y-axis $(x,y) \rightarrow (-x,y)$. Therefore, the image of $(-2,6)$ after a reflection in the y-axis is $(2,6)$.

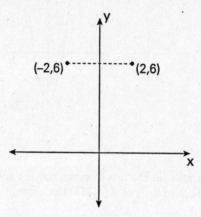

17. (3)

An isosceles trapezoid is a four-sided figure with two sides that are parallel and two congruent sides, AD and BC, that are not. Also, the base angles (in this case, $\angle D$ and $\angle C$) are congruent:

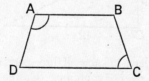

Look at the left side of the diagram first. Since AB and DC are parallel, AD looks like a transversal. Thus, $\angle A$ and $\angle D$ are interior angles on the same side of a transversal, and angles are supplementary (their sum is 180°). Since $\angle D$ is congruent to $\angle C$, the sum of the measures of $\angle A$ and $\angle C$ is also 180°.

18. (3)

All lines that are parallel to the y-axis have the equation $x = k$, so you can eliminate answer choices (2) and (4) right away. Here's a diagram of what the parabola and its axis of symmetry might look like:

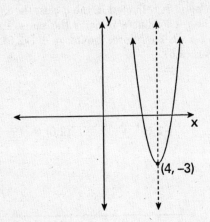

Since the formula for the axis of symmetry is $x = k$, you want to use the x-coordinate of the point $(4, -3)$. Therefore, the equation of the line is $x = 4$.

19. (4)

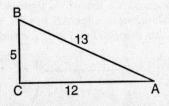

For this one, you have to know all three parts of SOHCAHTOA (Sine equals Opposite over Hypotenuse, Cosine equals Adjacent over Hypotenuse, and Tangent equals Opposite over Adjacent). In the diagram above, there are three ways to determine the measure of $\angle A$ using trigonometry:

$$\sin A = \frac{5}{13} \qquad \cos A = \frac{12}{13} \qquad \tan A = \frac{5}{12}$$

The only one of these that appears among the answer choices is the last one, which is answer choice (4).

20. (2)

To find the distance between any two points, use the distance formula:

$$d = \sqrt{(x_2 - x_1)^2 + (y_2 - y_1)^2}$$

In this case, $(x_1, y_1) = B(-7,2)$ and $(x_2, y_2) = E(1,8)$:

$$d = \sqrt{(-7-1)^2 + (2-8)^2}$$
$$= \sqrt{(-8)^2 + (-6)^2}$$
$$= \sqrt{64 + 36}$$
$$= \sqrt{100} = 10$$

21. (2)

The best way to work with this one is to consider the y-intercepts of the two lines. Both lines are written in $y = mx + b$ format, so you know that the first line crosses the y-axis at $(0,8)$, and the second line crosses at $(0,-6)$:

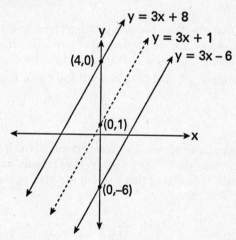

All the lines in the answer choices have the same slope (3), so you don't have to worry about the slope. Just find the point that is equidistant from the two y-intercepts by finding their average. The average of 8 and –6 is 1, because $\frac{8 + (-6)}{2} = 1$. Therefore, the equation of the line is $y = 3x + 1$.

22. (1)

Since the diagonals of a rhombus are perpendicular to each other, every rhombus is made up of four right triangles. The diagonals also bisect each other. Since SU and RP measure 12 and 16, respectively, then $ST = 6$ and $RT = 8$.

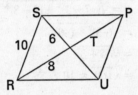

Concentrate on right triangle STR. You know the length of its two legs, so you can use the Pythagorean Theorem from here. You might also save a little time, however, if you recognize that $\triangle STR$ is a 3:4:5 right triangle. Thus, $SR = 10$.

23. (1)

This is a great question, because you don't have to do any math! All you have to know is the right formula to use. This is a basic combinations problem. There are nine roses, and you have to choose three. Use the formula $_nC_r$ and plug in $n = 9$ and $r = 3$. You get $_9C_3$. And that's it!

24. (2)

To find the number of possible arrangements of the letters in a word with n letters, in which one letter appears p times and another appears q times (remember that p and q are greater than 1), the formula looks like this:

$$\frac{n!}{p!\,q!}$$

POWWOW has six letters, but there are three W's and two O's. Therefore, you can express the number of arrangements as:

$$\frac{6!}{3!\,2!} = \frac{6 \cdot 5 \cdot 4 \cdot 3 \cdot 2 \cdot 1}{(3 \cdot 2 \cdot 1) \cdot (2 \cdot 1)} = \frac{720}{12} = 60$$

25. (3)

The length of a third side of a triangle must be larger than the difference between the two known sides and less than their sum. In other words:

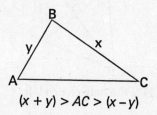

$$(x + y) > AC > (x - y)$$

Since the two known sides are 5 and 2, the length of the third side must be between 5 − 2, or 3, and 5 + 2, or 7. You can eliminate (1) and (2), because the third side has to be greater than 2, not equal to 2. You can also get rid of (4), because the third side must be less than 7, not equal to 7. The only remaining choice is (3).

26. (3)

The center of a circle is the midpoint of a diameter. Use the formula for the midpoint of a line segment:

$$(\bar{x}, \bar{y}) = \left(\frac{x_1 + x_2}{2}, \frac{y_1 + y_2}{2} \right)$$

For this problem, let $(x_1, y_1) = A(-1, 3)$ and $(x_2, y_2) = B(4, 1)$:

$$\bar{x} = \frac{x_1 + x_2}{2} \qquad\qquad \bar{y} = \frac{y_1 + y_2}{2}$$

$$= \frac{-1 + 4}{2} \qquad\qquad = \frac{3 + 1}{2}$$

$$= \frac{3}{2} = 1.5 \qquad\qquad = \frac{4}{2} = 2$$

The coordinates of the center of the circle are (1.5, 2).

27. (1)

The easiest way to solve this one is to remember that the diagonals of a rectangle are congruent. However, if that rule escapes you, use POE. Answer choices (2) and (4) can't be right, because the quadrilateral could be a rhombus. The diagonals of a rhombus bisect each other, so they're perpendicular, and they bisect the angles through which they pass:

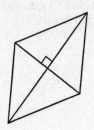

Answer choice **(1)** is the only choice left.

28. (2)

The ratio of the sides of a 45:45:90 triangle is $1:1:\sqrt{2}$. Since AC is the measure of one side of the triangle and BC is the measure of the hypotenuse, the fastest way to find BC is to multiply it by $\sqrt{2}$:

$$8 \cdot \sqrt{2} = 8\sqrt{2}$$

29. (2)

Before you do anything, you have to put the equation of the line in standard $y = mx + b$ form by adding $2x$ to each side:

$$y - 2x = 4$$
$$y = 2x + 4$$

The linear equation $y = 2x + 4$ is in standard form, so you know that the line's slope is 2. Since the slopes of any two lines are negative reciprocals (that is, their product is –1), any line that is perpendicular to $y = 2x + 4$ must have a slope of $-\dfrac{1}{2}$. Each of the answer choices is also in standard $y = mx + b$ format, and (2) is the only line that has a slope of $-\dfrac{1}{2}$. You already have your answer; you don't even have to deal with the point (2,4)!

30. (1)

To find the slope of the line between two points, use the slope formula:

$$m = \frac{y_2 - y_1}{x_2 - x_1}$$

For this problem, let $(x_1, y_1) = (-2, 4)$ and $(x_2, y_2) = (8, -1)$:

$$m = \frac{-1 - 4}{8 - (-2)} = \frac{-5}{10} = -\frac{1}{2}$$

31. (3)

Test each of the four operations by plugging in odd numbers and see which one always results in another odd number:

$5 + 3 = 8$ The sum of two odd numbers is even, so eliminate (1).

$5 - 3 = 2$ The same thing happens when you subtract two odd numbers, so (2) is out.

$5 \cdot 3 = 15$ Aha! Another odd number! Keep it.

$5 \div 3 =$ Eliminate (4), because $\dfrac{5}{3}$ is not an integer.

You've used the Process of Elimination to cancel three of the four choices, and there's only one left. The answer is (3).

32. (4)

There's a lesser-known formula for finding the area of a rectangle using the diagonals:

$$A = \frac{d^2}{2}$$

Since all squares are rectangles, you can use this formula for squares as well. The diagonals of a square are congruent, so plug in $d = 8$:

$$A = \frac{8^2}{2} = \frac{64}{2} = 32$$

If you never learned this formula, you can also determine the area of the square by finding the length of the sides of the square. Remember that all squares can be divided into two 45:45:90 triangles:

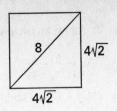

Since the hypotenuse of the square is 8, each side equals $\dfrac{8}{\sqrt{2}}$, or

$4\sqrt{2}$. The area of a square is s^2, so the area is $(4\sqrt{2})^2 = 16 \cdot 2 = 32$.

33. (4)

Focus your attention on the denominators. Three of the denominators are not in their simplest form, but (4) cannot be reduced any further.

POE is also useful. If you see that $x^2 - 1$ can be factored into $(x + 1)(x - 1)$, you'll have your first clue that answer choices (1) and (3) can be reduced further. Answer choice (2) can also be simplified, because $x^2 - 2x + 1 = (x - 1)^2$.

34. (3)

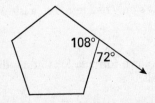

If a regular polygon has n sides, then the measure of each interior angle equals:

$$\frac{180(n - 2)}{n}$$

A pentagon has five sides; when you plug in $n = 5$, you can determine

that each angle measures $\dfrac{180(3)}{5}$, or 108°. Exterior angles are supplementary to interior angles, so each exterior angle measures 72°.

35. construction

This is about as simple a construction as there is. Take your compass, put the metal end on point C, and make an arc that intersects AC and BC. (Make sure that the distance between your compass points is smaller than side AC.) Label those points X and Y. Widen your compass a little bit, put the metal end on point X, and make a second arc within the angle. Then put the metal end on point Y and make a third arc that intersects the second. Label that point of intersection Z.

Now draw in ray CZ. This is the angle bisector.

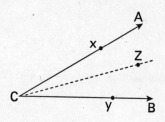

Part II

36. (−2,−3) and (2,1)

You should recognize the first equation as a circle, because the equation is in the standard formula $(x − h)^2 + (y − k)^2 = r^2$, in which (h,k) is the center of the circle and r is the radius. Therefore, the circle is centered at (−2,1) and has a radius of 4.

The second graph is a line, but you can't graph it until it's in $y = mx + b$ format. Tinker with it like this:

$$x − y = 1$$
$$−y = −x + 1$$
$$y = x − 1$$

Thus, the second equation is a line that has a slope of 1 and intercepts the y-axis at (0,−1). The resulting graph looks like this:

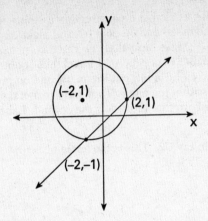

The points of intersection are $(-2,-3)$, and $(2,1)$.

37. a 4.5, −3.5

Whenever two fractions are equal to each other, you can cross-multiply:

$$\frac{x-3}{5} = \frac{2}{x+2}$$
$$(x-3)(x+2) = 5 \cdot 2$$

Use FOIL to combine the terms on the left:

$$x^2 + 2x - 3x - 6 = 10$$
$$x^2 - x - 6 = 10$$
$$x^2 - x - 6 - 10 = 0$$
$$x^2 - x - 16 = 0$$

You can't factor this, so you have to use the Quadratic Formula:

$$x = \frac{-b \pm \sqrt{b^2 - 4ac}}{2a}$$

This equation is in standard $y = ax^2 + bx + c$ format, and $a = 1$, $b = -1$, and $c = -16$:

$$x = \frac{-(-1) \pm \sqrt{(-1)^2 - 4(1)(-16)}}{2(1)}$$

$$= \frac{1 \pm \sqrt{1 + 64}}{2} = \frac{1 \pm \sqrt{65}}{2}$$

Substitute $\sqrt{65} \approx 8.06$ into the fraction and find the numerical values:

$$x = \frac{1 + 8.06}{2} = \frac{9.06}{2} = 4.53$$

$$x = \frac{1 - 8.06}{2} = \frac{-7.06}{2} = -3.53$$

When you round these off to the nearest tenth, as instructed, you get 4.5 and −3.5. Plug these values back into the original fraction to check your work.

b $\dfrac{840}{2002}$

The process for this question has two parts. There are fourteen students in all (six freshmen and eight sophomores), and you want to choose five of them. Use the formula $_nC_r = \dfrac{n!}{r!(n-r)!}$ and plug in $n = 14$ and $r = 5$:

$$_{14}C_5 = \frac{14!}{5!\,9!} = \frac{14 \cdot 13 \cdot 12 \cdot 11 \cdot 10}{5 \cdot 4 \cdot 3 \cdot 2 \cdot 1} = 2002$$

There are 2002 possible combinations.

For part two, you have to determine how many ways there can be two freshmen and three sophomores. Here, you use the combinations problem twice: You're choosing two freshmen out of six, and three sophomores out of eight):

$$_6C_2 = \frac{6!}{2!\,4!} = \frac{6 \cdot 5}{2 \cdot 1} = 15 \qquad _8C_3 = \frac{8!}{3!\,5!} = \frac{8 \cdot 7 \cdot 6}{3 \cdot 2 \cdot 1} = 56$$

To find the total number of combinations involving two freshmen and three sophomores, multiply these two numbers together: $15 \cdot 56 = 840$.

Therefore, the chance that a five-person combination will contain two freshmen and three sophomores is $\dfrac{840}{2002}$.

38. *a*

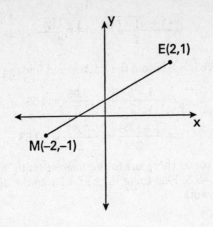

b S(−2,−7), T(7,−2)

Under the translation (x + 2,y − 6), each point shifts 2 units to the right and 6 units down. The image of M(−4,−1) under the translation is (−4 + 2,−1 − 6), or (−2,−7), and the image of E(5,4) under the translation is (5 + 2,4 − 6), or (7,−2). The graph looks like this:

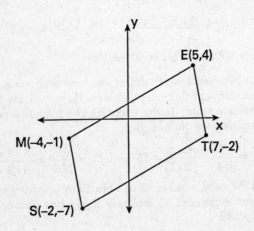

c   Yes

A parallelogram has two pairs of opposite parallel sides. To prove that *METS* is a parallelogram, you have to show that each pair of opposite sides are parallel. To do this, find the slope of each of the sides using the slope formula:

$$m = \frac{y_2 - y_1}{x_2 - x_1}$$

Slope of $\overline{ME}$:   Slope of $\overline{ET}$:   Slope of $\overline{TS}$:   Slope of $\overline{MS}$:

$$m = \frac{4 - (-1)}{5 - (-4)} \qquad m = \frac{-2 - 4}{7 - 5} \qquad m = \frac{-7 - (-2)}{-2 - 7} \qquad m = \frac{-1 - (-7)}{-4 - (-2)}$$

$$= \frac{5}{9} \qquad\qquad = \frac{-6}{2} \qquad\qquad = \frac{-5}{-9} \qquad\qquad = \frac{6}{-2}$$

$$\qquad\qquad\qquad = -3 \qquad\qquad = \frac{5}{9} \qquad\qquad = -3$$

Since $\overline{ME}$ and $\overline{TS}$ have the same slope, those two sides are parallel. The other two sides also have the same slope, so they're parallel as well. Thus, quadrilateral *METS* is a parallelogram.

39. a   S

✱	S	A	L	E
S	A	S	E	L
A	S	A	L	E
L	E	L	A	S
E	L	E	S	A

#	S	A	L	E
S	A	L	E	S
A	L	E	S	A
L	E	S	A	L
E	S	A	L	E

Find the identity element of the # function first. (Careful: Don't get careless and confuse the # function with the ✱ function.) If you look at the bottom column of the # table (with the *E* character at the far left), you'll see that the letters along that column match the headings above them. Therefore, *E* is the identity element.

The identity element is *E*, so you want to find the value that turns *L* into *E*. Look at the completed system: Since (*L* # *S*) = *E*, the inverse of *L* is *S*.

b A

The parentheses in this problem dictate the order in which you calculate this one. Work with the * table first, then move on to the # table:

$$(A * L) \# (E * S)$$
$$= L \# L$$
$$= A$$

c E

It's time to work backwards. You first want to find what character, when combined with L in the * table, yields A. Find A in the L column on the * table; since the L row and the L column converge at A, then $L * L = A$.

So far, so good. Since $L * L = A$ and $(x \# L) * L = A$, then $(x \# L) = L$. Now repeat the process on the # table. Look for the L somewhere in the L column; since the E row and the L column converge at L, then $E * L = L$. The answer is E.

d S, L

There's a nice fast way to do this one: Just try all four letters and see which ones match:

$S * S = A$	$S \# S = A$	Match
$A * A = A$	$A \# A = E$	No match
$L * L = A$	$L \# L = A$	Match
$E * E = A$	$E \# E = E$	No matchß

The only matches are S and L.

40. *a*

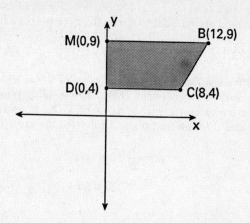

A trapezoid has exactly one pair of opposite parallel sides. To prove that two sides are not parallel, find the slope of each of the sides using the slope formula:

$$m = \frac{y_2 - y_1}{x_2 - x_1}$$

Slope of $\overline{AD}$:

$$m = \frac{4-9}{0-0}$$

$$= \frac{-5}{0}$$

$$= \infty$$

Slope of $\overline{BC}$:

$$m = \frac{4-9}{8-12}$$

$$= \frac{-5}{-4}$$

$$= \frac{5}{4}$$

Since $\overline{AD}$ and $\overline{BC}$ do not have the same slope, they're not parallel.

b **50**

This one isn't as hard as it could be, because all the measurements that you need are parallel to either the *x*- or *y*-axis. The formula for the area of a trapezoid is: $A = \frac{1}{2}(b_1 + b_2)h$.

The two *b*'s are the lengths of the parallel sides, and *h* is the perpendicular distance between them. These measurements are easy to determine using the graph: $AB = 12$, $CD = 8$, and $AD = 5$. Plug these values into the formula and solve for the area:

$$A = \frac{1}{2}(12 + 8)5$$
$$= \frac{1}{2}(20)(5) = 50$$

c **31**

Because three of the sides of this trapezoid are parallel to either the *x*- or *y*-axis, you can find their lengths easily; $AB = 12$, $AD = 5$, and $DC = 8$. You can find the length of the fourth side, *BC*, using the distance formula:

$$d = \sqrt{(x_2 - x_1)^2 + (y_2 - y_1)^2}$$

In this case, $(x_1, y_1) = B(12,9)$ and $(x_2, y_2) = C(8,4)$:

$$d = \sqrt{(8 - 12)^2 + (4 - 9)^2}$$
$$= \sqrt{(-4)^2 + (-5)^2}$$
$$= \sqrt{16 + 25}$$
$$= \sqrt{41} \approx 6.4$$

The perimeter of the trapezoid equals the sum of all four sides:

$$12 + 5 + 8 + 6.4 = 31.4$$

When you round this down to the nearest *integer*, as instructed, you get 31.

d 51

As the term *nearest degree* implies, you'll have to use a little trigonometry on this one. And, you'll have to add a line to the graph—a line from C that is parallel to AD like this:

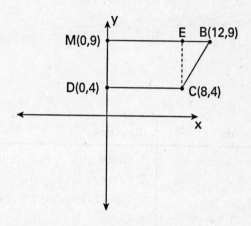

Call the new point *E*; now you can work with right triangle *BCE*. Quadrilateral *AECD* is a rectangle (because it contains four right angles), and opposite sides of a rectangle are congruent. Therefore, *EC* (the leg opposite ∠*ABC*) = 5. Also, *DC* and *AE* are both 8 units long, so *EB* (the leg adjacent to ∠*ABC*) equals 12 − 8, or 4. Now you have two measurements, so use tangent (the TOA in SOHCAHTOA):

$$\tan \angle ABC = \frac{EC}{EB} = \frac{5}{4} = 1.25$$

Hit "tan-1" on your calculator to find that the measure of ∠*ABC* is 51.34°. When you round this off to the *nearest degree*, as instructed, you get 51°.

Part III

41.

The sentences translate into symbolic form as the following:

$$\rightarrow C$$
$$(C \wedge D) \rightarrow \sim S$$
$$\sim F \rightarrow S$$
$$D$$
$$\sim F$$

Prove: $\sim P$

Statements	Reasons
1. $\sim F \rightarrow S$	1. Given
2. $\sim F$	2. Given
3. S	3. Law of Detachment (1, 2)
4. $(C \wedge D) \rightarrow \sim S$	4. Given
5. $\sim(C \wedge D)$	5. Modus Tollens (3, 4)
6. $\sim C \vee \sim D$	6. De Morgan's Law (5)
7. D	7. Given
8. $\sim C$	8. Law of Disjunctive Inference (6, 7)
9. $P \rightarrow C$	9. Given
10. $\sim P$	10. Law of Disjunctive Inference (8, 9)

42.

The plan: Opposite angles of a rhombus are congruent, and the sides are also all congruent. Prove that $\triangle VTW \cong \triangle STX$ using Angle-Side-Angle, and then use CPCTC.

Statement	Reason
1. $\angle RSX \cong \angle RVW$	1. Given
2. $RSTV$ is a rhombus	2. Given
3. $\angle RST \cong \angle RVT$	3. Opposite angles of a rhombus are congruent.
4. $m\angle RSX - m\angle RST = m\angle RVW - m\angle RVT$	4. Subtraction property of equality
5. $\angle TSX \cong \angle TVW$	5. Angle subtraction postulate
6. $TV \cong TS$	6. Definition of a rhombus
7. $\overline{VTX}$, $\overline{STW}$, SX, VW	7. Given
8. $\angle VTW \cong \angle STX$	8. Vertical angles are congruent.
9. $\triangle VTW \cong \triangle STX$	9. ASA $\cong$ ASA
10. $\overline{TX} \cong \overline{TW}$	10. CPCTC

EXAMINATION
AUGUST 1999

Part I

Answer 30 questions from this part. Each correct answer will receive 2 credits. No partial credit will be allowed. Write your answers in the spaces provided on the separate answer sheet. Where applicable, answers may be left in terms of π or in radical form. [60]

1 If $a \heartsuit b$ is defined as $a \heartsuit b = a^2 + b$, find the value of $2 \heartsuit 3$.

2 In the accompanying diagram of scalene triangle ABC, D and E are the midpoints of $\overline{AB}$ and $\overline{AC}$, respectively, and $DE = 7$. Find the length of $\overline{BC}$.

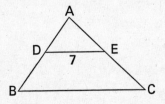

3 Using the accompanying table, compute $(I \ae E) \ae (R \ae D)$.

æ	R	I	D	E
R	I	E	R	D
I	E	D	I	R
D	R	I	D	E
E	D	R	E	I

4 In the accompanying diagram, $\overleftrightarrow{FABG} \parallel \overleftrightarrow{HCDI}$, $\overline{BC}$ and $\overline{AD}$ intersect at E, m$\angle GBE = 3x + 20$, and m$\angle ECD = x$. What is the value of x?

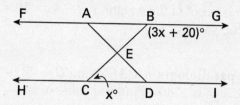

5 If the legs of a right triangle have lengths of 9 and 7, what is the length of the hypotenuse, expressed in radical form?

6 In $\triangle SUM$, m$\angle S = 75$ and m$\angle U = 43$. Which side of $\triangle SUM$ is the *shortest*?

7 In $\triangle ABC$, m$\angle A$ measures twice m$\angle B$. If an exterior angle at C measures 126°, find m$\angle A$.

8 The lengths of the sides of a triangle are 8, 11, and 14. Find the perimeter of a similar triangle whose longest side measures 21.

9 Find the slope of the line segment that contains points (–3,–1) and (1,2).

10 How many different five-letter arrangements can be made using the letters in the word "SLEEP"?

11 If 5 is a root of the equation $x^2 - kx - 10 = 0$, what is the value of k?

12 In parallelogram $CARS$, $m\angle C = 5x - 20$ and $m\angle A = 3x + 40$. Find the value of x.

13 Solve for x: $\dfrac{8}{x} - 2 = \dfrac{2}{3}$, $x \neq 0$

14 Find the area of a triangle whose vertices are $(4,8)$, $(4,3)$, and $(7,3)$.

Directions (15–35): For *each* question chosen, write on the separate answer sheet the *numeral* preceding the word the expression that best completes the statement or answers the question.

15 Which statement is logically equivalent to $\sim(\sim a \vee b)$?
(1) $a \vee \sim b$
(2) $a \wedge b$
(3) $a \wedge \sim b$
(4) $a \vee b$

16 The diagram below shows the construction of dropping perpendicular $\overline{PX}$ from point P to line ℓ. The arc drawn form point P intersects line ℓ at A and B, and the arcs drawn from points A and B intersect $\overleftrightarrow{PX}$ at C.

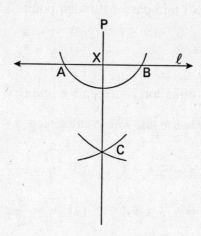

Which statement is *not* always true about this construction?

(1) $PA = PB$ (3) $PX = CX$
(2) $AX = BX$ (4) $AC = BC$

17 Which equation represents the locus of points equidistant from points $(4,2)$ and $(8,2)$?

(1) $x = 6$ (3) $x = 12$
(2) $y = 6$ (4) $y = 12$

18 What is the image of point (−5,4) under a reflection in the origin?

(1) (−4,5)   (3) (5,−4)
(2) (−4,−5)   (4) (−5,−4)

19 What is the equation of a line that is parallel to the x-axis and passes through point (3,5)?

(1) $x = 3$ (3) $x = 5$
(2) $y = 3$ (4) $y = 5$

20 Which equation represents a line that is perpendicular to the line whose equation is $y = \dfrac{2}{3}x + 4$?

(1) $y = -\dfrac{2}{3}x - 4$ (3) $y = -\dfrac{2}{3}x + 4$

(2) $y = -\dfrac{3}{2}x + 4$ (4) $y = \dfrac{3}{2}x + 4$

21 In the accompanying diagram of $\triangle ABC$, $\overline{BA} \cong \overline{BC}$, m$\angle ABC = 48$, $\overline{DA}$ bisects $\angle CAB$, and $\overline{DC}$ bisects $\angle ACB$.

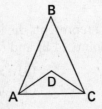

What is m$\angle ADC$?

(1) 48   (3) 114
(2) 66   (4) 134

22 Point (2,1) is the midpoint of a line segment whose endpoints are (3,2) and (1,*a*). What is the value of *a*?

(1) 1   (3) 3
(2) 2   (4) 0

23 A quadrilateral must be a parallelogram if one pair of opposite sides is

(1) congruent, only
(2) parallel, only
(3) congruent and parallel
(4) parallel and the other pair of opposite sides is congruent

24 The sum of $\dfrac{y-4}{2y}$ and $\dfrac{3y-5}{5y}$ is

(1) $\dfrac{11y-30}{10y}$ (3) $11y-30$

(2) $\dfrac{4y-9}{10y}$ (4) $\dfrac{4y-9}{7y}$

25 In right triangle *ABC*, m∠*C* = 90. If tan *A* = 10, what is m∠*A* to the *nearest degree*?

(1) 45   (3) 85
(2) 84   (4) 89

26 The distance between points $(4a, 3b)$ and $(3a, 2b)$ is

(1) $a^2 + b^2$ (3) $a + b$
(2) $\sqrt{a^2 + b^2}$ (4) $\sqrt{a + b}$

27 Which statement is logically equivalent to "If the traffic light is red, then the cars stop"?

(1) If the traffic light is not red, then the cars do not stop.
(2) If the cars stop, then the traffic light is red.
(3) If the cars do not stop, then the traffic light is not red.
(4) If the traffic light is not red, then the cars stop.

28 What are the roots of the equation $x^2 - 5x + 3 = 0$?

(1) $\dfrac{5 \pm \sqrt{13}}{2}$

(3) $\dfrac{-5 \pm \sqrt{37}}{2}$

(2) $\dfrac{-5 \pm \sqrt{13}}{2}$

(4) $\dfrac{5 \pm \sqrt{37}}{2}$

29 Which equation represents a circle whose center is $(4, -5)$ and whose radius is 8?

(1) $(x + 4)^2 + (y - 5)^2 = 64$

(2) $(x - 4)^2 + (y + 5)^2 = 64$

(3) $(x + 4)^2 + (y - 5)^2 = 8$

(4) $(x - 4)^2 + (y + 5)^2 = 8$

30 A classroom has 12 girls and 15 boys. If a committee of two students is selected at random, what is the probability that both students are girls?

(1) $\dfrac{_{12}C_2}{_{27}C_2}$

(3) $\dfrac{_{15}C_2}{_{27}C_2}$

(2) $\dfrac{_{12}C_2}{_{15}C_2 \bullet {_{12}C_2}}$

(4) $\dfrac{_{12}P_2}{_{15}P_2 \bullet {_{12}P_2}}$

31 Which equation illustrates the multiplicative inverse property?

(1) $b \bullet 0 = 0$ (3) $b + 0 = b$

(2) $b + (-b) = 0$ (4) $b \bullet \dfrac{1}{b} = 1$

32 If two consecutive sides of a rhombus are represented by $3x - 6$ and $x + 14$, then the perimeter of the rhombus is

(1) 10   (3) 72

(2) 24   (4) 96

33 If the graphs of the equations $y = x + 2$ and $y = x^2 - 3x + 6y$ are drawn on the same set of axes, at which point will the graphs intersect?

(1) $(-2, 0)$ (3) $(1, 4)$

(2) $(1, 3)$ (4) $(2, 4)$

34 Which equation represents the axis of symmetry of the graph of the equation $y = -x^2 + 4x - 2$?

(1) $x = 2$ (3) $x = -2$

(2) $y = 2$ (4) $y = -2$

35 What is the sum of the measures of the exterior angles of a regular hexagon?

(1) 60   (3) 360

(2) 120   (4) 720

Part II

Answer three questions from this part. Clearly indicate the necessary steps, including appropriate formula substitutions, diagrams, graphs, charts, etc. Calculations that may be obtained by mental arithmetic or the calculator do not need to be shown. [30]

36 *a* On graph paper, draw the graph of the equation $y = x^2 - 4x + 3$ for all values of x in the interval $-1 \leq x \leq 5$. [6]

   b On the same set of axes, draw the image of the graph drawn in part *a* after a translation that maps $(x,y) \rightarrow (x - 4, y + 2)$. Label the image *b*. [3]

   c State the coordinates of the turning point for the graph drawn in part *b*. [1]

37 Solve the following system of equations algebraically and check.

$$x^2 + y^2 = 40$$
$$y - x = 4$$

[8,2]

38 In the accompanying diagram, *STAR* is an isosceles trapezoid with $\overline{SR} \cong \overline{TA}$, *ST* = 20, *RA* = 30, m∠*SRA* = 40, and altitudes $\overline{SE}$ and $\overline{TF}$ are drawn

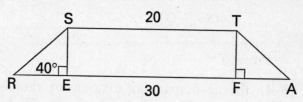

a Find *SE* to the *nearest tenth*. [4]

b Find *SR* to the *nearest tenth*. [2]

c Find the perimeter of trapezoid *STAR* to the *nearest integer* [2]

d Find the area of trapezoid *STAR* to the *nearest integer*. [2]

39 Emily receives a box of chocolates containing ten candies: 4 nut clusters, 1 peppermint, 2 jellies, and 3 caramels.

a How many different sets of five candies may Emily select? [2]

b How many of these selections will contain 2 nut clusters, 2 jellies, and 1 caramel? [3]

c What is the probability that a selection of five candies will contain 2 nut clusters, 2 jellies, and 1 caramel? [2]

d What is the probability that a five-candy selection will contain 4 nut clusters and 1 peppermint? [2]

e What is the probability that a five-candy selection will contain all caramels? [1]

40 *a* Given: $Q \rightarrow R$

$R \rightarrow T$

S

$\sim(S \wedge \sim Q)$

Prove: T [6]

b In the accompanying diagram of rhombus *ABCD*, *AB*=10 and diagonal *AC* = 10. Find the length of diagonal $\overline{BD}$ to the *nearest tenth*.   [4]

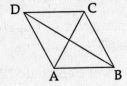

Part III

Answer one question from this part. Clearly indicate the necessary steps, including appropriate formula substitutions, diagrams, graphs, charts, etc. Calculations that may be obtained by mental arithmetic or the calculator do not need to be shown. [10]

41 Given: parallelogram $ABCD$ with $\overline{AB}$ extended to E, $\overline{DFE}$ intersects $\overline{BC}$ at F.

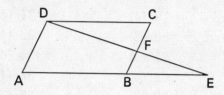

Prove: $\dfrac{AE}{CD} = \dfrac{AD}{CF}$ [10]

42 The vertices of quadrilateral $DEFG$ are $D(3,2)$ $E(7,4)$, $F(9,8)$, and $G(5,6)$. Using coordinate geometry, prove that

a $\overline{DF}$ and $\overline{GE}$ bisect each other.   [5]

b $DEFG$ is a rhombus.   [5]

ANSWER KEY
Part I

1. 7
2. 14
3. I
4. 40
5. $\sqrt{130}$
6. $\overline{SM}$
7. 84
8. 49.5
9. $\dfrac{3}{4}$
10. 60
11. 3

12. 20
13. 3
14. 7.5
15. (3)
16. (3)
17. (1)
18. (3)
19. (4)
20. (2)
21. (3)
22. (4)
23. (3)

24. (1)
25. (2)
26. (2)
27. (3)
28. (1)
29. (2)
30. (1)
31. (4)
32. (4)
33. (4)
34. (1)
35. (3)

Part II

36. *a* see explanations
    b see explanations
    c (–2,1)
37. (–6,–2) (2,6) Check
38. *a* 4.2
    b 6.5
    c 63
    d 105

39. *a* 252
    b 18
    c $\dfrac{18}{252}$
    d $\dfrac{1}{252}$
    e 0
40. *a* see explanations
    b 17.3

Part III

41. see explanations
42. see explanations

Tables of Natural Trigonometric Functions

(For use with Sequential Math – Course II Regents Examinations)

Angle	Sine	Cosine	Tangent	Angle	Sine	Cosine	Tangent
1°	.0175	.9998	.0175	46°	.7193	.6947	1.0355
2°	.0349	.9994	.0349	47°	.7314	.6820	1.0724
3°	.0523	.9986	.0524	48°	.7431	.6691	1.1106
4°	.0698	.9976	.0699	49°	.7547	.6561	1.1504
5°	.0872	.9962	.0875	50°	.7660	.6428	1.1918
6°	.1045	.9945	.1051	51°	.7771	.6293	1.2349
7°	.1219	.9925	.1228	52°	.7880	.6157	1.2799
8°	.1329	.9903	.1405	53°	.7986	.6018	1.3270
9°	.1564	.9877	.1584	54°	.8090	.5878	1.3764
10°	.1736	.9848	.1763	55°	.8192	.5736	1.4281
11°	.1908	.9816	.1944	56°	.8290	.5592	1.4826
12°	.2079	.9781	.2126	57°	.8387	.5446	1.5399
13°	.2250	.9744	.2309	58°	.8480	.5299	1.6003
14°	.2419	.9703	.2493	59°	.8572	.5150	1.6643
15°	.2588	.9659	.2679	60°	.8660	.5000	1.7321
16°	.2756	.9613	.2867	61°	.8746	.4848	1.8040
17°	.2924	.9563	.3057	62°	.8829	.4695	1.8807
18°	.3090	.9511	.3249	63°	.8910	.4540	1.9626
19°	.3256	.9455	.3443	64°	.8988	.4384	2.0503
20°	.3420	.9397	.3640	65°	.9063	.4226	2.1445
21°	.3584	.9336	.3839	66°	.9135	.4067	2.2460
22°	.3746	.9272	.4040	67°	.9205	.3907	2.3559
23°	.3907	.9205	.4245	68°	.9272	.3746	2.4751
24°	.4067	.9135	.4452	69°	.9336	.3584	2.6051
25°	.4226	.9063	.4663	70°	.9397	.3420	2.7475
26°	.4384	.8988	.4877	71°	.9455	.3256	2.9042
27°	.4540	.8910	.5059	72°	.9511	.3090	3.0777
28°	.4695	.8829	.5317	73°	.9563	.2924	3.2709
29°	.4848	.8746	.5543	74°	.9613	.2756	3.4874
30°	.5000	.8660	.5774	75°	.9659	.2588	3.7321
31°	.5150	.8572	.6009	76°	.9703	.2419	4.0108
32°	.5299	.8480	.6249	77°	.9744	.2250	4.3315
33°	.5446	.8387	.6494	78°	.9781	.2079	4.7046
34°	.5592	.8290	.6745	79°	.9816	.1908	5.1446
35°	.5736	.8192	.7002	80°	.9848	.1736	5.6713
36°	.5878	.8090	.7265	81°	.9877	.1564	6.3138
37°	.6018	.7986	.7536	82°	.9903	.1392	7.1154
38°	.6157	.7880	.7813	83°	.9925	.1219	8.1443
39°	.6293	.7771	.8098	84°	.9945	.1045	9.5144
40°	.6428	.7660	.8391	85°	.9962	.0872	11.4301
41°	.6561	.7547	.8693	86°	.9976	.0698	14.3007
42°	.6691	.7431	.9004	87°	.9986	.0523	19.0811
43°	.6820	.7314	.9325	88°	.9994	.0349	28.6363
44°	.6947	.7193	.9657	89°	.9998	.0175	57.2900
45°	.7071	.7071	1.0000	90°	1.0000	.0000	

Glossary

If a term you're looking for doesn't appear here, it may be defined in the Stuff You Should Know chapter. Otherwise, consult your math textbook.

A

abscissa   Another name for the x-coordinate of a point.

acute angle   An angle that measures less than 90°.

acute triangle   A triangle with three acute angles.

additive inverse   The opposite value of a number (which, when added to that number, yields zero). For example, the additive inverse of a is $-a$, because $a + (-a) = 0$.

alternate interior angles   Two interior angles that are on opposite sides of a transversal that intersects with two parallel lines.

altitude   A segment drawn from a vertex of a polygon (usually a triangle) that is perpendicular to the opposite side of that polygon.

associative property   Mathematical rule that states: $a + (b + c) = (a + b) + c$ and $a \cdot (b \cdot c) = (a \cdot b) \cdot c$.

axis of symmetry   The line that contains the vertex of a parabola and cuts the parabola exactly in half.

B

backsolving   The practice of plugging the answers provided on a multiple-choice test into the question to see which one works.

base angle   An angle that includes the base of a polygon (usually a triangle).

bisect   To cut exactly in half.

C

collinear   Located in the same line.

combinations   The number of ways you can choose a specific number of items in no particular order from a group.

commutative property Mathematical rule that states: $a + b = b + a$ and $a \cdot b = b \cdot a$.

complementary angles Two angles whose sum is 90°.

congruent The same size and shape (symbolized by ≅).

corresponding angles Two angles that appear in the same position when two lines are cut by a transversal.

D

denominator The bottom number of a fraction.

diameter The greatest distance within the circumference of a circle.

dilation The process under which the coordinates of each point in a figure are multiplied by a constant.

distributive property Mathematical property that states: $a(b + c) = ab + ac$.

E

equidistant The same distance away from a point or series of points.

equilateral triangle A triangle with three congruent sides and three angles that measure 60°.

exterior angle An angle that is formed when a side of a triangle is extended beyond the vertex of the triangle and is supplementary to its adjacent interior angle. (It also equals the sum of the triangle's other two non-adjacent interior angles.)

F

FOIL An acronym for First, Outer, Inner, Last, a process by which you multiply algebraic terms.

H

hypotenuse The longest side of a right triangle.

I

identity element   An element in a set such that the element operating on any other element of the set leaves the second element unchanged.

image   The result after a point or series of points undergoes a transformation.

intercept   The point at which a graph intersects one of the coordinate axes.

internal angle   An angle that lies in the interior of a triangle.

isosceles trapezoid   A trapezoid with two non-parallel sides that are congruent.

isosceles triangle   A triangle with at least two congruent sides.

L

leg   One of the two perpendicular sides of a right triangle.

locus   A set of points.

M

median of a triangle   A segment drawn from the vertex of a triangle to the midpoint of the opposite side of that triangle.

midpoint   The point equidistant from the endpoints of a line segment.

multiplicative inverse   The reciprocal of a number that is not equal to zero. For example, $\frac{1}{a}$ is the multiplicative inverse of a, because

$$a \cdot \frac{1}{a} = 1.$$

N

negation   The negation of statement t is the statement, denoted by $\sim t$ that has the opposite truth value of t.

negative reciprocals   Two numbers whose product is –1.

numerator   The top number in a fraction.

O

obtuse angle   An angle that measures greater than 90°.

obtuse triangle   A triangle that contains an obtuse angle.

operation   A process, such as addition or multiplication, by which numbers or variables are combined.

ordered pair   Two numbers written in a specific order (usually involving the coordinates of a point).

ordinate   Another name for the y-coordinate of a point.

origin   The point (0,0) on the coordinate axes.

P

parallel lines   Lines within the same plane that have the same slope and will never intersect.

parallelogram   A quadrilateral with two pairs of opposite sides that are parallel.

perfect square   A number or term with a square root that is rational.

perimeter   The sum of the lengths of all the sides of a polygon.

permutations   The number of ways in which a certain number of items can be displayed or arranged.

perpendicular lines   Two lines that intersect in a right angle.

plugging in   The process of replacing variables with numbers to turn an algebraic problem into an arithmetic problem.

process of elimination (POE)   Arriving at the right answer by eliminating all the other answer choices that you know are incorrect.

proportion   An equation you set up when the relationship between two pairs of numbers is the same.

Q

quadrilateral   A polygon with four sides.

R

radical sign   Another word for the root of a number (in this book, it means the square root and is denoted by the $\sqrt{}$ sign).

radicand   The number that appears beneath the radical sign.

radius   The distance from the center of a circle to the circumference of that circle.

rational number   A number that can be expressed as the quotient of two integers.

reflection   A transformation in which a point is "reflected" in a line, usually the x- or y-axis.

regular polygon   A polygon in which the sides and angles are congruent.

rhombus   A quadrilateral with four congruent sides.

right angle   An angle formed by two perpendicular lines that measures 90°.

right triangle   A triangle that contains a right angle.

root   A number that makes an equation true. For example, 2 and −2 are the roots of the equation $x^2 - 4 = 0$.

Rule of 180   The sum of the three angles in a triangle is 180°.

S

scalene triangle   A triangle with three unequal sides.

segment   A finite linear connection between two points.

similar triangles   Two triangles that have the same shape but not the same size (corresponding angles are congruent and corresponding sides are proportional).

SOHCAHTOA   Abbreviation for the relationships of the three main trigonometric ratios.

supplementary angles   Two angles whose sum is 180°.

system of equations   Two or more equations involving the same variables.

T

T-chart   A list of coordinates of a particular graph.

translation   A transformation in which you add to or subtract from the coordinates of a point, thus mapping it onto its image, which is a specific distance away.

transversal   A line that cuts through two parallel lines, thus creating several pairs of congruent angles.

trapezoid   A quadrilateral with exactly two parallel sides.

turning point   The point at which the graph of a parabola changes direction (also known as a vertex).

V

vertex   (1) The point at which the graph of a parabola changes direction (also known as the turning point); (2) the point of a polygon; (3) the center point of an angle.

vertex angle   The angle in an isosceles triangle that is not equal to either of the other two angles.

vertical angles   Two opposite angles formed by two intersecting lines.

ABOUT THE AUTHOR

Doug French graduated from the University of Virginia and has been working as a teacher, writer, editor, and course developer with The Princeton Review since 1991. He has taught classes for the PSAT, SAT, LSAT, GMAT, and GRE in the U.S., Europe, and Asia, and he has tutored math students in everything from fifth-grade arithmetic to BC calculus.

Doug also works as a freelance writer, draws cartoons, and does voice-overs. (He sounds a lot like that MovieFone guy.) His mom, however, has more talent in her little finger than he has in his little finger.

SEQUENTIAL MATH – COURSE II

Part I Score	. . . .
Part II Score	. . . .
Part III Score	. . . .
Total Score	. . . .
Rater's Initials:	. . . .

ANSWER SHEET

Pupil . . . .   Sex: ☐ Male ☐ Female   Grade . . . .

Teacher . . . .   School . . . .

Your answers to Part I should be recorded on this answer sheet.

Part I

Answer 30 questions from this part.

1	11	21	31 . . . .
2	12	22	32 . . . .
3	13	23	33 . . . .
4	14	24	34 . . . .
5	15	25	35 . . . .
6	16	26	
7	17	27	
8	18	28	
9	19	29	
10	20	30	

Your answers for Part II and Part III should be placed on paper provided by the school.

The declaration below should be signed when you have completed the examination.

I do hereby affirm, at the close of this examination, that I had no unlawful knowledge of the questions or answers prior to the examination, and that I have neither given nor received assistance in answering any of the questions during the examination.

_____

Signature

SEQUENTIAL MATH – COURSE II

Part I Score	. . . .
Part II Score	. . . .
Part III Score	. . . .
Total Score	. . . .
Rater's Initials:	. . . .

ANSWER SHEET

Pupil . . . .   Sex: ☐ Male ☐ Female   Grade . . . .

Teacher . . . .   School . . . .

Your answers to Part I should be recorded on this answer sheet.

Part I

Answer 30 questions from this part.

1	11	21	31 . . . .
2	12	22	32 . . . .
3	13	23	33 . . . .
4	14	24	34 . . . .
5	15	25	35 . . . .
6	16	26	
7	17	27	
8	18	28	
9	19	29	
10	20	30	

Your answers for Part II and Part III should be placed on paper provided by the school.

The declaration below should be signed when you have completed the examination.

_____

Signature

The University of the State of New York

REGENTS HIGH SCHOOL EXAMINATION

SEQUENTIAL MATH – COURSE II

Part I Score	....
Part II Score	....
Part III Score	....
Total Score	....
Rater's Initials:	....

———

ANSWER SHEET

Pupil .... Sex: ☐ Male ☐ Female   Grade ....

Teacher .... School ....

Your answers to Part I should be recorded on this answer sheet.

Part I

Answer 30 questions from this part.

1	11	21	31 ....
2	12	22	32 ....
3	13	23	33 ....
4	14	24	34 ....
5	15	25	35 ....
6	16	26	
7	17	27	
8	18	28	
9	19	29	
10	20	30	

Your answers for Part II and Part III should be placed on paper provided by the school.

The declaration below should be signed when you have completed the examination.

I do hereby affirm, at the close of this examination, that I had no unlawful knowledge of the questions or answers prior to the examination, and that I have neither given nor received assistance in answering any of the questions during the examination.

_____

Signature

The University of the State of New York

REGENTS HIGH SCHOOL EXAMINATION

SEQUENTIAL MATH – COURSE II

Part I Score	....
Part II Score	....
Part III Score	....
Total Score	....
Rater's Initials:	....

ANSWER SHEET

Pupil .... Sex: ☐ Male ☐ Female Grade ....

Teacher .... School ....

Your answers to Part I should be recorded on this answer sheet.

Part I

Answer 30 questions from this part.

1	11	21	31 ....
2	12	22	32 ....
3	13	23	33 ....
4	14	24	34 ....
5	15	25	35 ....
6	16	26	
7	17	27	
8	18	28	
9	19	29	
10	20	30	

Your answers for Part II and Part III should be placed on paper provided by the school.

The declaration below should be signed when you have completed the examination.

I do hereby affirm, at the close of this examination, that I had no unlawful knowledge of the questions or answers prior to the examination, and that I have neither given nor received assistance in answering any of the questions during the examination.

_____

Signature

The University of the State of New York

REGENTS HIGH SCHOOL EXAMINATION

SEQUENTIAL MATH – COURSE II

Part I Score	. . . .
Part II Score	. . . .
Part III Score	. . . .
Total Score	. . . .
Rater's Initials:	. . . .

ANSWER SHEET

Pupil . . . .   Sex: ☐ Male ☐ Female   Grade . . . .

Teacher . . . .   School . . . .

Your answers to Part I should be recorded on this answer sheet.

Part I

Answer 30 questions from this part.

1	11	21	31 . . . .
2	12	22	32 . . . .
3	13	23	33 . . . .
4	14	24	34 . . . .
5	15	25	35 . . . .
6	16	26	
7	17	27	
8	18	28	
9	19	29	
10	20	30	

Your answers for Part II and Part III should be placed on paper provided by the school.

The declaration below should be signed when you have completed the examination.

I do hereby affirm, at the close of this examination, that I had no unlawful knowledge of the questions or answers prior to the examination, and that I have neither given nor received assistance in answering any of the questions during the examination.

_____

Signature

The University of the State of New York

REGENTS HIGH SCHOOL EXAMINATION

SEQUENTIAL MATH – COURSE II

Part I Score ....
Part II Score ....
Part III Score ....
Total Score ....
Rater's Initials: ....

ANSWER SHEET

Pupil .... Sex: ☐ Male ☐ Female   Grade ....

Teacher .... School ....

Your answers to Part I should be recorded on this answer sheet.

Part I

Answer 30 questions from this part.

1	11	21	31 ....
2	12	22	32 ....
3	13	23	33 ....
4	14	24	34 ....
5	15	25	35 ....
6	16	26	
7	17	27	
8	18	28	
9	19	29	
10	20	30	

Your answers for Part II and Part III should be placed on paper provided by the school.

The declaration below should be signed when you have completed the examination.

I do hereby affirm, at the close of this examination, that I had no unlawful knowledge of the questions or answers prior to the examination, and that I have neither given nor received assistance in answering any of the questions during the examination.

_____

Signature

The University of the State of New York

REGENTS HIGH SCHOOL EXAMINATION

SEQUENTIAL MATH – COURSE II

Part I Score	....
Part II Score	....
Part III Score	....
Total Score	....
Rater's Initials:	....

ANSWER SHEET

Pupil .... Sex: ☐ Male ☐ Female   Grade ....

Teacher .... School ....

Your answers to Part I should be recorded on this answer sheet.

Part I

Answer 30 questions from this part.

1	11	21	31 ....
2	12	22	32 ....
3	13	23	33 ....
4	14	24	34 ....
5	15	25	35 ....
6	16	26	
7	17	27	
8	18	28	
9	19	29	
10	20	30	

Your answers for Part II and Part III should be placed on paper provided by the school.

The declaration below should be signed when you have completed the examination.

I do hereby affirm, at the close of this examination, that I had no unlawful knowledge of the questions or answers prior to the examination, and that I have neither given nor received assistance in answering any of the questions during the examination.

_____

Signature

The University of the State of New York

REGENTS HIGH SCHOOL EXAMINATION

SEQUENTIAL MATH – COURSE II

Part I Score	. . . .
Part II Score	. . . .
Part III Score	. . . .
Total Score	. . . .
Rater's Initials:	. . . .

————

ANSWER SHEET

Pupil . . . .   Sex: ☐ Male ☐ Female   Grade . . . .

Teacher . . . .   School . . . .

Your answers to Part I should be recorded on this answer sheet.

Part I

Answer 30 questions from this part.

1	11	21	31 . . . .
2	12	22	32 . . . .
3	13	23	33 . . . .
4	14	24	34 . . . .
5	15	25	35 . . . .
6	16	26	
7	17	27	
8	18	28	
9	19	29	
10	20	30	

Your answers for Part II and Part III should be placed on paper provided by the school.

The declaration below should be signed when you have completed the examination.

I do hereby affirm, at the close of this examination, that I had no unlawful knowledge of the questions or answers prior to the examination, and that I have neither given nor received assistance in answering any of the questions during the examination.

————————————————

Signature

The University of the State of New York

REGENTS HIGH SCHOOL EXAMINATION

SEQUENTIAL MATH – COURSE II

Part I Score	. . . .
Part II Score	. . . .
Part III Score	. . . .
Total Score	. . . .
Rater's Initials:	. . . .

ANSWER SHEET

Pupil . . . . Sex: ☐ Male ☐ Female   Grade . . . .

Teacher . . . . School . . . .

Your answers to Part I should be recorded on this answer sheet.

Part I

Answer 30 questions from this part.

1	11	21	31 . . . .
2	12	22	32 . . . .
3	13	23	33 . . . .
4	14	24	34 . . . .
5	15	25	35 . . . .
6	16	26	
7	17	27	
8	18	28	
9	19	29	
0	20	30	

Your answers for Part II and Part III should be placed on paper provided by the school.

The declaration below should be signed when you have completed the examination.

I do hereby affirm, at the close of this examination, that I had no unlawful knowledge of the questions or answers prior to the examination, and that I have neither given nor received assistance in answering any of the questions during the examination.

_____

Signature

The University of the State of New York

REGENTS HIGH SCHOOL EXAMINATION

SEQUENTIAL MATH – COURSE II

ANSWER SHEET

Pupil . . . . Sex: ☐ Male ☐ Female Grade . . . .

Teacher . . . . School . . . .

Your answers to Part I should be recorded on this answer sheet.

Part I

Answer 30 questions from this part.

1	11	21	31 . . . .
2	12	22	32 . . . .
3	13	23	33 . . . .
4	14	24	34 . . . .
5	15	25	35 . . . .
6	16	26	
7	17	27	
8	18	28	
9	19	29	
10	20	30	

Your answers for Part II and Part III should be placed on paper provided by the school.

The declaration below should be signed when you have completed the examination.

I do hereby affirm, at the close of this examination, that I had no unlawful knowledge of the questions or answers prior to the examination, and that I have neither given nor received assistance in answering any of the questions during the examination.

_____

Signature

The University of the State of New York

REGENTS HIGH SCHOOL EXAMINATION

SEQUENTIAL MATH – COURSE II

Part I Score	....
Part II Score	....
Part III Score	....
Total Score	....
Rater's Initials:	....

ANSWER SHEET

Pupil .... Sex: ☐ Male ☐ Female   Grade ....

Teacher .... School ....

Your answers to Part I should be recorded on this answer sheet.

Part I

Answer 30 questions from this part.

1	11	21	31 ....
2	12	22	32 ....
3	13	23	33 ....
4	14	24	34 ....
5	15	25	35 ....
6	16	26	
7	17	27	
8	18	28	
9	19	29	
10	20	30	

Your answers for Part II and Part III should be placed on paper provided by the school.

The declaration below should be signed when you have completed the examination.

I do hereby affirm, at the close of this examination, that I had no unlawful knowledge of the questions or answers prior to the examination, and that I have neither given nor received assistance in answering any of the questions during the examination.

_____

Signature

The University of the State of New York

REGENTS HIGH SCHOOL EXAMINATION

SEQUENTIAL MATH – COURSE II

_____

ANSWER SHEET

Pupil .... Sex: ☐ Male ☐ Female   Grade ....

Teacher .... School ....

Your answers to Part I should be recorded on this answer sheet.

Part I

Answer 30 questions from this part.

1	11	21	31 ....
2	12	22	32 ....
3	13	23	33 ....
4	14	24	34 ....
5	15	25	35 ....
6	16	26	
7	17	27	
8	18	28	
9	19	29	
10	20	30	

Your answers for Part II and Part III should be placed on paper provided by the school.

The declaration below should be signed when you have completed the examination.

I do hereby affirm, at the close of this examination, that I had no unlawful knowledge of the questions or answers prior to the examination, and that I have neither given nor received assistance in answering any of the questions during the examination.

_____

Signature

SEQUENTIAL MATH – COURSE II

Part I Score	. . . .
Part II Score	. . . .
Part III Score	. . . .
Total Score	. . . .
Rater's Initials:	. . . .

ANSWER SHEET

Pupil . . . .   Sex: ☐ Male ☐ Female   Grade . . . .

Teacher . . . .   School . . . .

Your answers to Part I should be recorded on this answer sheet.

Part I

Answer 30 questions from this part.

1	11	21	31 . . . .
2	12	22	32 . . . .
3	13	23	33 . . . .
4	14	24	34 . . . .
5	15	25	35 . . . .
6	16	26	
7	17	27	
8	18	28	
9	19	29	
10	20	30	

Your answers for Part II and Part III should be placed on paper provided by the school.

The declaration below should be signed when you have completed the examination.

I do hereby affirm, at the close of this examination, that I had no unlawful knowledge of the questions or answers prior to the examination, and that I have neither given nor received assistance in answering any of the questions during the examination.

_____

Signature

Expert Advice

Talk About It

Pop Surveys

Paying for it

www.review.com

THE PRINCETON REVIEW

Getting in

Word du Jour

Find-O-Rama School & Career Search

www.review.com

Finding it

Best Schools

www.review.com

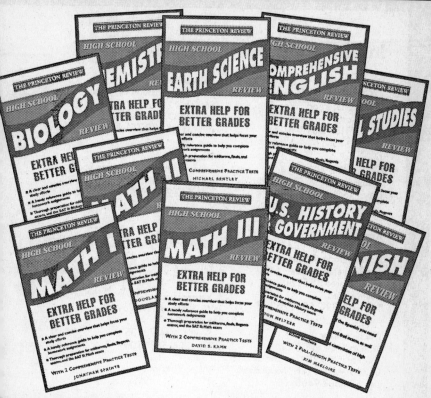

FIND US...

International

Hong Kong
4/F Sun Hung Kai Centre
30 Harbour Road, Wan Chai,
Hong Kong
Tel: (011)85-2-517-3016

Japan
Fuji Building 40, 15-14
Sakuragaokacho, Shibuya Ku,
Tokyo 150, Japan
Tel: (011)81-3-3463-1343

Korea
Tae Young Bldg, 944-24,
Daechi- Dong, Kangnam-Ku
The Princeton Review—ANC
Seoul, Korea 135-280,
South Korea
Tel: (011)82-2-554-7763

Mexico City
PR Mex S De RL De Cv
Guanajuato 228 Col. Roma
06700 Mexico D.F., Mexico
Tel: 525-564-9468

Montreal
666 Sherbrooke St.
West, Suite 202
Montreal, QC H3A 1E7 Canada
Tel: 514-499-0870

Pakistan
1 Bawa Park - 90 Upper Mall
Lahore, Pakistan
Tel: (011)92-42-571-2315

Spain
Pza. Castilla, 3 - 5º A, 28046
Madrid, Spain
Tel: (011)341-323-4212

Taiwan
155 Chung Hsiao East Road
Section 4 - 4th Floor,
Taipei R.O.C., Taiwan
Tel: (011)886-2-751-1243

Thailand
Building One, 99 Wireless Road
Bangkok, Thailand 10330
Tel: 662-256-7080

Toronto
1240 Bay Street, Suite 300
Toronto M5R 2A7 Canada
Tel: 800-495-7737
Tel: 716-839-4391

Vancouver
4212 University Way NE,
Suite 204
Seattle, WA 98105
Tel: 206-548-1100

National (U.S.)

We have more than 60 offices around the U.S. and run courses at over 400 sites. For courses and locations within the U.S. call 1-800-2-Review and you will be routed to the nearest office.